SICK SOCIETY

REIMAGINING
HOW WE LIVE WELL TOGETHER

ISBN: 978-1-7395607-5-1

Illustrator: Marie-Louise Welton. Email: trueman@reimagininghealth.com
Copyeditor: Lucy Warriner

First published 2024 by Boz Publications Ltd

Boz Publications Ltd.
71-75 Shelton Street, Covent Garden,
London, WC2H 9JQ, United Kingdom.
www.bozpublications.com
office@bozpublications.com

For Joshua, Amelia and Samuel,

I love you.
I see you.
You are always welcome home.

I hope this book contributes in some small way to reimagining a future for our society which is much more loving and kind. It's a bit of a mess at the moment, but it doesn't have to be. Remember in whatever you do, let love cause you to be outraged at injustice, to challenge the inevitability of the status quo and to actively create moral alternative ways of doing things.

Keep hope and faith alive in your soul.
Above all, choose love.

COMMENDATIONS FOR *SICK SOCIETY*

'Why are we living this way? In this heartfelt book GP Andy Knox draws on stories from his everyday community practice to suggest ways in which we might create health, in the place where health starts: our communities. These are important stories of hope and insight for everyone trying to create change from deep inside our health and welfare systems.'
Professor Hilary Cottam, Author and Social Activist

'This is a powerful and deeply personal book based on the author's experience as a GP where he has looked after so many people who have been failed by society. Full of anecdotes and insights, it challenges us all to put aside our cynicism, world weariness and feelings of powerlessness and do something to make the world a better place.'
Lord Nigel Crisp

'A brilliant book by Andy Knox. Not only does it make a powerful case for radically rethinking approaches to health and care delivery; it also takes the reader on a transformative journey of self-discovery and growth, stimulating practical ideas and challenging a fundamental shift in mindsets. Utterly captivating, mesmerisingly beautiful and deeply heart-wrenching. A must read for anyone wishing to improve health and care for the future.'
Professor Durka Dougall, Chair of The Health Creation Alliance

'This is a book which humanises health care, providing a radical and inspiring way forward for us to follow. It will leave you angry at times, it will uplift you and it will also give you a clear sense of how we can be healthier as individuals and as a society. Sick Society is a book that comes from the heart of an outstanding clinician whose practical compassion for his patients is simply overwhelming. Whether you are an "ordinary" patient, a clinician or a decision maker, I recommend that you read this book. It will remind you that all is not lost in our sick society and that there is a surprising solution ...'

Tim Farron, MP

'Sick Society *is a stark reality check about where we currently find ourselves. The problems we face are wicked. The solutions of the past are unable to help us navigate our way into the future we hope for. So, what must we do? We must, as Andy Knox implores us, ask some fundamental questions about the values upon which we are building our society. This isn't comfortable, but it is vital. As a GP and now leader of an Integrated Health and Care System, I know just how complex the task ahead of us really is in tackling the health inequalities in our society. We must begin by recognising the power of communities and choosing to deliberately work together with them differently. If you care about why this is important and how we might find a new way together, then this book is for you.'*

Professor Claire Fuller, CEO at Surrey Heartlands Health and Care Partnership

'I jovially told the NHS Assembly recently that if I could ask anyone in the country to be my GP, it would be Andy Knox. He is a doctor and leader, rooted in his community, driven by compassion and absolutely committed to tackling inequalities. I implore you to connect with the stories of the people you meet in these pages. This is what we see day-in and day-out in Primary Care. Our NHS and public services are overwhelmed. What can we do? We start by facing the reality of where we are and examining the values which underpin the status quo. We allow ourselves to feel outraged, to challenge the inevitability that things must be this way and find creative moral alternatives towards a reimagined future. This book is beautiful, challenging, heartbreakingly bleak and wide-eyed with hope. You may not agree with everything, and that's OK. But let's be determined to find

solutions to the problems we face and together build a kinder society.'

Professor Dame Clare Gerada, President of the Royal College of General Practitioners and Co-Chair of the NHS Assembly

'I have known Andy since he was a student studying medicine at the University of Manchester when he attended the church I was leading with Frank. I agree with him, society is sick.

'Reading these stories and looking around us at community life is proof of that. The system is broken in so many ways just like the man in the "Good Samaritan" account who was beaten and left at the side of the road.

'But the stories in this book also point to the fact that if we act, society can be made well again, and we can restore hope. Not everyone will agree with everything written in here, but it's important we keep wrestling with the issues and really listen well to each other.

'I am so proud of and grateful for Dr Andy Knox who is one of those people who believes in a different, more equal kind of society.'

Debra Green OBE, Founder of ROC – the community engagement charity

'As a local GP Andy has an amazing insight into how society functions and the way public services work to support people. He sets out a new approach to creating health rather than using the proverbial sticking plaster approach to address the deep injustices that exist. Fantastic read and packed with key lessons for government, public service leaders, community organisations and frontline teams.'

Professor Donna Hall, CBE, Chair of New Local

'Drawing on his experience as a general practitioner and a population health leader, Andy Knox offers a searing analysis of society's ills and *what must be done to address them. His anger and passion are palpable as he blends personal stories with references to other critiques to outline a manifesto for change. Knox's core argument is that we must rediscover the role of love in our lives and communities to have a chance of healing our fractured relationships. In a compelling read, he challenges each of us to play our part in the journey.'*

Professor Sir Chris Ham, Co-Chair of the NHS Assembly. He is Emeritus Professor of Health Policy and Management at the University of Birmingham, Visiting Professor at the London School of Hygiene and Tropical Medicine and Senior Visiting Fellow at The King's Fund where he was Chief Executive between 2010 and 2018

'Unknowingly, I read this book with two sets of eyes and two hearts. Firstly, through my lived experience of being broken through trauma, addiction, mental health and poverty ... Secondly, through my professional capacity – helping support thousands of people, break free from addiction, mental health, crime, and trauma ...

'Andy brings us back to what is integral to a system of support, and any interventions – that is LOVE. This is what is missing in our services, the basic need for people to feel loved and valued. Without this, services just provide an intervention that has no depth or weight to it. Without love and connection, the intervention is forgettable.

'This book is a blueprint of how to love and be loved. Amazing, passionate and an inspirational read.'

Dave Higham, CEO The Well Communities, Author of *Rat Hell to Rat Park*

'There are many incredible people who work in our health and social care system. Invisible heroes who support us day in and day out. This support contributes to the health, wellbeing and happiness of many different

communities in our society. General Practice, often seen as the gateway to the NHS, is one such place where many inspirational individuals provide kind and compassionate care to people from all walks of life that make up our incredibly diverse society. Dr Andy Knox is one of those people.

'His book brings to life the story of individuals who experience inequality and injustice. The numbers we hear about and read about every day are brought to life in full technicolour. Demonstrating that what you see in the consultation room is not always the full story but symptomatic of some of the issues within society today. This book illustrates something that is often unacknowledged in society today, and that is every human being is worthy of love, and together with love we can make things better.

'These stories do not just demonstrate the impact of truly listening and seeing people; but are also a call to action for us all. They show the power of empowering people to help themselves, the importance of translating complexity into simplicity, of working in collaboration and the benefits of true partnership with our communities. Although the stories in this book took me on a roller-coaster ride of emotions, laughter and tears I was left with one overwhelming emotion – hope. I am hopeful that these messages and the learning from these powerful stories reach more people across all the different parts of society culminating in a wave of positive change. It was a soothing balm to my soul. I am proud to call this man my friend and I stand right beside him. The revolution starts here.'
Fatima Khan-Shah, Associate Director, Long-Term Conditions and Personalisation, West Yorkshire Health and Care Partnership

'This book should be read by those who care about people and what they do, and about the places within which they live and work. Andy Knox is an insider who cares about people and the place where he lives. He is not into short-term fixes but long-term solutions. This book is full of insights from the coal face and should be read by those operating at the top, middle and

bottom of our NHS and public sector systems. It is full of human insights that really matter.'
Lord Andrew Mawson, OBE

'This book and its author inspire me to keep making the active choices that contribute to the overall wellbeing of Morecambe Bay, its surrounding conurbations and beyond to where my prayers and relationships take me. They can do the same for you where you are!'
Dr Roger Mitchell, Political Theologian and Activist

'I appreciate the honest, personal and professional perspective in this book. It challenges us all to care, to act, and to create space for understanding. Here's to less meetings and more practical action to tackle heath inequalities.'
Joan Saddler, OBE, Director of Partnerships and Equality, NHS Confederation

'Given the state of society this book is not a comfortable read, its frontline accounts from a local GP will open the readers' eyes to the challenges faced by so many in our communities. Andy Knox knows and loves the community he serves, and this book is his account of what he sees today and how he sees hope for the future. Love is the most powerful emotion, we need it as much as we need oxygen, and the author pens a path to a better world built from that love. I hope other parliamentarians and politicians pick up this book and reflect on the opportunities to build that world of love.'
Cat Smith, MP

'It is hard not to feel paralysed by the gravity of the multiple crises we face: the entangled realities of climate change, deepening poverty, homelessness, growing inequalities within Britain and between nations, war, and refugee displacements. As our political class and news media daily propagate fear, continuously scapegoating and blaming "others" for the state we are in, it is difficult not to respond with despair and anger. As people's trust in our political system to effect change frays, and democratic forms of accountability fail, it is easy to feel cynical and exhausted.

'In this book Andy Knox draws on his many years of experience as a frontline GP and medical leader, to carefully story the crisis we face. He details how the people he daily encounters through his practice navigate catastrophes and hardships, and examines how crises are experienced and embodied in ways that make his patients unwell in a variety of ways. There is no denying, as Andy describes it, that our society is sick. Yet, despite its challenging subject matter, this is not a pessimistic book. On the contrary, in guiding us through some of the abject realities endured by so many in our communities, by revealing the connections between individual stories of hardship and wider societal and structural injustices, and by adopting throughout an ethic of listening, Andy has produced a moving and deeply hopeful account of how we might effect change.

'Drawing on the wisdom of movements for social justice from throughout history, and across the world, Andy develops a multifaceted account of "love" as the foundational relation which connects us to each other and remains a wellspring of hope that things can change. For Andy, love is a human praxis and a politics that has the power to restore individuals and communities in the face of dehumanising systems and practices. Sick Society is a clarion call to rethink, reset, and crucially to regroup through participation in social movements for justice, and to practise what Andy wonderfully calls "love action". If you are seeking hope, I urge you to read and share this book.'

Professor Imogen Tyler, Professor of Sociology, Lancaster University

'This is an incredible book. Andy writes it as an NHS GP working on the frontline of healthcare and using his experience of his consultations to highlight the problems society faces. Through the eyes of his patients Andy cleverly weaves their huge challenges in life into each chapter and produces ideas and solutions we can all enact to make life better for the communities we live in. He also points out how politicians have failed society and must do much better to improve the lives of everyone in society. I highly recommend this unique book.'

Dr David Wrigley, NHS GP and immediate past Deputy Chair of the British Medical Association UK Council

CONTENTS

The author has taken great care to respect and maintain the confidentiality of his patients, whose stories have been told in this book. Names and key details have been changed, including places of work, and some stories have been amalgamated or amended. This maintains the essence of the issues described, whilst protecting the identities of those involved. There are exceptions to this, but only where there has been explicit consent for people to be named and their actual stories told.

A NOTE FROM THE AUTHOR

Dear Reader,

This book contains some stories which are not altogether easy to read. Some of them are sad or contain difficult themes. If you are struggling with your mental health, I would advise you to wait to read on until you are feeling more well in yourself. Perhaps you could read this alongside someone else, and discuss the chapters together.

It is possible that some chapters may trigger difficult memories. If this happens, please be gentle and kind to yourself, and seek help from friends, family or your own GP and their team.

I hope, however, that you will find deep hope in this book. Together, we can face the reality of our painful present whilst reimagining a future which is altogether much more loving and kind.

Andy Knox

ACKNOWLEDGEMENTS

When I set off writing this book, I had no idea how many people would get involved and help me along the way.

First and foremost, I need to thank my best friend, my wife, Kathryn. Thank you for helping me to know when the time was and was not to write. Thank you for loving me, patiently and faithfully. Thank you for encouraging me and calling me to be present. I am forever grateful for you.

Joshua, Amelia and Samuel – this book is for you. Thank you for bearing with all my blabbing on about it whilst I've been writing it.

Mum and Dad, thank you for cheering me on.

Lynn – for reading and rereading, rereading and editing, encouraging and spurring me on. Thank you!

Lucy, for your copyediting skills, patience and kindness. Your eye for detail is astounding. Thank you!

Andy, for bearing with me, for making me rewrite the whole blooming thing, a few times! For steering me through the ethical and ecological minefield that is publishing. Thank you!

Roger, Sue, Imogen, Trueman, Marijke, Andy, Paul, Cate, Hilary, Gill, Neil, Andrew, Lucinda, Julia and Chris for reading, discussing, sharpening and pushing me to write better, differently and with greater clarity. I am forever grateful.

To all those who read and were willing to endorse this book – I respect each of you more than is possible to communicate in these pages.

Thank you.

FOREWORD

This is an extraordinary book – which I am very glad to have read, and rather wish I had written. It is all about love; that 'transcendent love' which holds all of life together and is the deep foundation on which all health is built. When love is lacking, society is sick, and Andy Knox employs his diagnostic skill as a doctor to examine our western culture and expose its many inequalities and injustices. He longs for a future which is much 'more loving and kind' and offers us a prescription for working together to that end.

That does not make it a comfortable read. He challenges assumptions and pleads for deep systemic change. Describing our economic ideology as 'irresponsible, unkind and immoral' he suggests that our society is currently 'swimming in a sea of ubiquitous greed' which deepens the widening gap between rich and poor. Startling statistics confront us throughout the book – indicating, for instance, that half of all emissions from air travel are caused by only 1% of the population; that 1 in 10 of us have experienced more than 4 'ACEs' (adverse childhood experiences) at a cost to the economics of England and Wales of £43 bn p.a.; that working-age ill health costs the UK economy over £100 bn p.a.; and that 53% of all GPs says they are suffering with a work-related mental health issue. The status quo, he says, is broken and unfit for purpose, and a combination of individualism and an obsession with 'unbridled free-market capitalism' has hard baked social injustice into the way our society is set up.

Using numerous case studies from his own clinical experience, Dr Knox addresses an amazingly wide range of issues which include Community; Schools, Work; Money; Ecology (and Climate

Change); Parenting; Dignity and Freedom. He is invariably hard-hitting, passionate, and prophetic and his descriptive powers are frequently poetic. Each chapter (except the last of them) ends with several provocative questions, and there are plenty of suggestions for practical action. Above all, his deep compassion lends warmth and colour to what could otherwise be rather a bleak exposé, and his very articulate and accessible writing style gives momentum and pace to what could seem like a fairly lengthy thesis.

There are nuggets of insight and wisdom in every chapter. So for instance, he highlights the crucial importance of deep, attentive, and humble listening; emphasises the need for spiritual as well as physical and mental wellbeing; explores the value of giving – for the giver as well as the receiver; and explains why forgiveness is such an essential aspect of healing. There are many important reflections on medical ethics (including euthanasia, obesity, ageing, disability, and abortion) and fascinating observations about the connection between areas of economic disadvantage and ill-health.

Andy Knox has read widely and thought deeply. Not everyone will agree with all his conclusions, but few would dispute the fundamental belief which has motivated this remarkable treatise: namely that 'We are never well outside of love, or without love. If we do not love, we are not well.'

James Newcome
Bishop of Carlisle. Lead Bishop on Health and Social Care

PREFACE

WHY THIS BOOK?

A good friend asked me recently, 'How can you possibly have time to write a book?' I thought about it for a minute and let the question sit with me. In response, I found these words coming out of my mouth, 'I am too busy not to write this book.'

Both as a human being and a doctor, I honestly don't know if I have ever felt more hard-pressed, more stretched, more exasperated or perplexed! As we begin to find our feet after the first few waves of a global pandemic, our public services are completely overwhelmed. It feels like they are bursting at the seams. Many lives have been lost. There is such massive inequality and inequity in our society and staggering levels of injustice. We are in a cost of living crisis. People are struggling with their mental health. Refugees and asylum seekers flee from senseless wars, only to live in camps, drown in the sea or be held in merciless detention centres. Children go hungry and the poorest in our communities have little help available. Global temperatures are increasing. Wildfires are destroying homes. Devastating floods are claiming many lives. We are watching a climate crisis unfold before our eyes with untold human suffering. Things feel out of control.

However painful it might be, we need to sit, to pause and to allow ourselves to feel the pain of what is really going on in our communities and across this globe. I find that nigh on impossible to do. I'm the kind of person that wants everything to be joyful and happy all of the time. I love fun. I love adventure. I love taking time to dream and imagine about the possibilities of the future. Yet I'm learning to recognise that running away from the pain of our reality leads us into a false joy, a false hope and unrealistic expectations about how to fix things. Rather, we must allow ourselves to sit honestly with and feel the discomfort of our current experience. This will allow us to find an integrity and authenticity in the truth of our reality. From this place, we can uncover some of the reasons why we find ourselves where we are. When we face the truth, it allows us to ask better questions, to peel back the deeper layers. We can see behind the facades to the uncomfortable realities of what upholds our current status quo. Only then might we find a way forward into a future that is good for everyone.

All over the globe, slowly but surely a great awakening and reformation is beginning to take place. One of a similar importance to the Renaissance, the Enlightenment or the Industrial Revolution.

The status quo is broken and unfit for purpose.

It simply cannot make us well or restore the environment. Therefore, we need to ask ourselves some important questions.

- Why are we living this way?

- Why do we allow such senseless, societal injustice and environmental destruction to continue?

- How can we build a society that works for everybody within a sustainable ecology?

We must stop looking for simple answers to significantly wicked questions.

We need to quit kidding ourselves that we can continue with an economic model of growth-obsessed, unbridled free-market capitalism *and* reverse climate change or tackle the devastating inequalities we see.

It is time to get serious.

In writing this book, I am acutely aware of my privately educated, middle-class, white, male privilege. If these facts about me turn you off and you want to read no more – I completely understand. There have been plenty of books written by men of my ilk.

Yet as a human being, as a father, as a GP, as a previous director of population health and now as an associate medical director, I find so many reasons to be doing so. Not, I hope, out of blind arrogance, but with a sense of humility that I absolutely do not have the answers but do have many questions. I'm not writing this on behalf of any of the organisations I work for, and my words do not represent them. These are my own thoughts and ideas. As a father, I want my kids and their generation to know that there are many people who are hearing their anxieties and are taking them seriously. I want them to see that we are aligning with their passion to make the world new. To be trying to find some words to recognise both the gravity of our situation and yet find the audacious hope that we might be able to find some beautiful new possibilities together.

In my professional roles, I am tired of trying to put a sticking plaster over the superficial wounds that I see in people's lives or in our wider communities. For me, there is no integrity in continuing to tinker around the edges. Whilst there is no doubt that many small acts of kindness can change the world, we also need to challenge the very foundational values upon which we have built our society. The inequalities and inequities ravaging so many of our communities are staggering.

This book is my attempt to call out what I have been seeing in my consulting room and in our communities for far too long. We need to understand what needs our attention. What is it that needs healing? To find out, we have to look beneath the surface. The people turning up at the doors of the NHS are showing us uncomfortable truths. They are telling us, loud and clear, that things aren't working right now. If we accept the premise that we are deeply connected to each other and the planet we co-habit, then together we must face the fact that we are sick.

Our society is sick. Individualism is killing us.

I want to be part of a reimagining, an awakening and a movement for the change we need.

The journey into societal health is not going to be straightforward, easy or painless. It is going to require humility, honesty and determination. Health is deeply political, economical, ecological and sociological. It is created in and with communities and we need to reorientate ourselves towards this truth.

If we believe in a society that genuinely works for everyone, then we simply cannot remain as we are.

It was Archbishop Desmond Tutu who anecdotally said, 'There comes a point where we need to stop just pulling people out of the river. We need to go upstream and find out why they are falling in.'[1] The sad reality is this: we have created a scenario in the UK in which circumstances are causing people to fall into the river more readily and we are leaving them there to drown.

The truth is, there is a far deeper sickness baked into our society.

We are love sick.

What do I mean by that? Together, we will uncover what this means, why this is so and how we can respond.

Albert Einstein has been credited with warning us that, 'Insanity is doing the same thing over and over and expecting different results.'[2] We must be brave enough to examine what the data shows us. We need to hear the stories of those who are often ignored. We must ask ourselves some uncomfortable questions. I have written this book because I am tired of feeling as if I am on the back foot. I do not want to get people 'just well enough' to go on and keep on propping up the economy. No, we need something altogether different. We need our planet and our communities to be able to flourish.

My hope is to be part of a growing call to **realign and reorientate our life together** both now and for the future generations; towards a future of wellbeing for all people and the planet, **built on love.**

THE PARABLE OF
THE SINKING SANDS

I live in Morecambe Bay, in the North West of England. Morecambe Bay is the largest expanse of intertidal mudflats and sands in the UK, with some of the fastest and most voluminous tides anywhere in the world. It serves as a profound metaphor for where we find ourselves now.

If you stand on the southern shore of the Bay and look across to the majestic landscape of the South Lakeland Fells, the famous Lake District National Park, you see an enviable vista. It lifts your soul and creates a breathtaking sense of stillness, humility and hope.

Were you to try to cross Morecambe Bay on foot, you could easily find yourself in perilous danger. You would be caught in the sinking mudflats and overwhelmed by the speed of the spectacularly fast tides. Indeed, this happens to unprepared and unsuspecting people several times a year and thanks to the brave volunteers of the RNLI, Bay Rescue, the Coastguard and the Fire and Rescue Teams, people stuck in the mud are frequently saved.

Each year there is the opportunity to walk across Morecambe Bay with the help of a royal guide.[3] There is something deeply poetic about a group of people stepping carefully through the difficult terrain to find a way together to the other shore.

Perhaps right now, we are collectively stuck in the mud, we are sinking and maybe the panic is setting in. Every so often, we lift our eyes and see the distant mountains, wishing somehow that we could cross this terrain to the far side, but we are not even sure how to get unstuck let alone find our way across.

Well, maybe it's time for us to pull each other out and begin to lift our eyes again towards the future we know in our hearts is possible. We are going to tread through perilous and at times treacherous paths, avoiding pitfalls along the way and recognising that we have limited time before several metres of water could overwhelm us.

Yet we cannot remain where we are.

We find ourselves at an epoch, a *kairos* moment in time. **It is creating space for us to discover together how we get ourselves unstuck.** To find a way together, through practical action in the painful present, to an altogether more beautiful future, with love as our guide. So, lift your eyes to the mountains and let us refocus our vision to find fresh hope.

Why

are

they

falling

in?

INTRODUCTION

APOCALYPSE NOW?

As I write, the war between Russia and Ukraine escalates and the threat of World War III looms in our collective imaginations. People in Yemen are driven to starvation by a bitter civil war. Sri Lankans are running out of food and medicines. Western forces have withdrawn from Afghanistan, leaving mayhem. Tigrayan's suffer appalling violations in Eritrea and Ethiopia. New Zealanders are recovering in the aftermath of catastrophic floods. An earthquake has left desolation in Northern Syria and Southern Turkey. An enormous tide of refugees sweeps across the globe.

When we also examine the combined and devastating effects of the Covid-19 global pandemic, the cost of living crisis, the threat of global food shortages, the destruction of forests, the pollution of rivers and oceans, the alarming reality of climate change with its associated destructive weather patterns and staggering levels of social and financial inequality, it can feel like we are in an apocalyptic moment. However, an apocalypse does not mean the end of everything. A literal translation means to 'uncover, disclose, reveal'.[4] In other words, apocalyptic events expose things as they are. They cause us to question the legitimacy of the current order of things. But they always carry a sense of hope because an apocalypse opens up the possibility of an alternative future.

This is our moment to build a more loving world.

Time is still just about on our side.

A SICK SOCIETY

This book is an attempt to add my voice to the many who are calling for us to pay attention to our current reality. I hope to expose the status quo and reimagine a world of alternative and altogether more kind and loving possibilities. If you care about this too, no matter who you are, where you're from or how you spend your days, this book is for you.

The first 19 chapters introduce you to a person I know or have known, usually in my capacity as a doctor, but sometimes in my other roles. Each character represents people I have cared for in various ways, whilst I've worked in five different hospitals and four GP practices in three separate counties of the UK, and overseas. The stories reveal to us some much more significant problems than those issues the individuals originally present with. They expose the deeper sickness in our society: the sickness of our communities, our politics, our economics and our ecology. However, the confidentiality of my patients is something important to me. So, to protect them, I've changed the names of most of the people involved, except if requested not to. In most cases, I've also amalgamated several people into one and altered some details, so that each person remains anonymous. **Each story is therefore more like a parable. However, this does not make them any less true.** I am hoping that as you read and reflect, guided by some questions at the end of each chapter except the last, we can find some solutions together to the problems we face.

THE DEEPER LAYERS

As a GP, my job is to listen to people who present with various problems. I seek to understand what the problem is and what is important to them. We then go on a journey together to help them learn about what their symptoms might be telling them. We work out what the options are for treating the issue, improving their health and wellbeing or helping them face the reality of living with a lifelong or even terminal condition. Sometimes when a patient comes to see me, they want me to take their problems from them, but that isn't my job. I can be with them in their pain. I can help them sort through the difficulties they are facing in a way that makes most sense for them. Or I can help to strengthen their back, so they can carry their burdens more readily. But what if it is the way society is set up and the way we are living together that is making them unwell? To be honest, I feel tired of simply helping people cope with a day-to-day life that is stacked against them. I'm only interested in doing that, if we are simultaneously remaking and rebuilding society to be one that truly works for everyone.

The invitation in this book, is not to try simply to fix the individual in front of us at the start of each chapter, valuable though that is. Rather the encouragement is to listen more intently to the issues their story exposes about our shared, community life.

Social injustice is hard baked into the way our society is set up.

Structural and systemic disadvantages experienced by people are caused by biases, socioeconomic and political drivers. These lead to inequitable social realities, which cause unfair outcomes for the communities who experience them.[5] This needs to change.

Professor Sir Michael Marmot (Professor of Epidemiology at University College London, Director of the UCL Institute of Health Equity, and Past President of the World Medical Association) has already done decades of work, along with many others on the social determinants of health. We know that issues like poverty, disability, race, gender, poor housing, lack of access to good work, poor transportation and poor educational outcomes lead to poorer health.[6] I am wanting to dig even deeper – down to the roots of what holds these social injustices in place. You see, as Marmot puts it, 'If you want to understand why health is distributed the way it is, you have to understand society.'[7] The reality is that underneath the inequalities we see in society and the destruction of the climate, sit a set of values and practices which need exposing. Once we understand what is causing our deeper societal sickness, we can find ways of building a kinder and more sustainable world.

THE NHS IS ON ITS KNEES

I passionately believe that we need a thoroughly well-funded health and care system, freely available to all, paid for through taxation. However, the NHS at large is at breaking point.[8] Unfortunately, the impact of Covid-19 has made things significantly worse.[9] As we begin to recover in its aftermath, the clapping of the NHS heroes is fading into memory. Now people feel they are not getting the care they need.

GPs are seeing exceptionally high numbers of patients with increasing complexity, but different areas experience variable levels of access.[10] In some places there are long waits on the phone to get through to the GP. It seems some people find it difficult to get to see a doctor face to face. This is sadly not surprising, when due to failed workforce planning and recruitment/retainment strategies, there is a shortage of around seven thousand GPs in England alone.[11] This is felt most acutely in our areas of greatest need, due to a funding formula which makes it harder to recruit doctors into areas of higher disadvantage.[12] Hopefully the landmark NHS Long Term Workforce Plan will make a difference.[13]

At present, ambulances are queuing at the doors of our emergency departments and people are lying for hours on hospital trolleys, being treated and dying in corridors. It is becoming impossible to get the flow of people through the hospital, with high numbers of people 'blocking beds', unable to be discharged, due to a lack of social care provision. The overwhelming tide of people, needing help and care, continues to flood through the doors.

Doctors, nurses and other health and care professionals are feeling overwhelmed. They look at the catch-up work required after the Covid-19 pandemic and cannot comprehend how they could possibly work any harder. Both patients (people using the NHS) and professionals are understandably frustrated. The patients cannot get the services they both want and need. The professionals cannot offer the care and expertise they are trained to give. If they are not careful, they begin to blame each other.

The patients may be tempted to think the professionals are either being self-protectionist or lazy. The professionals might presume the patients are being over-demanding or lacking in understanding.

Unsurprisingly, given the pressures, there are high levels of burnout among staff.[14] Female suicide rate is highest among female doctors.[15] Nurses, midwives and doctors are referring themselves for mental health support at alarmingly high rates.[16] Many are planning to leave their career early.[17] This has been made even worse with the associated holes in our staffing levels.

In January 2020, before the Covid-19 pandemic even hit us, the NHS had a staffing shortfall of 100,000 people.[18] Despite this, incredible care happens in and through the health and care system every day through the tireless efforts of our brilliant teams. People are working long hours to serve their local communities with compassion. However, this is taking its toll. Morale is low and the system is creaking under the pressure. We cannot ignore the huge cost burden of our current model of health and care on the people who work within it. Nor indeed on the unpaid carers who prop it up, unnoticed, looking after loved ones, struggling on, whilst they care. We can still celebrate the good work being done, whilst facing into our reality that things need to change.

In a recent survey of nurses across the UK, conducted by the Royal College of Nursing, 57% of them said they are considering leaving the profession early due to feeling undervalued.[19] As a profession, in November 2022, they decided to strike for the first time in their history.[20] In a recent survey 53% of all GPs say they are suffering with a work-related mental health issue.[21] This is unsustainable. No matter how much resilience training we do, or compassionate leadership courses we create,[22] we are facing an enormous uphill struggle.

All of this has been made worse because the NHS and social care systems have been drastically underfunded for over a decade, counting for inflation.[23] We have one of the lowest spends per head of population on health and care of any G7 country.[24] However, a fully funded and staffed health and care service (though this is vital!), will still never be able to meet the needs of the population. The inequalities and inequities are staggering. The prescriptions we are writing cannot fix the deeper issues we are facing, and the workforce is becoming burnt out in the process of trying to do so. **This is because we continue to focus on responding to ill health, rather than creating a society of wellbeing.**

WHERE ARE WE NOW?

The truth is we are all part of a system and society which is not fully working.

This has been going on in cyclical loops for the last few decades. Every time a new political party takes power, the NHS (and care system) enters another cycle of reorganisation. In fact, the NHS currently finds itself in such a loop of change.[25] This one encourages more integration and has many positive aspects. An actual plan for social care, however, remains a nettle too difficult to grasp. Although the current government are trying to find a way through some political quagmire towards a funding agreement, there are no easy answers.[26]

The NHS is a phenomenal healthcare system. A crowning jewel of our collective life in the UK. However, the NHS prescriptions simply are not working for the levels of societal sickness we are dealing with. The truth is that the problems run much deeper and are far more complex.

DIAGNOSTIC SKILLS

So, I will be drawing on some of my skills as a diagnostician to delve a bit deeper and to listen to the signs and symptoms we are seeing. They are in ourselves, in our communities, in our neighbourhoods, and in our ecosystems. I believe we need to begin a journey of unlearning and rediscover a path towards true health and wellbeing for our society and our planet.

This means we have to look in some uncomfortable places. We have to explore some things that perhaps make us feel fearful, ashamed or deeply angry. But we must not allow these things to prevent us from reimagining a future which is kinder, fairer and altogether more loving. In this book, I'm going to be digging down and thinking about sociology, economics, politics and even theology.

Theology? God? Yes – and I'll tell you why. This is by no means a theological book. However, the development of Western thought, philosophy, society, politics and economics is closely entwined with the history of 'Christendom'. If we're going to explore concepts like power and leadership, we cannot ignore it. It is my contention that a particular reading of the Bible has given rise to some views of power which have stuck fast, even in atheist circles. If we don't understand what has shaped us and why, it can be difficult to offer a fair critique of the past and reimagine the future. In order to explore this as fully as possible, and to be true to my own faith journey, I have included these aspects. If this offends you or turns you off, then when you get to those bits, please feel free to turn the page and carry on without engaging with them. However, I suspect you will find them interesting, no matter what your faith persuasion may be.

LOVE

In writing this book, I am making some key assumptions about how the world works. In other words, I am hoping that you agree with me that **love is our deepest motivation, value and foundation.** I am hoping you are the kind of goodhearted person who is all too familiar with our current state of discontent and who wants to be part of co-creating a more loving way of being the family of humanity together.

I believe that everything that exists is because of love, and love holds it all together.

Love is the foundation and without it there can be no wellbeing.

We are never well outside of or without love.

If we do not love, we are not well. If we are not loved, we are not well.

It is, however, possible to be loved whilst being unwell and to be unwell and still be loving.

Love is what makes it possible to be well.

But what do I mean by love?

SOME DEFINITIONS

Love is a noun. It is a thing. It can be the love within family relationships, in friendships, between lovers or as a choice towards those who are not easy to love.

The highly influential writer, feminist and social activist, bell hooks, who died on 15 December 2021 at the age of sixty-nine, described love this way:

> *Imagine how much easier it would be*
> *for us to learn how to love if we began with a shared*
> *definition. The word "love" is most often defined as a noun,*
> *yet all the more astute theorists of love acknowledge that we*
> *would all love better if we used it as a verb.*[27] *(emphasis added)*

Valerie Kaur, lawyer, author, feminist and activist, describes love as 'revolutionary'.[28] Like Martin Luther King Jr and many others longing for social justice, Kaur sees love as a deep motivation and driving force for action.

In this book, I will mainly be using love as a doing word, a verb, an action. We could potentially call this action compassion. It is love which moves us to doing something.

THE SPACE TO REIMAGINE

Therefore, my questions are these:

- If love is our deepest motivation and that which holds all of life together, why is it that so much of our corporate life together is so unloving?

- What would it be like if we took love seriously?

- What if love were at the foundation of how we view people, how we build society, how we practise our politics, how we shape our economy and care for the ecology?

As you meet some of my patients and follow them out of the consulting room and into society, I am hoping to make space for you to sit with the pain of our current reality. I want you to recognise the implications of remaining as we are. Together we might build some more life-giving alternatives. What might this mean for you, where you live? What might it require of you in the various roles you play? Let's enter this conversation together from a posture of humility and try to avoid idealisation at every turn. Perhaps we can (re)awaken the deepest longings and dreams of our souls as we open up space for a reimagined future.

This book is full of frustrations and hopes, questions and ideas, deep listening and new discoveries, difficult diagnoses and hopeful possibilities. If you care about society and living well together on planet earth, then this book is for you! There is a growing and powerful movement of health creators. Together we must change the way we think about health and society. Health is made at home and in communities.[29] We can create a healthy society together.

In launching us into the rest of this book, I want to leave you with an image in your mind.

THE PARABLE OF THE OAK TREE

In the field opposite where I live, stood the most beautiful oak tree. Indeed, if a child were to try to draw a tree, they would probably draw something like this. With its strong trunk and full foliage, almost in perfect symmetry, it was something to behold. Visitors to our village could often be seen, getting out of their cars halfway down the lane, to take photos of this magnificent specimen. It looked immovable. Then something unexpected happened. On 26 November 2021, a hurricane blew in from the North East of the UK. This was a rare event. The vast majority of storms into the UK blow in off the Atlantic Ocean. This tree was well used to those kinds of storms. However, the wind blows where it will. And this tree, which seemed utterly stable, like it would stand for generations to come was blown down in one night. Sometimes, whole systems and ways of doing things can seem like they will last forever. Intransigent and immovable with root structures which make them unshakeable. But unexpected events can cause them to fall.

Do not believe that things must remain as they are.

The winds of change are blowing.

Do not
believe that
things must
remain as
they are

CHAPTER ONE
LOVE CHANGE

DROWNING

When I was four years old, my parents took my three brothers and me on holiday to Majorca. It was a gift to us as a family, as my dad was a preacher and we were not particularly wealthy. We stayed in a lovely villa, with terracotta tiles and a swimming pool. The skies were blue, the days were hot, and we spent most of the time (as I remember it) sucking on watermelon, looking for lizards and swimming. My younger brother, David, who was only one year old at the time, developed a very nasty bout of chicken pox whilst we were there. On one particularly hot day, he had a raging temperature. My parents were tending to him inside the house, trying to console him. I was splashing around in the shallow end of the pool, with strict instructions not to remove my armbands. My elder two brothers, Jon (seven) and Matthew (nine) were diving off the board and generally larking around.

In the deep end of the pool, I noticed the dinghy. It was red, white and blue and bobbing happily on top of the water. It looked so much fun. More fun than I was having on my own in the shallow end. So, I got myself out by the steps and half-ran to the deep end. I can't tell you why, but I took off my armbands. Then I jumped into the inflatable boat. Unfortunately, as I did so, it flipped over, and I was trapped underneath it and unable to swim. I remember, so vividly, trying to keep my head above water by kicking my legs. But it was no use. I was drowning.

My brother Jon saw it happen from the other side of the pool and shouted to my eldest brother, Matthew, who was on the diving board. He ran as quickly as he could to where I was. Leaning over the edge and grabbing me by the arm, he pulled me out of the pool, scratching my abdomen and legs as he did so. Jon ran to get my parents from inside. I don't fully remember what happened next, but I do remember coughing up a lot of water and being consoled by my very worried mum and dad. Around 30 years later, I had a similar experience.

DROWNING AGAIN

It was 21:30, on a Thursday evening in November 2012. I had just finished another long day. I was close to burnout. My workload had felt exhausting for too long. I turned off my computer, rested my head on my folded arms, and I wept. I was so tired; overwhelmed by the relentlessness of it all and wondering if I should walk away. It felt like I was drowning again. I had recently arrived in Carnforth, having decided to leave Manchester and move to Morecambe Bay with my wife and three children. I had left a highly successful partnership on the east side of Greater Manchester, in the post-industrial borough of Tameside. Our practice team had just won the North West RCGP[30] Practice Team Award of the year.

My new practice had a rule that you couldn't just enter into partnership. You had to spend a year as an associate GP first. This was to allow you to decide if you liked the practice enough to stay. It also allowed the practice team time to decide if they liked you enough to keep you on! So, I was an associate, and was therefore less able to affect the decisions being made in the practice. The whole practice team was working flat out and was under strain. We'd had a few GPs off sick. And then, when it felt like there was nothing left to give, we were given a new initiative. We were asked to take on a peer review of each other's referral letters. This was to ensure that each referral to hospital was necessary. It was an attempt to try and manage people's care more effectively in the community.

It felt like a straw that might break this camel's back. Just one extra little task to take on at the end of a long day. Having done two full clinics, with home visits in between, with no time for a lunch break; sorting through lab results, reading letters from various places; ensuring all associated tasks were complete and writing letters on behalf of patients who were beginning to have their benefits capped and slashed under the austerity policies of the time. I was shattered. Needless to say, the morale of the entire team was very low. We felt overwhelmed with the pressures we were under. Compassion fatigue had set in. I was getting very little time with my family and to make matters worse, I realised that I could not fix the problems that my community were facing. There seemed to be an uncontrollable tide of people coming through our doors, asking for help. With allied community services also facing the chop, it felt like we weren't helping people, but sending them away with a sticking plaster over deep wounds.

I made a decision that day that I wanted to understand how we might do things differently. It took me on a journey, following my patients out of my consulting room and into the wider community. As I did so, I had to learn to listen more deeply. I was challenged and changed in the process. I have discovered some deeply uncomfortable truths about the realities of inequality and inequity in our society. I was deeply humbled by people, as I heard their stories. I made clumsy mistakes based on wrong assumptions and said things out of turn. I had to learn new ways of thinking and working. Thankfully, I found that people were very kind and patient with me as I did so.

FROM HERO TO HOST

The change began for me in the community in which I live and work, in the town of Carnforth. I knew that things needed to be different, but I wasn't sure where to start. So, I drew on a learning experience I had back in 2010, in Bristol, with the 'Art of Hosting' (AoH) Network.

Perhaps my greatest learning from the AoH has been a foundational shift in my thinking about what leadership is for. I no longer think of leadership as needing to be a hero who can ride in on a white horse to try and fix things (usually failing, whilst hurting and disempowering people in the process). Rather, I see it now as learning to become a host.

Leadership has to me become much more about hospitality.

It is more about creating space for deep listening, great conversation, collective sense making and collaborative action. Having great questions, I've found, is way more powerful than trying to have all the answers. Starting with a posture of humility and vulnerability invites real participation.

So, rather than try and come up with the solutions to to my community's and my own problems (as I perceived them), I decided, instead, to host some community conversations. I started the only way I knew how, which was to hijack one of our patient participation groups. I asked the practice team if I could host the evening and we put a notice in the practice bulletin. I

51

had a question I wanted to ask, and it was this: 'If Carnforth was the healthiest town in England, what would it be like?'

This seemed to whet people's appetites a little. About thirty-five people turned up. I talked with them about the realities of the health inequalities in our town, some of the issues we were facing, what it felt like to be a GP and a recognition that we were not able to meet the needs of our community. I explained that I would like to have a conversation with as many people from the town as possible. I didn't have an agenda. I just wanted to listen and hear the community.

The mayor of the town happened to be at that meeting. He got in touch with me the next day and offered to invite people to a public meeting at the Civic Hall. I bit his hand off! We put some posters up, he sent out some invites, as did I. A further notice went in the practice bulletin and a couple of weeks later, we had 150 people in the room. Again, I explained some of the issues we were facing and then asked my question. We used a conversation technique called a World Cafe.[31] It's a great way of including everyone's voice and ensuring all can participate.

I got a real surprise that evening. I thought the community were going to tell me all about how health services could be improved. I figured they would hound me about wanting better access to GPs. I was expecting a berating of how we were failing them. But that's not how the conversation went at all. What I discovered was that here was a community with a real love of their town and the surrounding villages. They knew the area far better than I did, and they had plenty of ideas about how it could be a whole lot healthier (although they preferred the word 'well' to 'healthy').

There were five things, in particular, they agreed on.

Firstly, they were sick of the dog shit – pardon my language. It made them feel as though our town was uncared for.

Secondly, they wanted a place to sing together. This completely amazed me, especially as I love singing!

Thirdly, they wanted some new youth clubs. Service provision had disappeared, and the young people were bored. They perceived this was leading to problematic behaviour.

Fourthly, they wanted a mental health cafe, where people could simply meet up and support each other.

Finally, they felt there was a need for a befriending scheme for older people, who were lonely, isolated and needed help with their shopping.

They also wanted more conversations. This is Lancashire! You don't just talk in one evening and be done with it. Oh no! At the Civic Hall that evening was the head teacher of the local high school. She decided that we should have a conversation at her school sports celebration evening. Amazingly, 300 young people and their parents or carers joined in. Then local churches, the rotary club, the Women's Guild and all kinds of groups were wanting to listen and talk. In the space of a few weeks, over a 1,000 people were involved in a conversation and the town felt like it was buzzing with a renewed sense of hope.

Over the following months, with a bit of seed funding from the NHS, our town and district councils, and some charitable donations, all kinds of new initiatives were beginning. Nearly ten years later, most of them continue. Carnforth Community Choir was born. Community dog-poo wardens began a kind of vigilante clear up. A local church gave us their space once a week to start a mental health cafe. A neighbourly shopping scheme for isolated elderly residents began. Various youth activities were better advertised. Walking groups, knitting clubs, gardening groups, men's sheds, community transport volunteers – all kinds of wonderful things were starting to emerge.

TAKING IT WIDER

I began to realise that creating health in and with communities is a real passion of mine. So, whilst continuing my practice as a GP, I began to get involved in the world of NHS leadership. A few years later I became Director of Population Health and Engagement for Morecambe Bay and more latterly Associate Medical Director for Lancashire and South Cumbria Integrated Care Board (ICB). The practice of hospitality as leadership, participating with our communities to build health and wellbeing, sits at the heart of how I work. I love nothing more than opening up the space for a big conversation and seeing how it begins to catalyse change.

I remember sitting in a circle of recovering heroin and crack cocaine addicts a few years ago, in the town of Morecambe, which sits on the southern part of Morecambe Bay. There were about fifty of us together and I wanted to explore with them, what it means for us to be healthy and well together. I wanted to understand their perspective about how Morecambe could become a healthier place to live.

I sat on the floor, in the middle with my charts of paper, ready to write and draw as they talked together. For several minutes, there was an awkward silence. No one spoke a word. Eventually one of the guys plucked up the courage to say, 'Andy we have no idea what you're asking or what you're talking about.' Everyone gave a kind of nervous laughter. It taught me so much that day about the assumptions that we can make when we open up conversations together. Language really matters. Our starting place, even when we are the 'expert' in the room, even when we have much knowledge to contribute, needs to be from a place of humility. We need to be willing to listen deeply and to be changed.

The conversation developed into an exploration of the question. We discovered that we needed to work out together what the question was that we needed to ask. Once we had crafted a helpful question together, we had a much richer afternoon exploring the real issues in Morecambe and how we might find a way through them together. If we are going to build a society that works for everyone, we all need to have humility. That means being willing to unlearn some of what we think we know and learn from one another across our current lines of division. I often hear it said that we need to cede power to our communities because they see the issues that matter. Rather, I think, we need to recognise the incredible power and capabilities already within our communities. We need to be with them in the change that is needed. If we do this our systems will be truly community led, bringing the best of our expertise alongside them, when needed. In this way, our common resources can be distributed in a way that will help us tackle the inequalities we see.

CULTIVATING SOCIAL MOVEMENTS

When you consider how change has happened in society over the last 150 years most of it has been led by social movement. It has not come through top-down hierarchical powers deciding that things need to change. Rather, the structures shifted in response to the passion of the community.

The suffragettes fundamentally changed the rights of women, although we still have much to do. The civil rights movement began to undo the oppression of white supremacy in bringing dignity to the lives of millions of black people, indigenous people and people of colour. We are by no means there yet, but that social movement began to create a more just society. The LGBTQ+ movement has helped to break the stigmatisation around sexuality and people being able to express their love for one another, no matter what their orientation. The climate justice movement is building momentum and has caused a global awakening, and yet our environment is still in a perilous state and close to tipping point.

If we are going to build a more loving society, then it will take a social movement, or rather multiple movements joining together – something which has already begun. So, how are social movements cultivated?

The academic Valérie Fournier writes about three critical key ingredients:[32]

cultivate some outrage, challenge inevitability and build moral alternative economies.

I will now look at these three ingredients in turn.

CULTIVATE SOME OUTRAGE

For a social movement to begin we must create a sense of outrage about injustice and stir some passion to break people out of apathy. In other words, motivated by love, people have to care about the issue enough to want it to change. Perhaps one of the reasons why we are content to live with such staggering global and national inequality is because we simply don't care about it enough. But perhaps more than ever, our eyes are being opened to the realities of the great injustices within our society, and the damage our way of life is doing to the environment which sustains us. Perhaps our sense of loss, accentuated through the Covid-19 pandemic will serve as a motivator for change.

Dr Maya Angelou put it this way:

> You should be angry. You must not be bitter. Bitterness is like cancer. It eats upon the host. It doesn't do anything to the object of its displeasure. To use that anger, you write it, you paint it, you dance it, you march it. You vote it.[33] *(emphasis added)*

It is certainly true that the millennial and Generation Z ('zoomer') generations are being awakened with a passion around these core issues. They are increasingly convinced that capitalism does not hold the necessary philosophical basis or moral capabilities to fix the issues ahead of them. Just witness what is happening around the globe currently with the Extinction Rebellion and the Black Lives Matter movement. There is a huge amount of collective and corporate outrage and passion as demonstrations spill onto the streets and disrupt daily life in major global cities. Even on a small scale here in Morecambe Bay, we have found that by sharing information with our communities about the staggering health inequalities at work between different neighbourhoods, it creates outrage. Outrage that there is a 15-year life expectancy gap between our most affluent and disadvantaged populations. This sense of discontent and passion grows within people who quite understandably then want to be part of seeing the change we need. When I talk about outrage in this book, I am not speaking of hateful anger. Rather I am talking about a deep compassion, like a fire in the belly which motivate us into loving action.

CHALLENGE INEVITABILITY

Stirring passion or creating outrage is not enough. Outrage, if not harnessed or channelled well can be dangerous and destructive. Once this has been kindled, we must then put it to good use and begin to challenge inevitability. The truth is that things do not have to be the way they are. The more that this is called out, the more the stronghold of the status quo begins to be undone.

For example, in the case of the Black Lives Matter movement, it should not be inevitable that simply by being black in parts of the USA or UK you are more likely to be arrested, stopped and searched, incarcerated or die in police custody.

When we think about climate justice it is not inevitable that the earth temperature must rise by 3 degrees or even by a further 1.5. This must be challenged. It is possible to turn the tide. It is possible to make a difference if we act together now.

When we think about the staggering health inequalities at work across the UK, or indeed the globe, it is not inevitable that simply because you are born and grow up in one area that you should have a life expectancy 15 years less than someone who lives on the other side of the same city.

It is not inevitable that just because you are a black woman that you should have higher chances of dying in pregnancy,[34] or your child dying during the birth process.[35]

It is not inevitable that if you are a boy of any colour growing up in poverty in the UK that you will almost certainly perform significantly worse in your key school exams.[36]

In fact, it is not even inevitable that you should have to grow up in poverty in this country.

It is not inevitable that food banks will be a thing of the future. In fact, they must not be!

These deep systemic injustices are not inevitable.

Social movements begin to challenge this and to change the mindset that is deeply set in.

BUILD MORAL ALTERNATIVE ECONOMIES

Once we have created passion or outrage and challenged inevitability, we must then begin to create moral alternative economies. We need to set about doing things differently and working out what works and what doesn't. We need to be OK with failing and learning how to build on successes.

But we must act! We must try new things. We must try things we've tried before but in different circumstances.

Doing nothing is not an option. Otherwise, we see the truth exposed, but are somehow hypnotised into an apathetic state. The facades go back up and the familiar once again returns.

So, in the climate change movement, for example, the anger gives way to challenge which leads to new experiments. There are a multitude of new technologies being tried across the globe which will negate our need for fossil fuels. From solar to hydrogen, we are trying all sorts of things to ensure that carbon stays in the soil and the air becomes as clean as possible. We are beginning to grow a green economy.

Here in Lancashire, and across the UK, there is a social movement developing around health inequalities. Many have been woken up to the reality that different parts of our communities are suffering significantly worse health than others. The data that we can build from multiple sources can be given to community teams who can then build heat-maps of their areas and discover where inequalities lie. This data can then be shared with communities, and new initiatives to build health and wellbeing can begin.

CHANGE CAN HAPPEN!

I have come to love my job: both as a GP and in my wider focus around population health. But to do this work well, I have had to change. And I have had to believe that societal change is possible. However, it is not inevitable. Many people choose not to change and to kid themselves that change is not needed. Therefore, things remain unjust and unfair. It doesn't have to be this way.

If you and I are willing to change, then a multitude of new possibilities open before us.

I love the privilege of sitting in my consultation room and listening to people. I love understanding what is important to them and creating space for them to make good choices about what they want to do or how they want to live with the issues/illnesses they are facing. I love working with teams of people from all different sectors of society to build meaningful change with our communities. However, the more I do it, the more I realise that the kind of interventions we are making won't be enough on their own. Along the way, as I've focused on population health, I have learned to recognise the deeper societal diagnoses that are causing us to be unwell.

As you meet some people I have cared for, in the pages that follow, my hope is that you will feel a host of different emotions. I imagine they will stir some passion in you. I hope that you will say to yourself, **'It doesn't have to be this way.'**

I hope you will read with a sense of humility and curiosity. I hope you will, all the more, want to be part of co-creating a society that is altogether more loving and more kind. We have to start with recognising what is amazing about our communities and building from these foundation stones.

Cultivate passion
Challenge inevitability
Build moral alternative economies

REFLECTIONS

- *What's amazing about the community you live in?*

- *What creates a sense of outrage in you? What lies beneath this outrage?*

- *In what ways do you believe that our current reality is inevitable? How might you challenge this in yourself?*

- *What (else) might you want to begin to experiment with in creating alternative ways of building a community/society/world that is altogether more loving?*

- *Do you want to be part of a more loving society? If so, why?*

- *What needs to change for this to happen?*

CHAPTER TWO
LOVE PEOPLE

CRUSHED

I met Ricky on a Sunday night, at a soup kitchen one warm summer evening. Under the baseball cap, and straw like hair, was a dirty but handsome face. His hands shook slightly as he reached out to have his polystyrene cup refilled with hot chocolate. A faint smile revealed his broken and worn teeth. He looked older than his twenty-four years. The cares of the world weighed heavy on his shoulders. Here was a man who looked truly broken.

Over the next few weeks, I got to know Ricky's story. He had been in care from a very young age. He had been a victim of significant physical and verbal abuse from his stepfather, who was an alcoholic. His own father was incarcerated for domestic violence – something he had witnessed as a toddler. His first memory was seeing his dad beat his mum with a golf club. His mum, who had significant mental health issues, was unable to look after him and refused or was too scared to leave her new partner. Removed from his home by a social worker, he was taken into foster care. The placement broke down when Ricky kept running away. He found himself in the first of many care homes. He was sent for assessments with local Child and Adolescent Mental Health Services (CAMHS). He was given an initial working diagnosis of ADHD (attention deficit hyperactivity disorder). But with frequent violent outbursts towards staff in his home, he was moved to a new facility in a different county. This meant a new referral to CAMHS before he could get any help. The help never came, before he was moved on again.

At eighteen, along with a black bin liner containing all his possessions, he was moved into an HMO (house in multiple occupation). His support vanished – he was no longer under the remit of children's services. He had no support network and felt utterly alone. He tried to reach out to his mum, only to find that she had died from an overdose. He went to try to find his biological father. He knocked on the door of his house and introduced himself. His father looked at him and said, 'I never wanted you. I don't want you now.' The door shut in his face.

One of the residents in his HMO turned out to be a local heroin dealer and he found himself enrolled into gang culture. For a short while, he felt like he belonged. However, as his own drug habit kicked in, he could no longer keep up with his payments and the gang leaders lost patience with him. He found himself on the streets, unable to pick himself up. He was not considered a priority to his local council when it came to getting him housed. And so here he was, in a line of others without food and no place to rest his weary head. Ricky had a natural distrust of those trying to help him. Other than swinging by for food and extra clothing, he was understandably resistant to other offers of support. He found a safety on the streets which he couldn't access elsewhere.

A few months later, I was having breakfast one Saturday morning and reading the local newspaper. I read in horror that whilst sleeping in a wheelie bin, on a particularly cold night, his 'bed' had been collected by the city's refuse team. Not Ricky! No! Aged twenty-five, he was literally crushed to death amongst the rubbish of the city. **He died alone, like a piece of trash.** A dreadful and heartbreaking accident. Or perhaps the inevitable outcome of a life with so little love.

THE CONTEXT OF TRAUMA

I wonder how many people looked at Ricky and wondered what was wrong with him. Why couldn't he just make better choices and get his life together? To ask what is wrong with someone fails to be kind. It is better to remain curious than judgmental. How does shame help a broken person, or indeed anyone?

A more compassionate approach is to wonder what has happened to someone.

What is their story?

According to the charity Shelter, a person does not need to be sleeping rough to be legally homeless.[37] Homelessness has a broader definition.

The Housing Act 1996 defines a person as homeless if one or more of the following applies to them:[38]

- They have no accommodation available to occupy

- They are at risk of violence or domestic abuse

- They have accommodation but it is not reasonable for them to continue to occupy it

- They have accommodation but cannot secure entry to it

- They have no legal right to occupy their accommodation

- They live in a mobile home or houseboat but have no place to put it or live in it.

At the end of 2021, there were over 275,000 people in the UK who were classed as homeless (people who have nowhere to call home). This is approximately the entire population of Belfast.[39]

The number of those who were street homeless had risen to nearly 17,700; 2,700 of these were rough sleeping each night.[40]

The average age of death for a street homeless person is forty-six for a male and forty-two for a female.[41] During the Covid-19 crisis, deaths of homeless people rose by over a third.[42] **These are the marks of a sick society.**

Ricky's life was physically crushed in a rubbish bin. But he had been metaphorically crushed time and again before this. He was a victim of multiple 'adverse childhood experiences' (ACEs) or childhood traumas. ACEs are one of our most important public health issues, secondary only to poverty and climate change. So, I want to be clear about what they are, and how and why they affect people so profoundly.

The research done in the UK and USA focuses on ten ACEs.[43] Five of them are considered to be direct and five are indirect. These are not easy things to talk about and if you have been a victim of one or more of these, then please be kind to yourself as you read what is ahead. Take time to pause and only read on when you are ready.

The five direct causes of ACEs are:

• Physical abuse

• Sexual abuse

• Emotional abuse

• Psychological abuse

• Neglect.

The five indirect ACEs are:

• Living with someone who abused drugs or alcohol

• Exposure to domestic violence

• Living with someone who was sent to prison

• Living with someone with serious mental illness

• Parental loss through divorce, death, or abandonment.

There have been some wide-ranging studies across the UK and USA into the numbers of people who have experienced ACEs. Although amplified in areas of greater economic injustice or disadvantage, we also see stark statistics in predominantly white, middle-class areas. Depending on the study you read, between *50% and 65% of people have experienced at least one ACE. Shockingly one in ten of us have experienced more than four.*[44] The more ACEs we experience, the greater the potential impact on our physical, mental, social health and wellbeing. If you have experienced one ACE, you have a higher chance of being subject to several. If you experience more than four, your health and wellbeing is highly likely to be significantly affected. If you experience more than six then you have a 46 times higher chance of becoming an intravenous drug abuser, a 35 times higher chance of ending your own life and an overall *20 year decrease in life expectancy.*[45]

The toxic stress levels caused by trauma significantly change the way in which our brains grow and function. This has a profound impact on our day-to-day functioning. We get stuck in the fight-flight-freeze response due to our brains feeling under constant threat. In his book, *The Body Keeps the Score*, eminent psychiatrist Professor Bessel van der Kolk shows how our bodies literally experience the reality of these traumas.[46] So, we become *more likely to develop chronic pain, inflammatory conditions, heart disease, cancer and mental health issues.* Toxic stress alters the way our DNA works and therefore changes the genetic information that *we pass onto future generations.* As an example, domestic violence in pregnancy is predictive of child developmental issues. Offspring of the survivors of the holocaust or genocide are far more likely to develop chronic anxiety. This highlights just how important our family history is.

The impact of trauma on an individual can be profound. Yet we are poorly informed about its consequences and how it can affect a person's wellbeing. Take, as an example, a child in a school labelled as 'naughty' or 'disruptive'. What if their behaviour is a communication about an underlying trauma or an ACE they are experiencing? What if it is because they were 'triggered' by a loud bang or a particular word or smell without any conscious understanding? What if isolating them or excluding them compounds the issue? What if Ricky had been seen through trauma-informed lenses? Would he have received more compassion? Might he have had different help?

Ricky's story is an extreme example of what can happen as a result of ACEs. But in England alone we have over 78,000 children in care and rising,[47] at an eye watering cost to local government budgets, which have already suffered staggering cuts. Three quarters of these children have experienced more than four ACEs.[48] However, the reality of ACEs does not just affect those in the care sector. It is far more widespread, and ACEs are believed to cost the economy of England and Wales in excess of £43 billion per year.[49]

Our understanding of the type of ACEs is growing and we are yet to understand the full issues surrounding county lines, online child exploitation, modern slavery, bullying and cyber-bullying. But more than this, **we need to understand that the way our society functions is deeply traumatic for many people,** as we will discover.

Issues like misogyny, racism, poverty and hunger are having profoundly negative effects on people throughout our communities. Even places which could or should feel safe, like work and school can themselves become part of the traumatic experience.

So many of the problems we are seeing in society now, are as a direct result of things we could and should have prevented in the first place.

START WITH KINDNESS

This book is about love as a dynamic force for change. It is about reimagining. It's about creating the space for us to take stock of where we are. To help us re-examine our values and to think about how we reframe our relationship with each other. I want us to consider how we organise ourselves, distribute our resources and care for our ecology.

All of this starts with people.

It is individual people who make up our society. Our society in turn shapes those people. It is people who create and design the rules around how we relate to one another. People form our politics and give value and values to our economy. It is people who relate to their ecology and the ecology in turn interacts with them. So, if we're going to reimagine and co-create a society that works for everyone, improving the health of the population through tackling inequality, inequity and social injustice then it is with people that we must begin. People are important.

When I was training as a GP, I walked into my tutorial one day with my trainer, and I let out a long sigh. She asked me what was wrong. I explained that I had just seen one of my real 'heartsink' patients. A heartsink patient is a term doctors and nurses use to describe someone who comes back time and again with the same problem. They cause your heart to sink because it feels like nothing ever changes. My trainer stopped me in my tracks. She said, 'Andy I never want to hear the word "heartsink" come out of your mouth ever again. If your heart sinks when a patient walks into your room, then the problem is not with the patient, it is with your heart. Get a bigger heart!'

I do not think I will ever forget that conversation. It made me seriously reflect on my capacity for compassion and kindness. Professor of Organisational Psychology at Lancaster University, Michael West, talks about the need for compassionate leadership in all aspects of society, but particularly in the realm of health and care.[50] We need to create compassionate cultures for our own teams. We need to care for the carers so that they do not burnout or feel overwhelmed with the complexity of the problems that we see. For West, our number one role in caring for people is to look at them with kind and fascinated eyes. If we have genuine curiosity, if we seek first to understand, if we are willing to hold a space for the other in front of us, then we allow ourselves to step into the space of genuine kindness and compassion.

The truth is we have never walked in the other person's shoes. We have no idea what their life experience has been. We do not know what it has cost them to even get dressed that morning. We have no idea what battles they might be fighting that day. We do not know the traumas they may have experienced or the grief they may be carrying.

So, we need compassionate curiosity.

Therefore, with big hearts, open hands, gentle eyes and listening ears, kindness allows us the opportunity to honour them. What a privilege for us to bring our presence, our time, our attention and our empathy to another human being.

How do we love people in the context of trauma and its devastating impact on human flourishing? Love demands of us that we find a way. Understanding people and their story is vital.

If we're going to understand people and how to love them, we need to know how people develop. Abraham Maslow, an American psychologist, of Russian-Jewish heritage developed a theory called the 'Hierarchy of Needs'. It is a helpful way of explaining the human journey into health and wellbeing. What Maslow does particularly well is to highlight how we gain our sense of 'self'. To put it another way, it describes how we develop our 'ego' or personality.

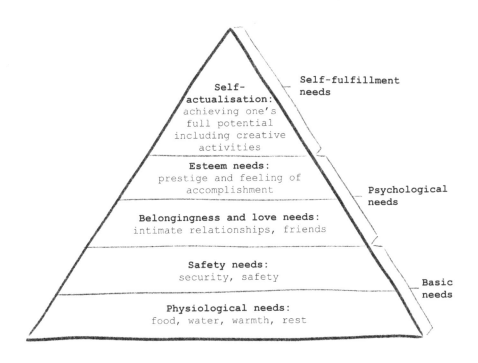

Figure 1: Diagram of Maslow's Hierarchy of Needs[51]

In the West, we have tended to focus on physical and mental wellbeing. However, I believe that spiritual wellbeing also plays a vital part. Although I think Maslow helps us to understand quite a holistic development of the human being, I think it leaves out some important aspects. I will explain a bit more about the framework Maslow built and why I think it needs some adaptation. I hope this will help us understand more deeply, what it means to become truly well.

RECONFIGURING MASLOW

Maslow's work has been fundamental in thinking about how human beings develop. It focuses on how we become well and flourishing individuals.

In his pyramid model,[52] he describes how from the moment we are conceived and all through our lives, we need to have our physiological needs met to survive. Once these are in place, we also need to be protected, to be safe. From this develops our sense of belonging and knowing we are loved. In turn, this builds our self-esteem, motivated by our ability to learn, develop skills and experience the sense of success. As we go on through life, with various motivational steps being fulfilled, we become energised and self-actualised to bring our full potential to the community around us. At this point is the opportunity to transcend into the place of becoming our best selves. Instead of being self-serving, we become a gift. So often though, this does not happen.

What I think is missing from Maslow's hierarchy is the idea of transcendent love. Transcendence literally means **'that which is beyond us'.**

So, in an ideal scenario, and I realise that this is absolutely and sadly all too often not the case, our lives begin from a place of love. Whether it's the ecstasy of the love making process in which we are conceived or simply the desire to co-create life with another as a celebration of our love, love forms us. Even if our own life started as the result of violence or abuse, somewhere in our story, even if in generations past, is the deep magic of love creating life. It is not all down to biological urges. There is something far more profoundly beautiful, which underpins our stories.

The creation of life itself is not only miraculous but is incepted and infused with love.

THE DIAMOND OF DEVELOPMENT

I have slightly adapted Maslow's pyramidal hierarchy into a diamond of development. In it, I emphasise the idea that we flow from love and our highest purpose is to become people of love, who perpetuate life in the communities and ecology around us and for future generations.

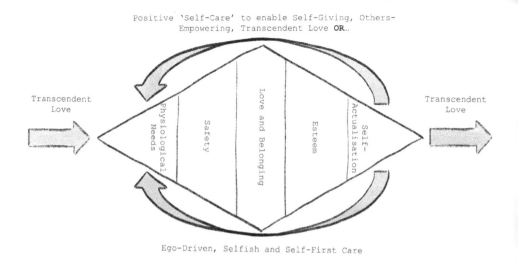

Figure 2: The Diamond of Development[53]

It is love that motivates the provision of our physiological needs and a safe environment. Love helps us to know that we are seen and that we belong in a family and community. Love gives us our sense of esteem, and provides the springboard for us to become actualised as a human being, able to flourish. The problem is that we can become, or are perhaps by nature, spectacularly selfish. Having become self-actualised, we can spend the rest of our lives ensuring that our own individual physiological, safety, belonging and esteem needs are met in an ever-repeating cycle, only to serve our own needs and wants.

The invitation to us is to move beyond individualism and our own ego-driven need for self-perpetuation and importance. We are instead invited to enter into the place of transcendent love. **To become a gift.** Our lives flow from transcendent love into transcendent love – we are born from that which is beyond us and live our lives into that which is beyond us – **becoming truly well and fully human in the process.**

For me, the source of this transcendent love is the community of God,[54] though I know many people do not see it that way.

LOVE IS FOUNDATIONAL

Every human being is inherently worthy of love. **The most basic human need is to be loved unconditionally, just for who we are.** There is much debate amongst psychologists about how the personality develops. Where they all agree, it seems, is that love is the deepest human need.

If we are to be well, then we must be loved. Therefore, love must infuse the ways that we think about our health and wellbeing. Our own wellbeing as human beings demands that love must be experienced from our earliest days. Love gives us a healthy sense of distinct 'self'. It is what nurtures us as we grow, holds us when we wobble, enables us to face the consequences of our actions, restores us when we fall, forgives us when we fail and embraces us when we are undeserving.

Unconditional love says, 'I am going to love you, no matter what.'

We need this from our primary caregivers – usually our parents, to begin with. However, where this is not possible, through death, illness or some other reason, it is vital that someone else steps in to provide this for us.

It is why we must, in my view, **be unashamed to talk about love as a core motivation** in our health and care systems, including our schools. *Knowing* we are loved is not enough. To be loved means to be seen.

We need to be seen, to be recognised and acknowledged as a person.

To be seen is to be known. To understand that our life has a meaning and a purpose. This is what developmental psychologists refer to as attunement. The gaze between a mother and her newborn child. A point of connection that begins to build a sense of attachment – the vital sense of belonging. Love means that we are seen as precious. And being seen as precious means that we can belong.

Someone asked me recently what three things I most want my kids to know. My answer was this:

1. I want them to know they are unconditionally loved.

2. I want them to know that I see them and honour them as a unique individual, who is therefore able to make and be responsible for their choices and actions.

3. I want them to know that they belong within a family and community – they are always welcome home.

For me, this is the foundation of what it takes to develop a human being and encapsulates the core of what it means to be a parent.

If we do not know our own sense of being loved, how will we learn to recognise that every person is worthy of unconditional love?

Belonging creates the space for us to be provided for and cared for.

This allows us to feel safe – knowing we are protected by those who love us. All of this builds our self-esteem, our sense of being precious – that we matter. Being honoured as a person allows us to develop a sense of purpose. This calls us to take responsibility for our own actions, choices and behaviours, developing our soul. We are therefore enabled to become a gift. As a gift, we are a net contributor to the community, economy and ecology in which we live. We become activated spiritual beings who bring life to our environments. However, throughout our development, we can be so easily knocked off kilter. Love brings us back to our centre.

It is my conviction, as a doctor, as a father and as a human being that **love is the deep foundation upon which all life and health is built.** So many of the issues I see in my clinic and which we see outworked in society right now are because people do not know that they are loved, just for who they are.

We have a severe lack of love in society. Therefore, we have a sick society. **We are, in fact, love sick.**

In the ideal setting, human beings are conceived in love, born out of love, nurtured in love, come to understand that they are unconditionally loved and so become themselves gifts of love within a community, economy and ecology which holds them in love. In so doing, human beings become participants in the divine nature itself. In my view, this is our ultimate purpose and hope. The sad truth is that for so many of us we do not know love like this in its fullest sense. I believe that every human being is worthy of love. At our best we become people of love.

Love is after all the most revolutionary force on the planet.

STARTING WELL

I started this chapter by introducing you to Ricky. If we're going to love people, then we need to create a world in which we proactively build wellbeing for our children and young people, by ensuring that they know they are loved. I want now to focus on things we can proactively do to protect children and young people from the long-term effects of trauma. Some may call me an idealist, but I'm also a realist. I accept that our society is broken and that far too many children do not grow up in a safe or loving environment, for lots of complex reasons.

I write this chapter at a time, when at the front of the corporate British psyche are two beautiful children, Star Hobson[55] and Arthur Labinjo-Hughes,[56] both tragically and brutally murdered in their homes by people who should have loved them. Of course, everyone needs someone to blame. So, we point our fingers at the ('evil') individuals who could perpetrate such a crime. We chastise the 'lazy or uncaring' social workers, who failed to protect them. We lambast the local governments for their funding cuts to social care provision. We blame austerity policies (though strangely ask for little account from those who dreamt them up). A loving world must be one in which children can grow up, knowing they are unconditionally loved, accepted for who they are, with a sense of belonging and security.

If we are to break the cycle of trauma and violence in society, we need to take some radical steps to do so. This is urgent. The recently retired Children's Commissioner for England has detailed how our looked-after children in England are being monumentally failed.[57] We need to cultivate a sense of outrage about the lack of love so many of our children experience. We need to challenge the inevitability of this situation and we need to create moral alternative economies to build a kinder future.

Thankfully, there is a growing global awareness of ACEs and their consequences. Wide reaching approaches like the 'Better Start' programme in Blackpool[58] are beginning to gain more ground. All of their services have been developed by Blackpool parents, for Blackpool parents. From pregnancy until the child goes to school, all kinds of community-led initiatives have been developed. Not only does this give children the best start in life but helps parents with the complex task of raising their children as well as possible, in a community of mutual support.

The Violence Reduction Network in Lancashire is taking a proactive approach to working with prisoners to think about the impact and consequences of their actions on their own children. Through reflective practice, it helps them re-engage with their children, whilst taking responsibility for their actions.

The New Beginnings Greater Manchester project in Stockport is led by Dr Jadwiga Leigh. It works with women, who have had their children removed and placed into the care sector. By enabling these women to talk about their own negative experiences, it helps them to understand why and how they have ended up being deemed 'unfit' or 'unsafe' to raise their own children. These reasons are often linked to substance misuse, but not always. This peer-reviewed programme is proving to be successful in helping these women to help heal each other and create a road for them to be able to receive their children back into their own homes.[59]

But we don't want help to only arrive when it's already too late. We desperately need to develop more parenting programmes, make them accessible and make it more normal and common to attend them. Parenting is the hardest job in the world. In a loving society, we need to help each other be better at it!

PROTECTION FROM TRAUMA

Of course, not all people who experience trauma or significant ACEs go on to have long-lasting physical or mental health problems. But why is this? What can make a difference?

In 2019, a team from John Hopkins Hospital in the USA, published a report in the *Journal of the American Medical Association (JAMA)*,[60] about what we can positively do for children that will create a life-long sense of wellbeing and offer some protection from the negative consequences of ACEs. They did a wide-ranging study and found seven key factors. We can't stop all negative experiences. But we can create safety nets as we entertain in our hearts and minds the possibility of a more loving world.

1. Creating space for children/young people to talk about their feelings with their family or a trusted family member.

2. Ensuring that children/young people feel supported by family during difficult times.

3. Helping children/young people to enjoy participating in traditions.

4. Giving children/young people a felt sense of belonging in high school.

5. Enabling children/young people to feel supported by friends.

6. Children/young people having at least two non-parent adults, who take genuine, kind interest in them.

7. Being protected by an adult and therefore feeling safe in their home.

In other words, the wider community can create a loving and protective environment for children, when their caregivers are unable or failing to do so. If Ricky had even some of these things, his life would have not ended up both metaphorically and physically crushed.

To be
loved
means
to be
seen

- *What about you? Do you know that you are loved – that you are seen and that you belong?*

- *If you've experienced trauma but never spoken to anyone about it, who might you be able to trust so that your experiences can be heard and validated?*

- *How might your own experiences of trauma continue to be shaping you now? Is this something you are getting help with, if needed?*

- *What of the wider reality of trauma affecting many people in our communities?*

- *What do we need to do to prevent trauma in our communities?*

- *How might we protect children from the long-term effects of trauma in our society now?*

- *How will we respond to the reality that we are love sick?*

We need to put love of our children and indeed all people at the very foundation of how we build a more loving and healthy society together. Only then can we learn to love life and enjoy it in its fullest sense.

Let's think together about what it really means to love and to be loved.

CHAPTER THREE
LOVE YOURSELF

BROKEN

Paul looked like a completely broken man. He sat down in the chair, like a shadow of himself. A mixture of tiredness, shame, embarrassment and deep pain fell across his forty-seven-year-old face.

'Hello Paul. How may I help you today?'

We sat in silence for a minute. Huge tears formed in Paul's eyes and dropped onto his pale denim shirt. Here sat a broken man. And so, I simply sat with him. Waiting. He lifted his head and pointed to a picture on the wall behind me. I turned round and saw something, which my daughter had bought me a couple of years previously. It is a simple picture of a rainbow on which are written these words: 'When you can't look on the bright side, I will sit with you in the dark.' For me it encapsulates a huge part of my work. Being with people in sad, fearful and difficult times.

'I remembered that,' he said, his voice shaking. 'I've only met you once before, a few years ago, when I brought my daughter to see you with her eczema. I saw those words and I remembered them. Well, ... I'm in the dark now, so I thought you might be able to help me.'

It transpired that Paul had tried to end his life the previous evening. He was prevented from doing so, by a passer-by, who managed to talk him away from the bank of the railway line. The kindness of this stranger and the cup of tea, which followed, had left Paul promising that he would book an appointment with his GP the next day. Like so many people I have met at the point they are thinking of ending their lives, Paul could see no way out.

Paul was a teacher. A good one too, with a big heart. He was working incredibly long hours, arriving at school early, staying late, dealing with complex safeguarding issues, and finding less and less joy in his work. Much of his lesson time was spent managing the behaviour dynamics of a mixture of teenagers. Some of them had significant trauma, unable to cope with the classroom environment. Others were acting up due to what he presumed to be too few boundaries at home. Some had mental health issues. Others were just deeply disrespectful. The day before, a fifteen-year-old boy had licked his face and posted it on social media. He would get a brief suspension, but the impact on Paul was profound. He felt abused.

'Of course, they're just kids. But sodding hell! When you give all you've got for them and this is what you get back. And then the bloody government only cares about the academic outcomes – in a school like ours! Ofsted gave us a shite report and so now the pressure is even more. But they forget you're a human too. Not a fucking slave. And all they seem to offer is more resilience training. Resilience training! We'll just pile more and more on you and teach you how to cope better. It's a joke.

'My wife got fed up with my working patterns and left me. I can't say I blame her. I haven't invested in our marriage like I'd have wanted to. But last night, after the boy licked my face, something just broke in me. It's like my whole world just imploded. I couldn't see the point anymore. I felt so tired. I couldn't remember why I give so much of myself to get so little back. The personal cost has been huge. I only get to see my own kids at the weekend. I'm so tired by then that I don't give them my best. I felt like there was no point living anymore.'

Suicide is most common in men aged forty-five to forty-nine. It remains the biggest cause of death for males in the UK under the age of forty-five. In 2020, there were 5,224 suicides registered in England and Wales.[61] There are many reasons why people can end up at the point of wanting to end their own life. This ranges from mental illness, financial ruin, drug, alcohol or gambling addiction, chronic illness and irretractable pain; to death by misadventure, bullying and loneliness. It is always a terrible and tragic loss.

If we are going to get to the root causes of suicide, both preventing them and ensuring that people on the brink of wanting to take their own lives receive the help they need, we must create the foundations for this to happen. We must build a society together based on love.

The journey to recovery for Paul began that day. It happened thanks to the kindness of a stranger walking his dog, who happened to be passing by and cared enough to intervene. It was made possible because Paul stayed true to his word to seek help and was brave enough to make himself vulnerable. As I simply held a space for Paul to tell his story, he began to go on a journey of self-discovery, which led to him making some choices about what he was going to live for. My job was to sit with him in the dark and to help him know that there was light at the end of the tunnel, even though he couldn't see it.

We were able to wrap care around him whilst he worked that out. This included support from the mental health crisis team, community chaplains, giving him some time off work, providing some therapeutic support, some helpful medication and practical lifestyle coaching. His head teacher gave him a phased return to work when he was ready and began to change the way behaviour was being managed in the school. I'm pleased to say that Paul is doing much better, though when I see him, I always check that he feels safe and isn't thinking of ending his life. Proactively asking about suicide doesn't increase someone's risk, it actively protects them.[62]

Sometimes it takes a life shock to help us examine why we keep living the way we do, as Paul experienced. These moments offer us the opportunity to (re)discover our own humanity, lovability and authenticity.

If we are going to be people of love, we must learn to love ourselves as we truly are.

Becoming people of love requires us to do our own (inner) work. I've personally found lots of help from *The Wisdom of the Enneagram*.[63] In a nutshell, the enneagram can help us to discover how our striving for love, from a place of insecurity and fear (which is the opposite of love) gives rise to our false self. Our false self is shaped by what we want people to know about us, the successful bits, the more acceptable parts. We are so desperate to be loved and to belong, that we present ourselves in a way that we hope will make us more loveable. When we discover that the world is not always loving and people let us down, we develop unhealthy coping mechanisms. Our 'personality type' or more accurately, our 'ego structure' develops to protect us from being rejected. And here lies our core issue: **we do not know who we are outside of love.**

Often, we try and externalise the problem. We blame others or society for being unloving. And don't mishear me – the problems are out there. The world is often an unloving place. But here is a truth found in all great religions and philosophical thought: the problem lies within us, also. The world is not loving, because we ourselves are not loving. **And we are not loving, not really, until we know that we are loved.**

If we are going to be compassionate, loving and caring then we need to be honest with ourselves about who we are. This is one of life's great questions. Who are you?

Facing up to our ego and what it is that we want others to believe about us, helps us dismantle our false self and become our true self. This requires us to step into the light. When we do this, we become more authentic and honest. We stop wearing the masks we have placed on ourselves in the hope that other people will find us somehow more acceptable. We stop wearing the masks that other people have placed on us, based on their own opinions of who they think we should be. When we face the reality of who we truly are, we are able to view ourselves and others with compassion and without judgement. And so, we become loving to those around us. We can begin to allow ourselves to be unconditionally loved, even if we have never experienced this before.

We do not learn to love ourselves so that we can become self-aggrandised, self-important and selfish. On the contrary, **we self-love and learn to self-care, so that we can bring our loving self to the community, economy and ecology around us.** Learning to love ourselves does not mean that we indulge every one of our own (selfish) desires.

Loving ourselves can mean needing to deny ourselves, so that we learn to live well in the context of the wider community. What I mean is that just because I want something, doesn't mean I can just go and get it, when it could hurt those around me.

For each of us, developing practices which care for our whole selves, is a key to our overall wellbeing. When we lean into the things that make our souls sing, keep our bodies nourished, our minds present and our hearts authentic, then we learn to become well.

CHOOSING LIFE-GIVING PRACTICES

Once we embrace this truth – the truth that we are unconditionally loved, we will be able to learn to do what is good for us and develop practices, which care for our wellbeing. I must be honest. I sometimes find it easier to be aware of all my flaws and failings than to be gentle and kind to myself. What does it mean to love ourselves? If we are going to self-care because we self-love, then we need to develop practices which help us. Personally, I find eight ways to wellbeing (yes eight, not the five ways to wellbeing that many may be familiar with[64]) helpful. They are simple, evidence-based and cover all bases. Perhaps if we stopped obsessing about needing the perfect six-pack or body shape and learned to celebrate the beauty in the diversity of who we are, then we would let go of much angst and unhelpful comparison. Here is my take on them.

1)   *Be active* – Get into your body. You have a body and your body needs good care. Using exercise to help you be more present in your surroundings is a good thing. It helps you feel much better through the release of endorphins into your blood stream. It means you are then more able to participate in life. So, what works for you?

One of my best friends runs ultra-marathons. To my mind, he is crazy. However, he loves it, and it keeps him well. Me – not so much. I will categorically never run a marathon, let alone an ultra one. I'm crossed between a hobbit and a cling-on anyway, so I'm not really built for it. What I do love though is walking with my springer spaniel, gardening and swimming. I'm also trying to get into yoga or pilates to help my core, because I've noticed some back twinges recently. So, loving myself means learning to listen to my body and work out what it needs. And I get it – I know what it is to have a very busy job and trying to juggle the work-life balance is nigh on impossible. That's why, for me, exercise must be both fun and practical. In the winter, I might do some high-intensity impact training (HIIT), but in the summer, I'm such a hot sweaty mess that I just feel horrific. So, I do what works, but in a way that honours my body as a vital part of me. It obviously depends on what your own body can do and cope with. It might be tai chi or chair-based exercises or a plethora of other things. Do what works for you.

2)   *Eat well* – There is little taught at medical school about nutrition. In fact, to me the lack of curriculum coverage on nutrition and trauma as two subject areas is quite frankly scandalous. But let me not get side-tracked, eating well is good for the body and the soul. What we put into our bodies is vital. It makes a difference to our physical and mental health and as we are increasingly

aware, to the wellbeing of the ecology itself. Many of our current eating habits are utterly toxic to our own bodies and to the earth itself, causing deforestation and climate change. There seems to be so much information out there and a new dietary fad seems to come to the fore on a weekly basis. So, what are we to believe? It completely depends on our body type, what our goals are, what kind of medical conditions we are already potentially living with and what is possible. What I will say though is four main points about our relationship with food.

Firstly, we are eating too much meat. I am perhaps the world's biggest meat fan – I love it. But I can't ignore the evidence on climate change if I'm going to be a person of love. So, as far as possible, I'm trying to be vegetarian on the working days of the week and allow myself meat at weekends.

Secondly, our diets are excessively full of sugar, carbohydrate and ultra-processed foods (UPFs). I am not against sugar and carbs, but I do think the evidence surrounding the rise in Type 2 diabetes is massively associated with the prevalence of them in what we eat on a daily basis. The issues here are complex. But if we limit our sugar intake and cut down on our carbs and UPFs, then we have made some good choices.

Thirdly, eating plenty of vegetables of different colours is seriously good for the microbiome, which lives in our gut. By choosing to eat well, we can change the environment of our own guts. This encourages good bacteria to live there. These work with us to keep us healthier.[65]

Fourthly, fasting is a good discipline both physically and spiritually. It allows our bodies to regenerate naturally, can help us with having a healthy weight and allows us to uncouple from consumerist greed. There are various methods of fasting and it's worth checking in with your practice nurse, dietician or health centre before you decide to do it, but it has many proven benefits and helps combat some of our unhelpful body cravings. Personally, I use intermittent fasting, and it works well for me. So, at certain times of the year, I tend to eat only between the hours of 14:00 and 20:00. Other people use varying time windows for when they eat. It differs for different age groups and body types. At other times I fast two days a week. However, I would counsel against fasting as a practice if you struggle with body image, have a complex relationship with food, or struggle with anorexia or bulimia. Only use practices which are genuinely life-giving.

3)   *Take notice* – For me this involves three things: learning to be present in the moment, learning to be grateful, and slowing down. I find it so easy to escape into my thoughts or get lost in new ideas and possibilities. Learning to be present and take notice for me has meant re-embracing the ancient Jewish and Christian practice of Shabbat, or Sabbath. Learning to rest on one day a week, switching off my screens and not engaging with social media, trying to do no shopping, whilst focusing on spiritual practices of silence, solitude, wonder and worship is incredibly life-restoring and helpful. For me, this is both individual and communal as an experience and something I utterly value. This can be as simple as sitting alone for a while and focusing on my breathing, or going for a walk with some friends, enjoying the outdoors. It is also well known that gratitude is a great combatant of anxiety.[66] When we learn to be grateful for what we have, we are less inclined to be worried about what we lack. Gratitude keeps us healthier than moaning and complaining ever will.

We have a saying in health and social care, which I think is used across the whole of the public sector, when thinking about rolling out new projects. It is the phrase 'at pace and scale'. Those four words alone are, in my opinion, responsible for an enormous amount of overwhelm, burnout and low morale in our society. We need to stop doing everything so fast. As John Mark Comer implores us in his book *The Ruthless Elimination of Hurry*, we need to get into the slow lane, learn to rest, learn to take days off, learn to switch off so that we can be present to all that is around us.[67]

Love does not happen 'at pace and scale'. Slowing down allows us to take stock and reassess how we are doing in aligning with our core values. There is so much disconnect between the values we want to live by and how we are living. This is because of the sheer pace we run at. When we slow down, we take notice. When we take notice, we begin to see that we need to think about our resources very differently. If we are going to build a loving and kind world together, then we need to give space for relationship. This is the antidote to consumerism.

4)   *Connect* – In his book, *Fractured*, Jon Yates paints a devastating picture of just how divided our society has become. We are now divided, perhaps more than ever before across all categories: rich and poor, old and young, Labour and Tory, Brexit and Remain. The lines of division are racial, economical and educational, and the gaps are widening all the time. If you don't believe me, read his book – it's very provocative. Yates suggests that the reason we are so divided now is that we have destroyed any sense of a 'common life'. He suggests there are two main culprits for this. Firstly, we have chosen, almost entirely, to spend increasing amounts of time with 'people like me'. Secondly, the sheer pace of transformational change has left us with little that

connects us. The growing distance and difference between us (geographically, sociologically, politically and economically) are causing us to become less healthy, less safe, less creative, less productive and less prosperous.[68]

Connection has therefore maybe never been so important. It's worth just noting how important friendship is to our wellbeing. We are living in an epidemic of loneliness. Loneliness leads to a huge increase in both physical and mental health problems. It is considered by medics to be as bad for a person's health as smoking. It leads to higher blood pressure, increased obesity, a weaker immune system, anxiety, depression, dementia and early death.[69] Yet 70% of people in the UK do not know their neighbour's full name.[70] One in five of us don't even feel we could call on any of our neighbours for help in a time of need. This is really sad.[71]

Social media was supposed to be this great connector of people around the world. It has left us *more* divided, increasingly siloed and even more entrenched in our own positions.[72] In fact, algorithms designed by the social media giants have cynically manipulated us, by targeting us and driving us towards more extremes.[73] More than ever, if we are to build a society with love at its core, we must pull on the power of friendship. But we must go further than just being friends with people who are 'like me'. In fact, to break our divides we must start by crossing over the road and choosing to build relationships with people who are fundamentally different to us. Only then can we start to heal our deeper wounds and find a new way forward for humanity together. More on this later.

5)   *Give* – Being generous with our time, gifts and resources is seriously good for us. It promotes social connection, reduces our blood pressure, reduces levels of stress and mental illness, and

leads to a happier and longer life.[74] However, rates of volunteering and associated clubs have fallen hugely over the last decade.[75] We are also becoming less generous with our money.[76] By giving to others, by caring for others, by loving others, we are doing ourselves good! It is a beautiful and virtuous cycle. As we give, we receive. We know this. Perhaps in our increasingly fractured world, we are forgetting it. It is well worth remembering and something we will look at again as we consider being cared for and caring for others.

6)   *Keep learning* – Keeping our minds active is excellent when it comes to improving our mental health and overall wellbeing. It can ward off dementia and help to connect us with other people.[77] Learning to dance, for example, has profound benefits to our physical and mental health.[78] So where is it in our school curriculums? Learning to play a musical instrument is likewise brilliant for health, wellbeing and cognition.[79] Learning a foreign language is also good for us and connects us to people who are by definition different to us.[80] Yet we see a demise of these things among our children and young people and across society as a whole. Learning new things is good for us and part of what it means to self-care.

7)   *Sleep* – Insomnia is on the rise and for those suffering, it is leading to more ill health.[81] Taking sleep seriously is vital for our wellbeing. Matthew Walker's book *Why We Sleep* lays out for us why sleep is such a vital part of our lives, why we need to stop fighting it and what we can do to improve it.[82] Sleep hygiene (looking after our bedtime routine) is a big part of helping us do this. Having a bedtime and sticking to it, turning off our screens for at least an hour before we want to sleep and practising relaxation before we go to bed can all help us embrace this restorative gift

to our bodies and minds. Letting our bodies rest is loving and kind, both to ourselves and those around us. We all know too well what it is like to try and live on too little of it. Our bodies really do need around eight hours per night for us to function at our best. So, guarding it needs to be a priority, though for parents of young children, this is easier said than done!

8)   *Have fun* – Do the stuff that makes your soul happy! Laugh more, go and watch some comedy, be a bit more childlike. Play some games, go to more parties, be silly, let your hair down, dance and sing like no one is watching and let life have a bit more zest to it! Life is not supposed to be dull and boring. It's OK to enjoy it. Maybe you just need to permit yourself to do that a whole lot more.

We can't go on simply excusing our own behaviours or patterns of thinking.

It is true that we are loved, just as we are. But love also requires us to change.

STRUTTING

Shortly after I qualified as a doctor, I was walking down the street one day in my dapper new suit, feeling quite pleased with myself, and strutting a little. From behind me came a voice of a chap called Adrian Nottingham, who was, until recently, serving as the

Mayor of Stockport, in Greater Manchester. Back then, he was a church pastor and something of a mentor to me. I waited for him, and we walked together for a little while exchanging niceties and catching up on life. As we were about to go our separate ways, he paused for a moment looked me in the eyes and said, 'Andy now you've got this new suit, and that stethoscope around your neck, just watch how you walk. Strutting really doesn't become you.'

I don't think I will ever forget that moment. In a moment of deep kindness and compassion for who I am, Adrian took the time to challenge me and confront my ego. He reminded me that arrogance is never a good look on anyone. He encouraged me to remember humility. The truth is that humility is vital if we are ever going to do our own internal work and become loving people. We have to confront our own ego, as we explored in Chapter 2. Humility allows us to do this and to keep on growing as people. To keep on doing our work even when it's painful. To seek help, to get therapy, to recognise where we are broken and allow ourselves to be healed, so that we can become more whole.

Paul, whom we met at the start of this chapter, realised that he had been getting too much of his self-worth from his work. Yes, there were significantly unjust external factors affecting him, which we will come to later. But first, he needed to invest in his own wellbeing, so that he could become a life-gift to others. This started by realising he'd hit rock bottom and asking for help. The starting place in learning to truly self-love, is humility. Paul's journey was not only about learning to love himself but about letting others love him too. Part of his stepping into the future was learning to stop having to fix the problems of all the kids in his school, burning out in the process. Instead, he had to learn to accept the help of others, including friends, family, therapists and colleagues. When we recognise that we need the love and help of others, that we're not supposed to try and be well on our own, then we can find our way to greater wholeness.

Come to love your true self

- *And so, what does this mean for you? What masks do you wear that stop you being humble, vulnerable and honest?*

- *Do you know that you are unconditionally loved, just for who you are? How do you know this? If you have children, do they know this too?*

- *What practices do you need to develop to better self-care?*

- *Does self-care lead to you being more selfish or more able to love others?*

- *Did you know that self-care is a kindness to those around you? In what ways can you see this outworking in your own life?*

When you learn to love your true self and therefore attend to and care for your whole self, you are more able to be a life-giving gift to your community and society as a whole.

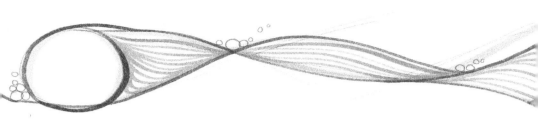

CHAPTER FOUR
LOVE RECEIVED

HUGGED

Peggy Hardcastle was a lady with some significant health issues. She came to see me fairly regularly and to be honest, there was not much I could do for her underlying condition. I could, however, try to help her manage some of the things it was causing. One day at the end of our consultation, she paused. She looked at me and thought for a moment. Then she said, 'Andy, do you mind if I ask you something?'

'Of course,' I replied, chirpily, though hoping to myself that it wasn't anything major, as I was already running late.

'Are you OK?' she asked.

'Wow, Peggy, I wasn't expecting that question. That is really kind of you to ask me. If I'm honest, I'm pretty weary. I'm working long hours; I'm not getting as much rest as I would like, and it feels relentless at times.'

I wasn't sure how appropriate my honesty was, but she slightly caught me off guard. So, I qualified it. 'That doesn't mean that I'm too busy for you, Peggy. I don't want you to think that you should not come and see me.'

'Oh no,' she replied in her warm, Wolverhampton accent, which always made me feel at home, 'I didn't take it that way. Would you mind if I gave you a hug?'

'That would be ever so kind. Thank you.'

And so, she did. A warm wholehearted hug. Then she put her hands on my shoulders and looked me in the eyes and continued.

'No, thank you. I want you to know that I'm grateful to you. And it's OK for you to receive that back from me. I also want to assure you of something. I am a Quaker. When I pause in a moment of quiet, I will hold you in the light.'

What a beautiful thing to be told. I love that idea of being held in the light.

It gave me such a sense of strength. One of the things people in the caring professions are very good at is caring for others. However, my experience tells me that they are generally very poor at recognising reciprocity. Simply being more aware of when our patients or clients are giving us care back can be restorative. It could be anything from a little wink to a gentle touch or a thank you card. Rather than just shrugging it off, taking a breath and letting it sink in is a positive experience.

I have found that being awake to this idea has improved my mental and physical health and increased my sense of work satisfaction. The truth is this doesn't just apply to doctors or other clinicians. **It applies to all of us.** If we allowed ourselves, we would recognise that **there are many words and actions of love towards us, which perhaps go unnoticed.** Acknowledging and accepting this is part of **letting ourselves be loved by others.**

LETTING OUR GUARD DOWN

Dave Higham is the Chief Executive of a LERO (a Lived Experience Recovery Organisation) called 'The Well Communities'. This LERO has some fantastic outcomes; as a director I have had the privilege of watching many people come through a journey of recovery from drug and alcohol addiction. Dave has a beautiful saying:

> *'We are going to love you,*
> *until you learn to love yourself because*
> *you can have a life beyond your wildest dreams.'*

I've seen dozens of people at absolute rock bottom utterly resist and then choose to allow themselves to be loved. I've witnessed their journey through the 12-step programme,[83] with no judgement from the team, who themselves have walked the same journey. Each of them testifies to the power of love, something which many of them have never previously experienced.

REVISITING ACES

Having the humility to let our guard down and admit our need for the love of others takes real courage.

When we consider Ricky whom we met in Chapter 2, and the deep impacts of trauma in his life, we find someone who had (understandably) built up so many walls, that he had no idea how to let anyone love him. The consequences were devastating. Psychologist and advisor to the Scottish Government, Professor Warren Larkin has done some important studies into enabling people to talk about their adverse childhood experiences (ACEs) or trauma with a trusted health professional. His REACh study (Routine Enquiry about Adversity in Childhood) found that simply giving someone the space to talk about their own story and the things they went through in childhood can have a hugely positive effect on their wellbeing.[84]

When we tell a trusted other about our own traumas, it breaks the cycle of shame. It makes us feel heard, validates the difficulty of our experience, and breaks down the walls of self-protection we have built. It enables us to dare to receive the love we crave but are wary of.

Many of us, who have experienced difficult things in childhood and adolescence, never talk about them. Sometimes that's because we can't remember the experiences – they happen to us before our memories fully form. However, more frequently we bury them or hide them away because we don't want to talk about the deeply painful realities. Maybe we don't know how to, or we're worried about what might happen to us, or to the people who caused us the pain if we do. How do you start a conversation like that anyway? Are you going to just blurt it out to someone? What on earth will you do if you just start crying in the middle of a restaurant when you talk to your girlfriend/boyfriend/partner/friend about what happened to you? What about all those complicated associated feelings of shame, guilt, fear, thoughts of rejection? So, we keep the lid on, even though it's to our own detriment because we don't know how to bring it into the open.

And herein lies the starting place. It's vital that we learn this in the world of health and social care, but we all need to hear this incredible truth. Various studies have shown that it takes 9–16 years for people to be able to talk about trauma/abuse they experienced, but most never do. Psychiatrists Read and Fraser have been cited as finding that of their patients struggling with mental health issues, only 8% of them volunteered that they had experienced ACEs. However, when they were deliberately asked about their life story, 82% then talked about ACEs.[85]

We find it almost impossible to speak about without help, but when someone asks us about what we have lived through, it peels the sticking plaster off the deep wound and allows us to begin talking about our pain. And here's something remarkable. Dr Vincent J. Felitti found in a study of 140,000 people that simply by routinely asking all patients about ACEs, they saw significant reductions in visits to the GP and in the use of the emergency department by those people.[86]

What does that mean?

It means that **giving someone the chance to talk about their journey,** what they have been through, breaking the cycle of shame, fear and rejection is, in and of itself, **deeply healing.**

Knowing that you're not a freak, knowing that it wasn't your fault, knowing that it doesn't mean that you yourself will become an abuser/alcoholic/poor parent; many more realisations can make a significant difference to a person's wellbeing. Maybe it doesn't have to wait for a GP surgery or a counsellor's chair. Maybe, just maybe if we all allow ourselves to be cared for and care enough to ask each other deeper and more caring questions, we can help to heal each other. I know this is true of my own journey and that of many of my friends.

But let's not be naive. For some of us, the experiences we have had are so horrific that we are stuck in a moment, and we can't get out of it. This is where good therapy comes in. I wonder if we invested more in therapy and less in drugs to numb our pain, how much more healed we might be – perhaps more expensive in the short term, but overall, the cost is far less, both for the individual and society as a whole. Medication is helpful though, and as a doctor, I see it as a useful option. Therapeutic help can take many forms. Unfortunately, many of the waiting lists are very long, and private options are too expensive for most people to afford. Funding into both prevention and treatment is hugely important. However, getting to the place where we are willing to face up to the pain of our own journeys and receive the care of others is a vital step to building a more loving society.

But we don't need to have walked through a major trauma to recognise that we need the love of others. Throughout my life, I can see how many people have loved me, even when I was my most difficult or proud self. My opinions and perspectives have been changed so much by people who have chosen to reach across the divides that I myself, or our society have created. **When we allow ourselves to be loved by those who are different to us, we enter into the possibility of being made new.**

THE GOOD SAMARITAN

Perhaps the most famous story of all about what it means to be loved by our 'other' is one told by Jesus of Nazareth, recorded in the Gospel of Luke. Here I am quoting from a translation of the Bible called *The Message*:

There was once a man traveling from Jerusalem to Jericho. On the way he was attacked by robbers. They took his clothes, beat him up, and went off leaving him half-dead. Luckily, a priest was on his way down the same road, but when he saw him he angled across to the other side. Then a Levite religious man showed up; he also avoided the injured man.

A Samaritan traveling the road came on him. When he saw the man's condition, his heart went out to him. He gave him first aid, disinfecting and bandaging his wounds. Then he lifted him onto his donkey, led him to an inn, and made him comfortable. In the morning he took out two silver coins and gave them to the innkeeper, saying, 'Take good care of him. If it costs any more, put it on my bill — I'll pay you on my way back.' What do you think? Which of the three became a neighbor to the man attacked by robbers? The one who treated him kindly, the religion scholar responded.

Jesus said, Go and do the same. (emphasis added)

Luke 10:30b–37

Here I attempt a retelling of it in modern British society. Once there was a man called Clive. He was a happy go lucky guy and loved nothing more than enjoying a few beers with his mates before watching Millwall play football. He loved to sing at the top of his voice in the stadium but didn't agree so much with this taking the knee malarkey, in fact he had booed players from the stand when they did so.

Clive had no problem with having what he thought of as a bit of a joke after matches. He would sometimes put horrendous racist comments on social media feeds, under a pseudonym. One night, after watching England play against the Netherlands at Wembley with the St George's flag painted on his face and his England shirt proudly on his back, he was wandering back home. On the way, he got jumped by a group of guys. He was stabbed, left unconscious bleeding by the side of the road. He'd had a baseball bat to his head and was in a bad state. The gang of youths ran off not caring how he was, but £50 richer and with a mobile phone to sell.

Along the road came a local councillor. She saw Clive, lying in the street, but thought he was just very drunk – tutted to herself, made some internal assumptions about him – and walked on her way, checking that no one else was watching her. Then a retired vicar walked along. He was in a huge hurry because he was on his way to help at a homeless shelter and was already late. He thought to himself, 'I can't be any later. The queue for the soup kitchen will be massive by now and they need a Good Samaritan too,' and so he ran past, pretending not to see.

A couple of minutes later a taxi pulled up and out jumped a man called Abdul. He was a first-generation refugee who had escaped Afghanistan during the terror of the Taliban because he wanted his daughters to have an education. He pulled Clive into the back of his cab, leaving blood stains all over the seat and drove him to the nearest emergency department. They were met by a nurse from Poland. She would soon be returning there, as her husband could no longer find work in the UK, and they could not afford to stay. This would leave the hospital with an even worse staffing problem. She assessed the situation quickly and soon Clive was in a bed in the resus area being checked over by David, a trans male doctor. Together these people, all of whom Clive had deeply prejudiced views about, saved his life.

MISSING THE POINT

We are encouraged to be Good Samaritans. To be those who will go out of our way to help others, even those that many would walk by or refuse to help. We are encouraged to be do-gooders, to be model citizens, to show charity and help the weak.

The theologian Samuel Wells, who has spent much of his life working amongst the poorest communities both in Philadelphia and now in London, contradicts this usual interpretation. In his book *A Nazareth Manifesto*, he argues that the point Jesus was trying to make here was not that we should be like the Good Samaritan. *Rather, we are, in fact, like the man beaten up on the road.* 'You are in the gutter. You are stripped, beaten, and half dead. Stop pretending.'[87]

Whether we choose to recognise it or not we each have our own brokenness, our own pain, lying helpless by the side of the road and desperately in need of our 'other' to help transform and save us.[88] For some of us, this takes the form of trauma that needs healing. For others of us, it is behaviour patterns we can't break free of. For all of us it is rooted in fear and shame. Fear that we might be found out and rejected. Shame that causes us to believe we are, at our core, unlovable. So, we wear masks to conceal the naked truth about ourselves, hoping we might be somehow accepted by those around us.

The invitation of love is to let our guard down, to take our mask off, so that we can allow ourselves to be accepted truly as we are. Only when we are humble enough to recognise our own sickness and weakness, can we begin our own journey into true humanity. It is only when we **stop trying to project an image of ourselves** to those around us which seems somehow more palatable and **allow ourselves to be loved and embraced just for who we are, that we can become fully human and agents of this same kind of love.**

Allowing ourselves to be loved means letting our walls down. Accepting we are weak requires humility and vulnerability. This takes courage. Without it though, we deny our own deepest need. And so, we risk significant burnout. We risk missing out on life itself. However, if we are awake to the possibility of love, then we find we can receive it from a myriad of people, in multiple ways. Peggy, who has since very sadly died, helped me to remember this. I will miss her hugely and am very grateful for the life lesson she taught me.

Peggy is her real name. Her family wanted me to tell her story and I am glad to remember her in this way.

I will
hold you
in the
light...

- Are you able to recognise yourself as the person beaten up on the side of the road?

- How do you feel about your own weakness and vulnerability?

- How does it feel for you to receive love from others?

- If you find it difficult to receive love, why is this so? When did you last pause to recognise the love someone gave you?

- What stops you allowing yourself to receive love from others who are not like you?

- How might you let your barriers down?

- How much more might your emotional tank be filled if you let others love you just for who you are, without the need for pretence?

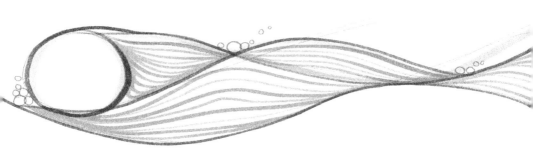

CHAPTER FIVE
LOVE GIVEN

BRUISED

Zoya seemed distracted. She'd come to see me to review her medication, but she was not her usual chatty self. Zoya is amazing – one of those women who everyone respects. She has this big, broad smile and a real zest for life. But not today. Today she seemed beaten, maybe even downtrodden. I asked her what was wrong.

The previous evening, her fourteen-year-old daughter, Miryam was out in town, getting a McDonald's. She was attacked by a gang of boys, from their own neighbourhood. They put her on the floor, repeatedly kicking her and calling her racist names. Zoya was seething and deeply hurt. They were making out like the Manchester bombings were somehow her fault. That she was a jihadi simply because she was wearing a hijab.

'How is it like this? Why do the papers print such rubbish about us?' Zoya asked. 'Why is so much hatred stirred up? That man, who did such terrible things. He was no true Muslim. Anyone who prays, or attends mosque, they would not think that way. Miryam was born here. She is a British citizen. She went to school with these boys. How can this be happening?' There was such exasperation in her voice.

'I am so sorry, Zoya. I don't know what to say. This should not be your experience. You should not have to feel like this. I am especially sorry for Miryam. Is she OK?'

'She is shaken up. She has a few bruises, nothing too bad. But she feels so confused. She just can't understand what happened.

She has been crying and crying. She was supposed to be out celebrating with her friends. She never saw this coming. I mean, over the years, there have been bits of name calling. But school have always been great. They've been straight in there with helpful interventions. Nothing like this though. Where has this come from?'

'What will you do? Have you called the police?' I asked.

'I have, but there is no CCTV and unless Miryam is willing to report them, there is little they can do. She doesn't want to do that – she thinks it will make things worse. And right now, I'm inclined to agree. I will have to deal with it myself.'

'Oh, OK. Do you have a plan?'

'I do. I'm going to love them. I'm going to knock on their doors this evening – they know me, and I know their mothers. I'm not going to give into fear. So, I'm going to invite them all to my house for a BBQ tonight. I believe in love, and I believe in accountability. So, we will eat together and then we will talk around the fire. You know me. I'm a community builder. And you don't build community by building up walls of hate. But you also have to have difficult conversations because without truth we are never really free to love. If we are ever going to all live well together, then we must choose truth and then we have to choose forgiveness. What other way is there?'

I was blown away. What an amazing woman!

Racism and racist abuse are well and truly on the rise in the UK. It is a stain on our life together and needs to be rooted out. Hate crimes against Muslims and Jews are significantly worsening.[89] The more we become entrenched in our siloed communities amongst people 'just like me', the worse it becomes. We live in a divided society. Our society is sick because people are divided. We do not love one another. **We are love sick.**

What Zoya did was remarkable. She made a conscious and deliberate choice to love against what her heart would have naturally wanted to do. However, what she chose led to something far more restorative for her community than she would have dared to believe or imagine. It took her some serious guts to go knocking on the doors of the boys who had done this to her precious girl. She had to hold her hands tightly behind her back so that she didn't slap them across the face when she saw them. She fought the tears back as she invited them over and watched their faces redden as they realised; they were found out. But as she and her husband sat round the fire with those young men, and they shared their story of what it was like to be them in their community, something changed. These youths received a kind of love and grace they were entirely unused to. It didn't fit with their understanding of how life works.

Zoya told me that each of them had eyes filled with tears and they each apologised to Miryam in turn. Miryam and her parents were able to forgive them. They also asked them to change. Those young men received something truly beautiful from Zoya and her husband. Something we don't hear about that often these days. They received mercy. It turns out that their merciful approach had transformative power. Not only did they learn something profound, but Miryam was able to walk around feeling safer, knowing that she had four people with a new understanding and respect of her.

BECOMING A GOOD SAMARITAN

Once we have owned our own brokenness and need of the 'other', we have the opportunity to become like the Good Samaritan. However, until we learn that we are unconditionally loved, (perhaps by ourselves, perhaps by others, perhaps by God,) we will continue to operate from our false self because we feel a need to prove ourselves. Unfortunately, and perhaps unwittingly, this leads to the oppression of others because we feel the need to compete with or dominate them. But once we know we are loved, we are able to love ourselves in a way that enables us to deny ourselves and give ourselves for the sake of others. Having been transformed by compassion, we become able to cross the road, and love the one who might be most difficult for us to embrace. This is what it means to love our enemies. When we learn to love each other like this, we can begin to create real wellness together in society.

Surely our hope for every person is that they can become true to who they are and a gift to those around them. **Deep, connected relationships – that is what community is about.**

It's fairly easy to love others who are like us. Not always, for sure, but loving others comes naturally to most of us. We fall in love; we love our parents or caregivers (even when that relationship is abusive – at least until we wake up to the cost of it). We love our families and our friends. We tend to love people who are like us and there is even evolutionary hardwiring that makes it so. In fact, we are more likely to help them out too. Loving people who are not like us, who are other to us, who are mean to us or who are our enemies – this is much harder.

This is costly love. A deep, conscious, gutsy choice kind of love. Love then is an act of the will, an action – it does something.

THE POWER OF FORGIVENESS

A few years ago, I had the privilege of doing some work in Sierra Leone. Whilst there, I met a remarkable young man called Idrees. He was seventeen years old and living in an orphanage. Most of the other children in the orphanage were severely disabled and had profound learning disabilities, but not Idrees. He was tall, eloquent and handsome, but had a severely disfigured right hand.

During the appalling war, which happened when he was just 18 months old, his village was raided by the Liberian troops. To save his life, his parents hid him in a bush hoping to come and rescue him at a later stage whilst they hid. Both his parents were massacred along with the rest of their village and when the troops discovered Idrees, for some inhuman reason, they took his right hand and plunged it into boiling oil. Left alone to cry, he was eventually found and united with a great aunt, who realised that given his disability, he would never be able to contribute to the economy of the household. So, when he was around five years old, she left him on the streets to beg. He was found by a social worker and taken to the orphanage where I met him, some 12 years later. I talked with him as I examined his hand and asked him what he wanted to do when he was older. He looked me straight in the eyes as he replied:

'I want to be a peace builder. I want to work for the UN. I want to go and work in Israel and Palestine. I want to help people know that it is possible to forgive. It is possible to be reconciled and live well together.'

I remember my eyes filling with tears instantly at such a remarkable statement. Here was a young man left disabled and outcast from his community by people who killed his parents, and yet he had found a way not only to forgive them but was determined to help others learn how to do this too.

'You see,' he continued, 'what hope is there for peace if we do not forgive? We have had to learn that here, in Sierra Leone. Hatred and bitterness will only ever lead to more fighting. Who wants to live like that? What good will ever come of it? Besides, I am a Christian. And when Jesus said we are to love our enemies, I think he meant it.'

I was deeply humbled.

LEARNING TO FORGIVE

There are many times when people come to see me as a GP, and I cannot find a physical cause for their pain. There are various other conditions when people have what we call 'medically unexplained symptoms'. For others, they can get stuck in a rut with their mental health and feel unable to get out of it.

In the West, we are not as comfortable as we might be in dealing with the concept of spiritual health. Our spirit, the true essence of who we are, can also suffer damage and ill health, which in turn can lead to physical and psychological manifestations of that same pain. One of the things I have seen time and again as one contributing factor is when someone is finding it difficult to forgive a past hurt. There is good evidence that forgiveness can help improve our physical, mental and spiritual health.[90] I wonder how much more healed we would be as people and as a society if we made the choice to forgive more readily.

Love enables us to forgive. And love is not a gooey emotion. It **costs** us. It is a **gritty** and **courageous choice.** But when we make that choice, it sets us free from bitterness to choose life and sets the one who has hurt us free to receive life, even if we perceive they are deserving of something less.

So, how do we do it? Well, it is a conscious choice.

More to Life[91] has outlined a helpful six-step process, which can be used if one is struggling to forgive. This can be used with a person face to face or done alone. It can be especially important if the person who you need to forgive has already died or you are not in contact with them. I have adapted it here:

1. Visualise the person – either sit with the person or sit in a room by yourself (or with a friend to help you) and visualise

the person you need to forgive in an empty chair opposite you.

2. Vocalise – say out loud the reason why you have been resenting this person. 'I have been resenting you for ...' This is different to 'you made me feel ...' This is an opportunity to factually state what it is that they did which hurt you. Naming our pain is important.

3. This step is difficult. It is an invitation to recognise why you have been holding onto your resentment. The truth is, we only hold on to unforgiveness because we gain something from it in some way. Maybe it allows us to continue with our hate or anger. Maybe it allows us to justify certain behaviours we have developed as a result, but here is the next statement: 'The gain for me in not forgiving you has been ...'

4. Then it's time for the reverse. 'The cost to me of not forgiving you has been ...' And this could be a number of things. It could be a manifestation of your emotional pain as physical pain, which you have carried in your body. It might be that you've not allowed anyone else to get close to you and so you have a deep sense of loneliness. Perhaps you've felt angry for years and it's just held you back from so much.

5. Then, a hard line. 'Please forgive me for not forgiving you until now.'

6. Finally, 'I forgive you.'

I have seen many of my patients and friends walk this journey over many years. Every time it is both internally and externally transformational. If it's needed in your life, I hope you find it helpful.

One patient of mine recently fed back to me that she realised that before she forgave anyone else, she needed to forgive herself. She felt deep shame and anger towards herself for some of her own choices. So, she practised the forgiveness process in the mirror. She described it as life-changing. She learned to look at herself as someone who deserved compassion for the mistakes she had made. Self-care begins with self-compassion. It's OK to be kind to ourselves. Learning this enables us to practise the same for others.

If we are going to **love people,** especially our other or our enemy, I believe there are **two key practices** that we need to develop. **The first is forgiveness,** both for ourselves and those who have hurt us, as we've discussed. **The second is learning to cross the divide.**

CROSS OVER THE ROAD

The story of the Good Samaritan reminds us that every human being is our neighbour, no matter what their gender, sexuality, politics, religion or race may be. Loving them is a big part of becoming fully human ourselves. In our increasingly ghettoed, siloed and divided society, we need to cross over the road deliberately to build relationships with those who are other to us.

Here in Morecambe Bay, there is a beautiful movement among women, called 'East meets West'. In the aftermath of 9/11 and the 7/7 bombings, a woman called Liz Bagley was concerned that Muslim women in our City of Lancaster, might be getting a rough deal. She had absolutely no Muslim friends and in 2005, having recently retired as a teacher, she visited a local school and asked if any of the Muslim mums would be willing to have a coffee with her. Ruqsana, a mother of five children was willing to do so. She told Liz about how it felt to be a Muslim woman in the UK and together they decided that things needed to change.

As a result of this cup of coffee in 2005, a thriving group now exists which bridges cultural, ethnic, religious, national, political, philosophical, economic and educational boundaries. Women have established loving friendships which have stood the test of time and are bringing real healing across the dividing lines of our society.[92] The group creates a deep sense of mutual respect and welcome for new people arriving in the city region especially for refugees and asylum seekers, who experience generous hospitality. It is staggering how one cross of a dividing line can have such a beneficial and catalytic effect.

My own experience teaches me that we are most changed and learn to love most when we are willing to encounter our 'other' and really listen to them. When this happens, we learn to see them as human, and we begin to think differently about them. We start to care about the injustices they are experiencing.

The word 'conversation' has the same root as the word 'conversion'. When we listen and talk with those different to us, we are both changed in the process.

Getting to know our 'other' doesn't mean that we will all become the same. We can live together well in a world which celebrates our diversity and difference without there being lines of division. Love enables this to be possible. I am not a relativist. I don't believe that all beliefs are the same. As a Christian, for example, I don't believe what my Muslim or Sikh or atheist friends believe. But that doesn't mean that I can't be friends with them, or that I can't be challenged, changed or encouraged by them. On the contrary, my faith for example, has become deeper, more real, more honest and humbler as a result. Love of the other doesn't cause us to lose our sense of identity; it strengthens and shapes it. I am, only because I am in relationship. I exist in the context of community. If everyone in that community was just like me and saw the world as I do, how boring would that be? My faith celebrates and finds meaning in the context of difference.

DARE TO DREAM

Of course, **there is huge love at work in our world each and every day.** We see it and experience it everywhere. It is, without a doubt, the most powerful force there is. People are loving each other and this beautiful earth we co-habit together, against the odds, every single day. All life flows from it.

So let us dare to imagine together a world that is determined by it.

We start by learning to love ourselves for who we truly are, not who we want others to believe us to be. When we face up to the root issues in our lives and dismantle our ego structures and projections, we become our true selves in the process. We become life-giving spirits, transformed by love itself. Humility, vulnerability and authenticity, practised with wisdom and self-compassion allows us to do this. They also help us to view others with kindness, recognising the pain, privilege, trauma and complexities of each other's journeys. This allows us to both be loved by others and love others across the dividing lines of our society. Zoya's example encourages us, not only to believe it, but to see how it is possible!

Love as the foundation stone

- *How many friends do you have, who are genuinely different to you?*

- *Have you formed opinions about certain people groups, based on what the media or reality TV feeds you?*

- *Have you formed opinions about trans people and their place in society without knowing anyone who is transgender?*

- *If you consider yourself to be White British, how many Muslim friends, for example, do you have?*

- *Have you ever bothered to understand a bit about Islam? Just as with Christianity, in Islam although the core beliefs are the same, there are a variety of theological, cultural and national perspectives, which can have a profound effect on how it is practised. And yet as a group, Muslims are generally tarred with the same brush by certain parts of the media. How might you need to challenge your own views?*

- *Are you aware of your own privilege and prejudice that both consciously and subconsciously cloud your ability to see people as they really are? If not, and you care about building a more loving and kind society, maybe it's time to cross over the road and do some listening. It will be good for your health and wellbeing. Could we dare to hope for a more loving world?*

- *Would you dare to imagine with me what it would be like if we placed love as the foundation stone of how we do life together?*

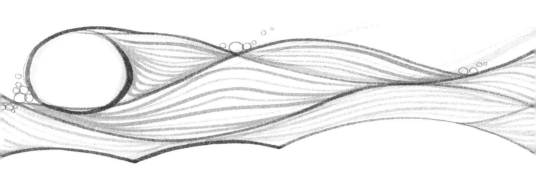

CHAPTER SIX
LOVE DIGNITY

UNDIGNIFIED

It was time for my lunchtime ward round of one our local nursing homes. I looked through the list of the usual suspects the sister wanted me to see and noticed a new name. Elsie, ninety-three years old. She had been discharged from hospital the day before. The nursing staff from the home reported that she'd had a fresh bleed from her back passage and would require an examination.

Bleeding from the back passage may be caused by several different factors. It might be as simple as a haemorrhoid, something more complicated, like diverticulitis or colitis, or perhaps a more sinister problem, like bowel cancer. I would need to examine her and take some stool samples and blood tests to send to the lab. I therefore made sure that I had gloves, KY jelly and an apron in my bag and I set off.

Thankfully, Moorland View is a good quality nursing home, run by an excellent nurse manager, Molly, who knows every patient by name. Molly knows each story, knows the family and their situation, and has a thorough care plan, including resuscitation status. This means she knows whether a person or their power of attorney wants them to have cardiopulmonary resuscitation, should their heart stop beating. Molly was busy talking with a family when I arrived. So, Angela, one of the other nurses took me around.

When we arrived in Elsie's room, she was lying on her bed. She had muscle wastage, contracted limbs and was doubly incontinent. I explained to Angela and the care assistant, Jodie, that I would need to examine her. This would mean I would need to feel her tummy and also inside her rectum.

Although she couldn't understand me, I introduced myself to this little, elderly lady. I explained what I would need to do. I asked her to let me know if anything was hurting her. The nursing staff kindly helped to calm Elsie, and carefully helped me to position her. We wanted to be as respectful and kind as possible, for what is quite an undignified examination at the best of times. Firstly, I gently palpated her tummy. Then we rolled her onto her side. I had a look around her back passage. She had some external haemorrhoids. I gently and carefully inserted my gloved and lubricated finger inside her rectum and tried to feel for anything concerning. She was very constipated, and the rectum was full of faeces. I couldn't feel much else, other than hard stool.

As I withdrew my finger, some of her poo flew out of her bottom and hit me on the forehead! Splat! Angela and Jodie tried to keep straight faces, but then both had a fit of the giggles.

'Please wipe my face!' I begged. 'Sorry love,' replied Angela, 'did you say something?' 'Oh dear, Angela,' giggled Jodie. 'He seems to be shit-faced!'

They were both roaring with laughter. They weren't being unkind. Sometimes, working in these environments can be pressurised and when something funny happens, however inappropriate, laughter can be a vital outlet. So, peeling my gloves off carefully, I went and got paper towels for myself and gave my face and hands a really good wash.

Elsie's stool samples and blood tests came back OK. I treated her constipation, which was giving her overflow incontinence. The next time I saw her, she was visibly more comfortable.

A DIGNIFIED END?

In 2022, there were over 400,000 people living in care homes in the UK, supported by over 750,000 staff.[93] In recent years, various news reports have detailed some harrowing stories of poor and inappropriate treatment of elderly citizens in both nursing and residential care homes. However, my experience is that incredible care and love is given to people towards the end of their lives by people who are paid very little for long hours and emotionally difficult work.

I know from experience in my own family, the trauma and tiring work involved in caring for someone who has dementia and how it becomes impossible without the significant support of home care, or indeed admission to a care home. I have also seen so many of my elderly patients become full-time carers for their loved ones, with very little effective support around them. This leads to exhaustion and increased risk that they too become much more unwell in the process of providing care.

Elsie had been living in a residential home, prior to her admission to hospital. But her care needs were far too great for her to remain in residential care. So, following her discharge from hospital she had been assessed as needing a nursing home placement. She arrived with a DNACPR (do not attempt cardiopulmonary resuscitation) form in place, but no care plan had been handed over. This would take a week or two to put in place.

Advanced dementia is a palliative illness. There is no cure for it. A few weeks after I first met her, Elsie developed a chest infection. She was seen by the out of hours GP over a weekend and started on some antibiotics. But when I saw her on the Monday lunchtime, it was clear that she was deteriorating.

I was faced with the choice about whether to try and treat her with yet another, slightly stronger set of antibiotics, admit her back into hospital, or to let the infection take its course. I didn't feel more oral antibiotics would work. She was very weak. What good would a further trip to hospital be? Perhaps it would prolong her life by a few weeks. But it was more likely that she would die on a hospital ward, cared for by people who have never really known her. Or worse still, she might end her days on a hospital trolley in the corridor of the emergency department. Withdrawing treatment would mean that Elsie would die peacefully with dignity, and we could support her well whilst this naturally took place.

I spoke with her niece, Carol, who lived over 200 miles away. We talked about her quality of life and the recurrent nature of these infections. We talked about the kind of lady that Elsie was before her dementia and what she would have wanted. We agreed that we would not give the antibiotics and that we would care for her well as she died. Elsie died two days later, without pain, as Carol held her hand. When I saw her to verify her death, Elsie's face seemed relieved.

Elsie calls us to pay attention. Here was an elderly woman, who had previously been a formidable head teacher. Now she was emaciated, unable to make any free choices. She was unable to feed herself, unable to manage her own bowels or bladder, unable to communicate, lonely for many hours each day and cared for by people she had never met before. This did not make her life unworthwhile. And indeed, she gave the opportunity for the best of humanity to be found through those who cared for her. People are not valued or valuable because of what they do or how much they contribute to the economy. People are loved, simply because they are. This is why we care so intently for our children who live with profound disabilities.

Covid-19 has, perhaps, awoken us all to the fragility of our own lives. There has been a corporate awakening to the reality of our mortality. In his brilliant book *Being Mortal*, Atul Gawande explores the complex situation we find ourselves in.[94] We are in danger of focusing so much on having a long life that we fail to give enough thought to the importance of having good deaths. Death does not need to be filled with fear or pain. It is the one certainty which faces us all.

I want to make it clear that I am not a proponent of euthanasia. I think it is fraught with complexities and difficulties. I do understand the arguments made in favour and have huge sympathy for them. However, if we're going to apply an ethic of love and care around the end of life, we need to ensure that we have a much more grown-up discussion about the reality of death. We need to think much more about the quality of someone's life rather than quantity of it. We need to ensure we allow people to die well with excellent palliative care. Our hospices must therefore be adequately funded.[95]

There is nothing wrong with allowing death to take its course at the right time, rather than prolonging life, simply because we can. Allowing people to die naturally, would help us with some of our social care crisis, whilst providing better and more compassionate care. Just because we can give recurrent courses of antibiotics for urinary tract infections or chest infections in the elderly with dementia, doesn't necessarily mean that we *should* do so. When people with advanced dementia are becoming more unwell in a nursing home or residential care setting, perhaps we shouldn't be so readily admitting them to hospital. Rather, we should have more active care plans in place, based on and respecting the autonomy of the person concerned. These now form part of routine care in England, but perhaps they are not explicit enough in many cases. Care planning needs to be done early to ensure we are able to respect a person's wishes in their final weeks and days of life. We need to recognise that people can die well whilst being loved and cared for without prolonging life unnecessarily.

Our society is sick because people are sick and are sometimes prevented from dying with dignity.

One of the important roles of GPs and nurse practitioners in community settings is to ensure that our elderly citizens have compassionate and caring discussions about their wishes surrounding their own deaths. But as death can sometimes be sudden or unexpected for any of us, it's worth us all having more conversations about this. I have cared for many people who have died far too young. This is always difficult and heart wrenching. But even when the conversations are painful and filled with sadness, we need to think about how we die well.

One way to do this, for example, is through a Death Cafe.[96] For many this might sound like an odd name and an unfamiliar concept. However, several of these are held every year around the UK. We need to ensure that financial and spiritual needs are thought about and planned for so that when death approaches, as it must for all of us, this happens in a way which is good for the person themselves, their family and professionals or friends who care for them. I can tell you from experience it makes it far less distressing and more compassionate to do it this way.

Social care provision, especially for our elderly citizens, remains poorly funded and often inadequately provided. Those who can afford it get a lovely lot, whereas many families are left struggling for help. Although the social care system in the UK, is as old as the NHS, it has received a far more meagre slice of the funding cake. In fact, funding fell by around 10% during the years of austerity economics,[97] making it an even deeper hole to climb out from. As a result, the care home market is unstable. There are significantly less nursing home beds available in the UK than there were ten years ago.[98] However, the proportion of our elderly population, as a percentage of the whole, is rising.[99] We have failed to plan adequately for this moment, and it is putting huge pressure on the NHS and social care system. We must now face it together.

In the meantime, beautiful new initiatives are on the rise to ensure people can die well and with dignity, surrounded by love. The Compassionate Communities Network[100] in Scotland is gaining real traction and is spreading to other parts of the UK. Compassionate Inverclyde, for example, describes itself as a movement built on kindness. Community members have an on-call system to ensure that no one in the district dies alone. They also put together boxes of helpful and practical items for whenever someone who lives alone is discharged home from hospital. It started because a lady called Alison felt passionate about the issue, began to challenge the inevitability of the situation, and dared to imagine how it could be different. Soon people joined her, and it has become an incredible force for good.

But people with lots of other commitments don't have time to pick up the full care burden being asked of them, due to a social care system that simply isn't working. There are no easy solutions to this conundrum. There is no way that someone like Elsie could have been cared for at home. But there are alternatives for many people, with the right kind of care planning in our communities.

DIGNITY IN OLDER AGE

In a loving society, we do not just want our elderly citizens to have a 'good death'. Rather, we want them to age well and to be honoured later in life.

Sir Muir Gray has done some wonderful work in recent years, pioneering the Live Longer Better course through the Optimal Ageing Programme.[101] As we grow older, our muscles become weaker, and so activity is important to help us maintain strength. Social isolation also becomes far too common. So, belonging to various groups and having plenty of hobbies becomes all the more important. Volunteering, contributing wisdom and love to the rising generations, becomes a beautiful point of reciprocity. Community and/or dementia choirs can be a great source of joy. Walking clubs and gardening groups, likewise, keep a sense of belonging. Faith groups host many activities for older citizens and are particularly able to bridge the divide of ethnicity and economic status.

Cities and towns themselves can become great places for elderly people to thrive. Greater Manchester, in the UK, is one example of an Age Friendly City.[102] This is a great aspiration for any city to reach towards and ensures that from conception to grave, life can be lived well.

We also need to think through the kind of environments our elderly citizens want to live in and what is affordable. Many of our elderly citizens struggle with the concept of residential and nursing homes from a cultural perspective.[103] If we are to see more people living in their own homes, we need to value care as a profession much more highly. We will also need to employ the use of household evidence-based technology more readily to help with issues around safety. From detecting falls and analysing faeces to prompting medication use, smart tech is gaining momentum.[104] However, this will not be without its challenges and must not replace the beauty of human contact and companionship. Whatever we develop, we have to solve the funding conundrum for social care somehow. This will have to be done through some form of taxation and that won't be easy for any of us to swallow. But we are living longer with more complex needs, and this costs us more than we are currently spending.

GENERATIONS TOGETHER

In the Netherlands, there have been successful experiments in multigenerational living for students in elderly residential homes. The students are able to live at a significantly decreased rent, in exchange for their help with care and daily living tasks. Both the students and older residents report that this improves their sense of wellbeing.[105] In both the USA and UK, there has been an explosion in the number of nursing homes opening their doors to pre-school children for a raft of activities, including reading, painting and singing.[106] Again, faith groups can also be places of great intergenerational cohesion, as found in the report on cohesive societies by the Faith & Belief Forum.[107] The Church of England has recently set out a radical reimagining of care, inspired by the Christian faith.[108]

More than ever, we need to bridge the generational gap. Our society is perhaps more divided than ever from the baby boomers to Generation X and millennials. This is not good for community cohesion and leads to greater prejudice and ageism.[109] We need to turn our hearts collectively to the elders. Likewise, we need the elders to turn their hearts towards the rising generation. The question for all of us, as we approach the later years of our lives, is what kind of legacy will we leave?

What does it mean for us to be good ancestors?

What does it mean for us to pour out our love for the next generation, so that our ceiling becomes their floor? Perhaps a gardening metaphor is better than a building one. So how does our seed ensure it bears fruit in a hundred years' time?

If we are to see life perpetuated in the flow of love through the generations, **we must live in such a way as to ensure that life flows through us.** We must **invest our wisdom, our time, our resources** and **our gifts** for the sake of those who follow us. Even if you do not believe in any kind of after life, surely you believe in the goodness of human and planetary life flourishing long into the future. So, how do we live well now to ensure this is the case?

Of course, some people have had to cut ties with the generation above or below them, due to abuse or other destructive behaviours. This is always difficult and costly and usually requires real bravery. The drawing of boundaries is a way of remembering to self-love, so that those affected can be a source of love for others and not drawn ongoingly into toxic relational dynamics. However, there remains something important about having other significant relationships across the generational divide.

Increasingly, we must develop ways of living well together. In particular, we should honour our elderly citizens and ensure they are cared for well in their later years so that when their time comes, they may die with dignity.

- *Why are intergenerational friendships important?*

- *Do you have any friends who are significantly older or younger than you, other than your family? If not, why not?*

- *How might we begin to repair some bridges and close the widening gap between the generations?*

- *How will we create a society of mutual respect?*

- *What can be done to create environments for storytelling, listening and learning from one another?*

- *Tough though it may be, if you are young(ish) have you ever had a conversation with anyone about what would happen if you died suddenly? If you were to die tomorrow, what kind of legacy would you leave? If you are in your later years, or living with the sad reality of a terminal illness, have you made a care plan with your GP?*

- *Have you had those difficult conversations with your family or loved ones about your wishes? Have you thought about what is important to you? Do you know what kind of funeral you would like? Have you made a will?*

- *Do those most important to you know that they are loved by you? Have you put right the things that you need to?*

- *Will you die knowing you are forgiven and that you have been forgiving?*

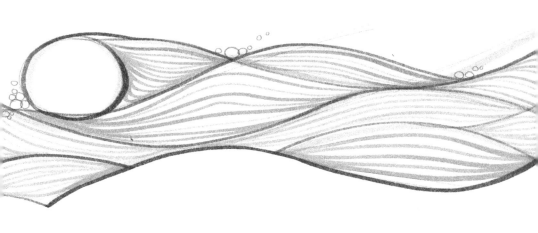

CHAPTER SEVEN
LOVE COMMUNITY

TERRIFIED

'Andy,' there was a knock at my door. 'I know you've finished your surgery, but I wonder if you could just see this lady. She seems really terrified.'

'Sure. Do you want to bring her in?' I responded.

Mary-Jo walked gingerly into my room. She was obviously in pain and winced as she sat down.

'Hello. How may I help you?' I asked.

'I was hoping for a lady doctor. Is there no lady doctor available?'

'I'm so sorry, not at this branch surgery, but I could book an appointment for you with a female GP tomorrow, if you'd prefer, at our larger site?' I offered.

'No, no, it's OK, doctor. I'm here now. I should have come much earlier. The thing is, doctor, it's my breast. It's terribly painful. Don't tell me it's anything serious.'

I asked some questions and listened as this fifty-seven-year-old woman told me more about how she was feeling. She'd first noticed a lump in her right breast around six months previously. She had tried to ignore it. But now she was in too much pain to do so any longer.

'Do you mind if I ask why you've waited so long to come and see us?' I enquired, gently.

'Well, the thing is, that when I was nine, I was having some problems down below and my Mam took us to see the GP. I had to lie down on his couch, and he pulled the curtain round. My Mam stayed on the other side. He sexually assaulted me. I just froze. I was terrified, petrified. He flashed me as well. Since that day, I have never let anyone see me naked – I've just felt too ashamed.'

'Oh Mary-Jo. I am so very sorry. That should never have happened to you. I don't know what to say. I am so sorry.'

'Well, I've never told anyone before. He's dead now – the bastard.'

It was no wonder that Mary-Jo had never trusted a doctor again. Here is an example of toxic masculinity, sexual exploitation, the abuse of power and its devastating effects.

She had also not attended any breast screening. This was in part due to her utterly awful experience at the hands of her abusive childhood GP. It was also because the Gypsy, Roma and Traveller community tend to have a lower take-up of breast screening than other ethnic groups,[110] which I will explore. It was also clear, given her pain, that I would need to examine Mary-Jo's breast. I expressed to her that I knew this would be difficult and might cause some unpleasant memories for her. With her permission, I asked one of our nurses, Lucy, to help as a chaperone. I gently explained to Mary-Jo exactly what a breast examination would entail. I explained that she could ask me to stop at any point if she felt uncomfortable. She gave her consent to go ahead. With Lucy's kind help, she undressed to her waist and lay down on the couch. We did all we could to help her relax.

As I peeled down the blanket, I could immediately see what we were dealing with. Her right breast had a fungating tumour, which was breaking through the skin. It looked incredibly sore. Her lymph nodes in her armpit were also prominent, a sure sign that the cancer had already spread. Lucy helped her redress and then sat down next to her as I talked through with her my concerns. A few days later she was seen in the breast clinic and the diagnosis of an advanced metastatic breast cancer was officially made. Six months later, she was dead.

If we allow ourselves to take a step back from this deeply troubling and heart-breaking story, we see a wider reality of the health inequalities being experienced across the UK. Although life expectancy has been increasing for those in our wealthiest communities, it is a different story for those in our economically poorest ones. The gap in healthy life expectancy is widening.[111] The Gypsy, Roma and Traveller community experience far worse health outcomes than many other communities.[112]

CO-CREATION

One of the things that has most helped in my role as an associate medical director, focused on population health, is to see how data can expose things in our communities that we are perhaps unaware of. By layering up data from multiple different sources including general practice, acute hospital trusts, mental health trusts, district councils, county councils and what was Public Health England, we can create quite extensive geographical maps of the kind of health issues our communities are facing.

One of the things we discovered in Lancaster and Morecambe, for example, was that Gypsy, Roma and Traveller women are significantly affected by breast and cervical cancer. They are dying from these cancers far earlier than other women in our communities. This is a social injustice.

We wanted to understand why they are not accessing the screening programmes available on the NHS. Smear tests can detect changes in the cells of the cervix before they ever become cancerous. Mammograms can pick up breast cancers before they become more problematic.

Rather than just coming up with a programme that we thought would make a difference, we decided to build a different kind of relationship with the women not accessing these services. We wanted to learn more about them and their customs and see how we needed to change our relationship with them and our approach to working with them. The Gypsy, Roma and Traveller community are one of the most stigmatised, misunderstood and racially abused communities in the UK.[113] They are the butt of many jokes[114] and huge assumptions are made about them and their customs without very much real understanding.

So, having taken the time to build some relationships, I met with some of the women from this community in a place they felt comfortable and listened to the issues they were facing. Then, with the help of the team at Co-create,[115] the Clinical Director of the Primary Care Network and a care co-ordinator, we shared with them some of the concerns we had around what the data was telling us. As we listened to their response, we gained some understanding of what it feels like to be so stigmatised as a community. We heard some of their concerns and fears about engaging with the health service at large. We learned about some very negative experiences and racist abuse they had suffered. We began to see why women from this community did not want to engage with health screening programmes.

For Gypsy, Roma and Traveller women it is vital to have a female doctor, with a definite sense of continuity of care so that trust can be established. We also did not realise that women would never discuss their own private health, particularly around gynaecological issues or breast health, in front of a male. This is just a taboo issue within their community. There was also a lack of awareness of what screening programmes fully entail, why they are important and how they can make a real difference. There are also quite high rates of illiteracy, due to low completion rates of education and so traditional NHS leaflets inviting them to appointments usually remain unread.

As we began to break down the barriers between us, we were able to include community leaders in helping us to begin to change this story. We worked with them to rethink and redesign how we could do things more effectively. We now have some real champions within this community who understand the issues involved and are working with us to ensure that our screening rates increase. Together, we can detect any issues sooner and prevent unnecessary early deaths. If we had not had inclusivity as a core value in how we worked, I doubt whether this would ever have changed. However, **the truth** is that most communities, **especially those who experience the worst health outcomes, are not included in decisions** made about the issues **which affect them most.**

HOW DOES YOUR GARDEN GROW?

It is rare for true social change to start from people in positional power. However, our communities are often desperate for social change and are full of excellent ideas about how this can happen. Unfortunately, they are often disregarded and thought of as part of the problem rather than being allowed to participate in the solution. The most dynamic social change maker I know is Professor Hilary Cottam. Her book, *Radical Help*, is an absolute must read for anyone who wants to participate in the work of social change in and through, not only the public sector, but society at large. The way that she worked in the town of Wigan – for example alongside then Chief Executive of the Council, Professor Donna Hall, former Leader of the Council, Lord Peter Smith, and previous Director of Public Health, Professor Kate Ardern – fundamentally changed the social fabric of that place.[116] Cottam's work is so extraordinary because it always starts with deep listening to communities. Her passion is to take the original hopes of the welfare state and make them fit for the twenty-first century.

In one very moving story in her book she talks about a small group of families who were high users of services, but frustratingly never seemed to change their behaviour.[117] This cost the public purse a lot of money. Cottam gathered into a room all the people who had worked with them over the previous decade. She asked them to map out all the different interventions that had been done with these families. It was a staggering amount of work, and an enormous cost financially but for almost no benefit. So, then Cottam and her team listened to those families and asked them what they wanted from life, what their dreams were and challenged the inevitability that their lives would always be stuck in a rut. Having done this, she began to ask them who they would need around them to support them to help them to find this way forward. Amazingly, they could identify four key professionals who they needed to have around them with a sense of consistency. It is often the case that social workers change on such a frequent basis that they never build a sense of relationship or trust with the families they are trying to help.

All of Cottam's work is based fundamentally on the principle of human relationship. This is why it is so powerful. Once the teams were established to work with these so called 'problem families', the changes began to take place. There was less petty crime, less fallout with neighbours, increased attendance at school, the parents were able to find work and stay in employment and their finances became more stable. These families stopped being considered a burden to society and found that they themselves could become net contributors. Interestingly and importantly, this way of working is also considerably cheaper!

In essence, Cottam is asking us to think differently about how we 'grow the good life', putting relationships at the heart of how we do this.[118] This leads us well into the imagery of growing a garden.

The truth is that communities are messy and complicated. As I write, I'm in the middle of a garden project. I know what I want my garden to be like, but it's not going to happen overnight. It takes some real careful thought and design. Not only do I need a plan – which I have to hold lightly, because of various unpredictable factors – I also require tons of patience! The garden I can see in my mind's eye will take years to flourish. That doesn't mean

I can't enjoy its beauty now. It still has many lovely aspects I can celebrate, whilst I get on with the work of participating with nature in cultivating of the space.

If we want life to flourish in our communities, we need to put down the spanners and hammers and pick up the trowels, forks and seed shakers!

We need to be much more proactive in how we create health and wellbeing together in our communities.

The good life includes being able to contribute to society and receive from it with a sense of reciprocity – giving and receiving. If we focused more on this principle of growing the good life in our communities how much fuller might our lives together be? To make this possible, Cottam implores us to be bold in our design, connect multiple forms of resource, create new possibilities and be open in our approach. By having **strong relationships** with the communities we serve, **really listening** to what their needs are and then thinking about how we **co-design and co-create solutions,** we will be able to meet these needs together with them.

Cottam is calling for much more relational and integrated care at every level of society. Her invitation is for us to stop and think about how disintegrated, disconnected, siloed and wasteful so much of our system working is. We need to unlearn some of our current methodologies and find more collaborative, connected and integrated ways of working. Recent legislation in health and social care is creating integrated care systems across England, trying to create environments in which local government, the NHS, the community, voluntary, faith sector and other key partners like the police and fire service, work together to serve the needs of the population. But we will not see the social change we need through public sector bodies alone.

NEW LEADERSHIP

The issues we are facing in society now are so complex and chaotic that we cannot keep trying to find solutions for them in our old methodologies. These are clearly failing us. The levels of destitution on our society are demonstrating this. The experience of Mary-Jo highlights just how broken things are. The injustice of this must surely make us outraged, cause us to challenge the inevitability and begin to create moral alternative economies together. This is going to take a new kind of leadership.

As the independent New Local think tank put it, 'We've tried a centralised, state-led approach. We've tried a privatised, market-led approach. They're not working. We need a new approach – empower communities to lead.'[119] But this will only work if those communities are loving. The old paradigm of white male patriarchal pyramidal leadership is entirely broken, defunct and ineffective for the future we so desperately need together.

We need to create a much more diverse, collaborative, collective, consensus-building, emotionally intelligent, kind, empathic, restorative, inclusive and anchored approach, **rooted in the creative commons.** This kind of leadership holds space for coalition building, holds steady the deep motivation to bring about real change and will allow us to build a loving society together.

A SOCIETY OF FRIENDS

Personally, I love the idea of being a Society of Friends. This is a title by which the Quaker movement is known but surely does not exclusively apply to them. Friendship, motivated by love, creates an incredibly strong environment in which we can tackle systemic injustice and find a new way through together. The early Quakers had three core principles of how they lived together, much like the earliest Christians.[120]

Firstly, they had a sense of *radical wonder or worship*. They had a childlike wonderment at God and/or the world around them, vital in bringing both a sense of gratitude and a deep awareness of the abundance available for all.

Secondly, they held a value for *radical justice*. In other words, they made sure that within their society of friendship, there was no one who lacked. They shared together, and when they died, they made sure that everyone had an equal tombstone.

In a Society of Friends there doesn't need to be a sense of hierarchy or insecurity over importance or role. We are born equal, and we die equal and so radical justice ensures that this equality remains through the course of life. That doesn't have to mean equal pay or communism, which is simply another form of control. But it does mean learning to deeply honour each other as human beings and a radical review of how we think about economics.

Thirdly, they had a sense of *radical friendship*. This meant a beautiful sense of inclusion, crossing the dividing line. Friendship fosters a desire to look out for each other, to treat each other with deep respect and kindness. Friendship ensures that no one is shut out of the circle. Friendship helps us to be well. Friendship means that we belong.

We need to challenge the inevitability of division between communities, between the haves and have nots or even between the North and the South. Wherever we can create the **moral alternative economy of friendship** in our society, crossing the dividing line, embracing our other and being changed in the process then we must do so.

There are loads of great initiatives that can help us, like the Big Lunch.[121] There are all kinds of ways we can volunteer and get stuck in.

CULTIVATING COMMUNITY POWER

Social change is inevitable. Creating the kind of social change we want to see, something more equitable, with love as the core foundation, is entirely possible. Positive societal transformation means communities need to find their voice, to understand each other and believe their own true power. It needs humble, compassionate leadership which is not afraid or insecure.

If ever we are to see real transformation and a sea change in inequity, giving power away and truly ceding it into community is vital.

Community power must then be cultivated and developed. However, **it isn't straight forward, it isn't easy and will unfortunately meet lots of resistance.** Resistance can be within us as imposter syndrome, self-doubt or disempowerment. Or it can be external, from those in positions of power who do not know how to let go of their own power or embrace humility.

To build real power in communities, we need to share with our communities the data we hold about them. It belongs to them after all because it is about them. But this is only part of the picture. We need to hear the stories in our communities about what is strong, not what is wrong. And we need to hear the uncomfortable truths on our streets and in our homes. Community journalism is something which can help us to hear. We need community organisers, field builders and participatory leadership, building agency and power. It takes time, energy and commitment. It can be exhausting but taking time to develop this kind of knowledge is vital. Its rewards will be a much kinder, participatory and therefore equal society.

STAYING WELL AS SOCIAL ACTIVISTS AND CHANGE AGENTS

Anyone who wants to see a more loving society and wants to be part of the change can be called a social activist and change agent. So, in this context of complexity and chaos, how do social activists and social change makers stay well and keep their energy alive? Dr Chris Erskine, who wrote his PhD on exactly this, gives us four key pointers to stay well in the process of social change making, in his short film *The Incomplete Activist*. My summary of his work is as follows.

Firstly, it's important for us all to be *kind to ourselves*. Sometimes in the work of social activism and change, we can feel like hypocrites and full of contradictions. Cutting ourselves some slack, recognising that we are complex people who mess up sometimes is important. We are part of a society which is sometimes directly opposed to our social activism.

So secondly, we need to be able to *laugh at ourselves* and the world around us and keep a good sense of humour.

Thirdly, we need to *regularly surround ourselves with beauty* and to keep that sense of wonder alive.

Fourthly, we must *remember that we are deeply and unconditionally loved* and surround ourselves with people who love us just for who we are, not for what we do or achieve. This allows us to steward our passions more effectively and be part of the change that we so long to see.

Mark-Jo's life speaks to us. She calls us to be community builders who belong to each other. If we are going to cultivate a loving society, we must ensure that no group is left behind or excluded.

Together we must co-create a society of friends.

Co-design
and
co-create
solutions

We need change. The values at the heart of our societal structures need to shift.

- *What if love was at the heart of our social structures instead?*

- *What would this have meant for Mary-Jo?*

- *What would it mean for the Gypsy, Roma and Traveller community, and other people groups who experience abuse in the UK?*

- *What difference might it make in breaking systemic cycles of injustice for families trapped in poverty and powerlessness?*

We really can build a more loving society together. The size of the issues can feel overwhelming. Slowly but surely love will seep into all parts of society and the change we long for, built on the values we hold dear, will be made manifest. We will continue to explore how this is possible.

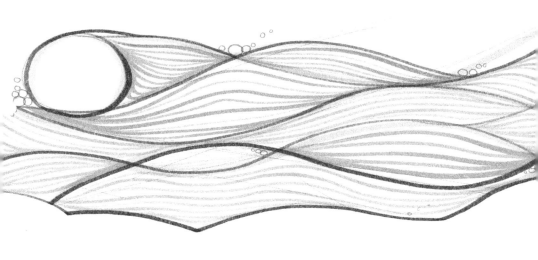

CHAPTER EIGHT
LOVE SCHOOL

EXPLOITED

Laura sat down and sighed. Gesturing towards her daughter, she said, 'Help her out, will you, doc?'

Faye, her daughter, folded her arms and bowed her head. This was not going to be a straightforward consultation.

'Well, thank you both for coming along here today. I guess that you both may have things to say and it's important that I get to hear from both of you. If you prefer, Faye, I can speak with you whilst Mum waits outside, or we can all stay in together. What would work best for you?' I asked, subtly shifting the power dynamics in the room.

She shrugged.

'OK, well, why don't we try staying in all together to start with and see how that works. But at any point, we can change that if we need to. So, how can I help? Who'd like to talk first?'

Faye pulled her phone out from her bag and began to play on it.

'I'm sorry Faye,' I began, 'but if we're going to talk then I'm going to need you to put that away.'

She reluctantly put the phone down and rolled her eyes.

I let the awkward silence unfold. It's something you have to learn to do as a GP. All too easy to fill the space.

'Come on, Faye. We talked about this. Tell him what happened,' Laura encouraged.

'She doesn't get it,' ventured Faye. 'She doesn't know what it feels like.'

'OK ... what doesn't she get?' I replied.

'Basically, Dr Knox,' her mum began, 'she sent a naked photo of herself to this boy at school. And now he's shared it with some of his mates, and they've shared it with theirs, and it's been seen by over 6,000 people. She tried to ask the boy why he did it. You should have seen the abusive messages she got back. I've never seen anything like it. Now she's really anxious, cutting herself and refusing to go to school. I've tried to work out why she did it in the first place. Maybe she's trying to find the love she's lost from her dad.'

Faye's dad had walked out on them a few years ago. Now he had a new partner and had two children with her. He'd broken off contact with Faye. So, the previous Christmas, Faye made a real effort and went round to see him. He opened the front door, but he wouldn't let her in the house. She had told her dad that she loved him and would like to spend time with him. He told her that he had a new family now and shut the door in her face. There may be complexities for him that I know nothing of, but no father should ever treat their child this way.

Every time she thought about going to school, she would have a panic attack. Getting out of bed and getting dressed some days felt like too much of an effort. The school was concerned about her attendance rate and had tried various things to try and coerce her in. However, there was little understanding of whom and what she was avoiding. The relationship was becoming very strained, with several letters home. She had tried to attend a few times, but sitting in a class, with people looking over their shoulder and sniggering had triggered such a visceral response for her that she couldn't possibly stay seated in that environment. Emotional outbursts were only making things worse. She had no idea how to cope with her racing heart, sweating, tight chest and internal rage.

'Oh Faye, I am so sorry. That sounds horrendous. It's no wonder you don't want to go back to school. How are you feeling?' I asked.

'I don't know. I feel dirty. And angry. And just like, totally embarrassed. I just can't believe he did it. I thought he was different. How can I ever show my face there again? I mean, I've got friends who post photos of themselves like that, and they can just laugh it off. But not me. I'm not like that. I just hate myself so much for doing it. I can't believe I was so stupid. I just want it to end.'

'Is that why you're hurting yourself?' I questioned.

'Yeah – I guess it's a way of punishing myself. It's not bad.' Faye showed me some superficial scratches on her arms.

'Does it get so bad that you feel you don't want to carry on living?' I continued.

She nodded.

'Have you ever thought about taking those feelings any further?

Have you ever thought about ending your life?' I carried on with the questioning.

Her mum looked away, wiping a tear from her cheek. She handed me a note.

'I found this on her desk. That's why I knew we had to come and see you.'

It was a goodbye letter to her mum.

Faye had planned to take an overdose. She'd found a combination of pills, including some pain killers her mum used for back pain. Had she taken them, it would almost certainly have been fatal. Thankfully, her mum had knocked on her bedroom door just as she'd finished writing it. She told Faye it would break her heart. They'd had a good cry and she'd persuaded her fourteen-year-old daughter to tell her what was going on. It wasn't only this incident. It was the pressure she was feeling at school to do well. It felt to Faye like it had all become about the exams. She felt like she was in a factory and there was no joy in her education. This double whammy of stress and now humiliation just felt like it was impossible to overcome. But she didn't know how to tell anyone. So, she'd bottled it up. And seeing no other way through, her conclusion had been that she needed to take her own life. What an utterly tragic end that would have been.

We need to face a difficult truth about our education system. School isn't working for many girls right now. It isn't working for many boys either. I could tell you countless stories of major delays in diagnoses of ADHD (attention deficit hyperactivity disorder) and ASC (autistic spectrum conditions) because of poorly designed mental health pathways and funding issues. The toll on families is unbearable and unsafe. I could detail the impacts of poor mental health provision in school settings and the impact it has on young people and staff. I could highlight how poor behaviour is often a communication from a child or young person of traumatic experiences happening in their life. What they need is relational connection and good boundaries, not punishment. Tragically in many of these cases boys and girls are recurrently or permanently excluded from school. But I want to avoid getting too sidetracked here. Let's keep our focus on Faye.

SEXUAL EXPLOITATION

The truth is, across the UK, by the age of seventeen, 7% of our young people have attempted to end their own lives. A quarter of them have self-harmed by the same age. We have a growing mental health crisis, **and our current solutions are not working.**

Schools are pulsating with the strain of the issues they are having to deal with each day. Suicide rates amongst our young women are now the highest they have ever been.[122] Faye was a victim of sexual exploitation, by a boy she had developed a close and trusting relationship with. Never before have we encountered a generation with such an unrealistic view of healthy sexual relationships.[123] The number of children and young people accessing pornography is startling.[124] As a result of the associated unrealistic expectations around sex, pressure around behaviours like sexting, are becoming more common.[125]

Naively, Faye didn't think in her worst nightmare, that the picture she sent to her boyfriend, via Snapchat, would become a source of such utter humiliation. She became a victim of sexual exploitation, and it made her feel like life was no longer worth living. Her spirit was wounded, her soul traumatised, and she was experiencing the regular reality of this in her body through panic attacks. This caused the desire to give physical expression to her psychological pain, through self-injury. She was experiencing the classic response to trauma – fight, flight and freeze – sometimes in combination. And she had no idea how to process it. All she knew was that she desperately wanted it to stop and to feel safe.

Thankfully, from that day forward, we were able to get Faye some good help, through a combination of excellent therapeutic support, superb input from the police, the school safeguarding and pastoral teams, and some whole-school interventions led by the head teacher. She was able to reintegrate into school and is doing much better.

TOXIC MASCULINITY

Faye's story also **highlights our urgent need to talk about the toxic aspects of masculinity and male sexual violence in our schools and wider society.** Over 50% of eleven-year-old boys are reported to have watched hardcore pornography,[126] an industry itself filled with sexual violence against women, many of whom are trafficked as sex slaves. The expectations of how it is acceptable to relate to peers as objects is a real problem. It was not just one boy's cruelty that led to Faye nearly ending her own life. It is, rather, a mindset which has grown within male subculture which is abusive and unacceptable.

We say we live in a free and fair democracy, but the evidence tells us something very different about what it is like to be female in our society.

The 'End Violence Against Women' campaign's report makes particularly grim reading.[127] It highlights how 20% of girls under the age of sixteen have experienced sexual violence, 50% have experienced sexual harassment and the *majority* of our young women feel regularly pressured to send nude photos of themselves to boys.

There is a real problem through all parts of society. Consider this: at the time of writing this chapter, 56 of the UK's sitting MPs, including three ministers, were under investigation for sexual harassment.[128] This misogyny must stop, but how? It is men who must take the prime responsibility to change it. Around half of women do not feel safe on our streets, compared to 19% of men.[129] We must listen deeply to the profoundly negative consequences of male sexual behaviour and its effect on women. We must confront our own attitudes and behaviours and change them. We must teach our young men how to treat young women with kindness and respect, not to objectify them. We must stop excusing testosterone as a hormone which cannot be controlled. We are not talking about consensual, and mutual sexual practice here. This is exploitative, abusive and violent.

Our schools are sick because our society is sick. **Our society is sick because it is love sick.**

BIOPOWER

It's all too easy to point the finger solely at social media for the rise in young people's mental health issues. For sure this is playing a part through growing issues with addiction to screens.[130] We also need to feed a new value set into social media platforms, to confront the lack of responsibility they are taking[131] and see them grow their potential as a force for good.

Alongside the new pressures of social media, exam pressure and a lack of support for students with their mental health is also having a profound effect. This has been shown in a wide-reaching survey of girls and young women in the Girlguiding movement.[132]

The overemphasis on academic outcomes rather than the wellbeing of students needs a total rethink.

We have a current system which sees end of year exams as the best form of assessment. This doesn't work for the majority. For someone like Faye, are attendance figures prioritised over wellbeing? How have we become so unable to hold space for recovery and healing? How do we create the kind of schools where a trauma-informed, compassionate culture enables our children and young people to be well whilst also helping them learn?

There is such a disconnect between the departments of education and health. What would our school curriculums be like if they put the health and wellbeing of children/young people and the planet at the core of them? How might this transform the typical school day? Perhaps, only more local integration can solve this conundrum, pushing back against the increasing detachment from local communities in schools. In the meantime, we are treating our children as fodder for the economic machine. It is what Michel Foucault described as biopower.[133] This really matters, especially as it is affecting those from our most disadvantaged backgrounds in a disproportionately negative way.[134] As long as we make education about league tables, outcomes and numbers, we dehumanise our children and young people. Our society is sick because our education system is sick. **It is love sick.**

MIND THE GAP

When we examine how poverty affects children from within different ethnic groups in the UK, we find staggering disparities. Think about this: 50% of Black British,[135] 47% of Pakistani British, 42% of Bangladeshi British, 32% of Chinese British, and 20% of White British children are growing up in poverty.

Poverty matters when it comes to education. The notion of social mobility is failing, especially when it comes to grammar schools. A recent report shows that 25% of grammar schools are admitting almost no children from disadvantaged backgrounds. This leads to a widening gap in educational outcomes, further imbedding societal inequalities.

A recent report for the Education Committee in the UK Parliament highlighted that white boys from poor backgrounds are doing particularly badly when it comes to education, with only one in ten making it through to university.[136] However, a report for the Social Mobility Commission shows that black boys from poorer backgrounds have higher exclusion rates and perform particularly badly in maths. Although white boys do badly in terms of educational outcomes, it is young people from Black and Asian backgrounds who most struggle to find long-term employment.[137]

Sadly, in my view, our schools have become very unhealthy places, working towards perverse outcome measures, which are arbitrary at best. Physical education is decreasing and so are the fitness levels of our young people.[138] Increased performance measures have seen a decrease in the provision of an artistic curriculum.[139] This leads to less regulation for young people and may be related to worsening mental health issues.[140] Our schools have also become places of great division and are leading to widening inequalities.[141]

We see so much love at work in our schools every single day, but it is being squeezed hard by an uncaring system. This system is seeing the funding gap between independent and state schools widening. Young people at independent schools are given 90% more funding than their counterparts in state schools,[142] benefitting from tax breaks funded by the whole population.[143] In the state sector, teachers have experienced a huge pay squeeze[144] whilst dealing with more complexity, and our young people are experiencing social injustice. Our society is sick because our education system is sick. **It is love sick.**

TEACHERS

Our teachers, who, in my opinion are undervalued and underpaid for the great service they bring to our children and young people, are like workers in the NHS, burning out and experiencing high levels of stress with the rising tide of this overwhelm. Teaching should be highly esteemed as a profession of great importance. Yet, a third of all new teachers are leaving the profession within five years of joining it.[145] **We need a radical rethink about whether we believe children are a real priority within our society.** If so, we need to make teaching a more joy-filled profession.

FOLLOWING PAUL INTO SOCIETY

If we follow Paul, the teacher, whom we met in Chapter 3, out of the consulting room and back into his school and our society, we discover some troubling truths. Paul's journey towards near suicide was not only attributable to his lack of self-care or inability to apply better resilience techniques. A recent survey has shown that over 40% of teachers in the UK plan to quit their job within the next five years.[146] The same is true in many jobs across the public sector. We have an education system, which is expecting so much more of our teachers, but with limited resources. There are hugely difficult behavioural issues for teachers to contend with on a daily basis, often linked to the ACEs we discussed previously. The focus on exams, over and above wellbeing, is creating huge stress, both for teachers and pupils alike. We need to be sure that we are not simply creating working cultures that expect people to 'grow a spine' whilst the way we practise politics and economics makes it nigh on impossible to stand up under the weight of the top-down pressure.

It seems our schools are not working for our young people or our teachers. Something needs to change. We need our schools to be trauma-informed, integrated, compassionate places of learning, in which our teachers are honoured for the great work they do and trusted to deliver it well. If we want our schools to be places of true flourishing, then we must value teaching far more, as a profession, whilst creating the space needed for our teachers to live well and love themselves. When we do this, we allow them to invest in themselves so that they can pour their own love into the rising generation.

There are many signs of hope across the UK. The Witton Park Academy in Blackburn is doing great work in being a truly compassionate, trauma-informed school.[147] The Cabot Learning Federation in Bristol is working to ensure greater equity and a truly inclusive approach to education.[148] The Oasis Trust is focusing on the social justice aspects of education and achieving fantastic results through Oasis Community Learning.[149] We just need more of it everywhere if we're going to have an education system that is fit for the future.

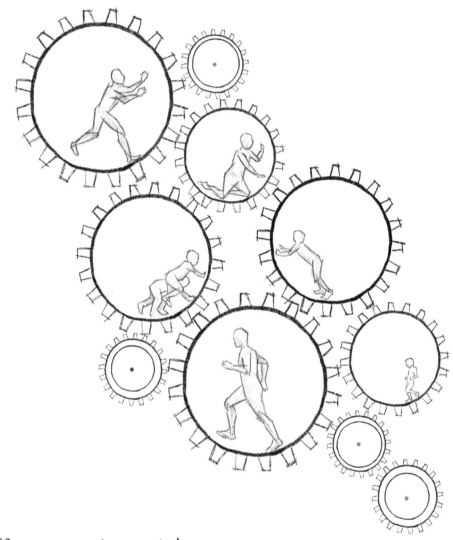

We are treating our
children as fodder for
the economic machine

- *When fathers walk away from the family home, it is the women who are left with the greater economic burden and higher proportion of the childcare.[150] What might life have been like for Faye if her dad had stuck around?*

- *What do you think it would feel like for Faye to be part of a society in which women feel safe, are not sexually exploited and have truly equal opportunities?*

- *Are you willing to challenge the inevitability of sexual violence in our society and be part of building a moral alternative economy in which misogyny plays no part?*
  - *What does this mean for you personally?*
  - *How might you need to adapt your own language or behaviours?*
  - *Who or what might you need to more actively challenge?*

- *What if we build our education system on different values in which children do not feel like they are fodder for the economic machine?*

- *How do we ensure that schools are part of the solution in tackling societal inequalities rather than exacerbating them?*

- *What if we put love into the heart of our education and learning systems? What would they be like?*

- *What would it mean for our children and young people's wellbeing?*

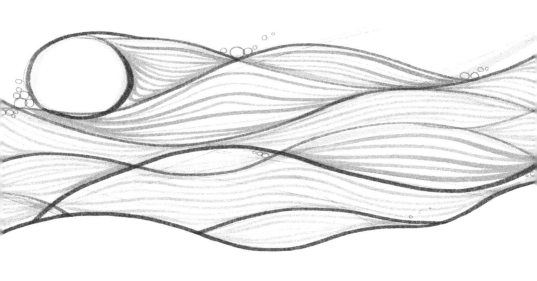

CHAPTER NINE
LOVE WORK

MISSED

Tariq staggered into my room. He swung the left side of his body round as he did so. I'd never met him before and was impressed by his big frame. He is what my eldest son would call 'a unit'. Somewhat scruffy, he sat down with a grunt. The kind of grunt that is a mixture of unfitness and being fed up.

'I want to know when I can get my licence back,' he started.

'OK, well, tell me some more about you and I'll see if I can help you answer that question,' I replied.

'I drive coaches. At least I did, until this happened. Now they're saying I can't drive for a long time. What does that mean?'

Tariq was forty-eight. He had left school at sixteen with few qualifications (another mark of how the education system fails many). His parents had both died when he was relatively young and he was estranged from his sister, who now lived abroad.

He'd always had to fend for himself and had had a variety of jobs. 'Brought up not to be a scrounger,' he'd been a coach driver for a local company for the last ten years or so. He loved this job. He'd taken trips all over Europe and loved the banter he had with the passengers. He worked long days and rarely took time off. The company felt like family to him. He had few other friends and lived in a one-bedroom council flat.

He had almost no time for exercise and smoked like a chimney. He had an unhealthy diet, mainly consisting of high sugars

(Lucozade), carbohydrates (rice and chips) and saturated fats (ghee in takeaway curries, and pastries). The road is not exactly full of nutritious options in motorway services. Without realising it, Tariq had developed Type 2 diabetes, linked to his obesity. If not treated, this easily leads to lots of other health problems.

Three weeks before seeing me, he woke up one morning, unable to move the left side of his body and with a drooping face. He'd suffered a massive stroke in his sleep. It could be put down to a combination of his genetic risk, his lifestyle and sleep apnoea (a condition in which you stop breathing for significant periods when asleep). But I think there are some deeper and wider issues which lay at the cause of this terrible incident. He was now discharged from hospital on a bunch of new medication. I was the first GP he had seen since he saw someone about acne as a teenager.

Maybe he was a pawn in a big travel company. Even if he mattered to the team, with his big personality and love of the long road, they certainly squeezed as much work as possible out of him, without many days off or time to self-care. Maybe I'm being unfair. Either way, he was a ticking time bomb, which had very sadly gone off. A clot had formed in his blood stream caused by high cholesterol and high blood sugars. It had fired into his brain and now only half of his body functioned properly. He would never be able to drive a coach again. The DVLA simply wouldn't accept the risk or the liability. Tariq's life was forever changed, with profound consequences for his future.

It did not need to have been this way.

WORK MATTERS

The social activist, author Professor Hilary Cottam, has explored the future of work in a series of blogs. The welfare system in the UK has a key assumption at the heart of it: good work. But good decent work is hard to find. Many people are having to do several jobs to keep up. At a national and global level, there is massive social injustice involved with a significant undervaluing of large parts of the workforce.[151] All the while our long working hours are killing us, according to the World Health Organization.[152]

What do workers want? They want decent pay for starters! They also need predictability in place of insecurity, a sense of purpose (not the same as workplace values) and freedom from surveillance. In other words, they don't want to be slaves to the algorithm, or fodder for the economic machine. They want to be able to care about green issues, but low paid work means that in reality this is impossible. They want to be able to live a real and good life outside of work that gives them space to breathe and to care.[153] And care is a huge issue! One in four of us in the UK are carers of some sort.[154] Yet the vast majority of this goes unnoticed and has to be squeezed in by exhausted people at the end of long working days. Most of this care falls to women, many of whom are being pushed out of work and into poverty in order to provide care for loved ones.[155]

The problem for many of us is that our current education and supposed 'lifelong learning' opportunities do woefully little to adequately prepare us for the world of work. We rely far too much on an industrial model in our schools and colleges, when completely new forms of curricula are needed. And we need new, flexible forms of work which take account of life transitions, technological developments, ecological impacts and economic shifts. Local government, more than national, has a huge role to play in this and can help create the conditions where the change we need is possible. But this cannot be done without adequate funding and the kind of leadership that is visionary enough to recognise that we are in the moment of an enormous shift.[156] Society is sick because many of our workplaces our sick. **They are love sick.** They fail to care enough for the workers.

JOY IN WORK

If we're going to build a society that is healthy, well and full of love, then our workplaces need significant transformation. In many companies, worker wellbeing is mostly an afterthought at best. This is true in both the public and private sectors. I have already mentioned the high burnout and low morale of staff in education and the NHS. The same is true in industry in which workers are often vastly underpaid on insecure contracts.

Profit does not have to matter more than people. This is a false economy.

However, there are some excellent examples out there already, with high employee satisfaction and wellbeing rates, like Unilever.[157] Buurtzorg is a model of care with a new way of thinking about how nursing services can be run. It was established in 2006 in the Netherlands and is now active in twenty-five countries. Its founder, Jos de Blok, describes how by starting with listening to patients' perspectives, systems and structures can be simplified.[158] This kind of model is much more enjoyable to work in for the nurses and allows them to be highly creative and flexible in how they do their jobs. With its flat management structures and high worker participation, it boasts 87% staff satisfaction rates. What if worker wellbeing was taken more seriously? Some businesses have been experimenting with a four-day working week. Although skepticism was high that this would be beneficial, the results have been staggering. Higher productivity and profits for the businesses and happier, healthier staff.[159]

How very different might Tariq's life be now, had his workplace taken more of an interest in his health and wellbeing, rather than just clocking him in and out? If they had paid him a real living wage, what might this have enabled around the choices available to him to live a healthier lifestyle? If he had been given days off and allowed time to rest, would he have suffered such a terrible stroke at such a young age?

A few years ago, I was seated in the Excel Conference Centre in London learning about global health systems. I was particularly struck by a presentation of a study from the Institute for Healthcare Improvement (IHI) in the USA led by a hero of mine, Professor Don Berwick. The study had researched which health systems around the world were the most excellent, safe and sustainable.[160] They found several common and key factors. However, **the most important thing they found** across the globe, in all kinds of different settings **was the creation of what they termed a 'culture of joy'!**

Even though their findings applied particularly to the world of health and care, they could apply to any workplace or community.

I love this idea. The idea that our workplaces could become places of wellbeing if we fostered a culture of joy together. A culture of joy is a culture in which we find joy in our work, even when that work is difficult or emotionally draining, because it connects to a deep sense of purpose and togetherness.

THE ROLE OF LEADERS

Leaders need to do five things, in particular, if they are to create a culture of joy.

Firstly, leaders need to show their teams appreciation. It is vital that we say thank you to each other and show our deep appreciation for the work that we do and the things we achieve together. It's one of the things teams often say is lacking and yet it's not very difficult to find time for. Even the small thank-yous matter. There is a great movement in the NHS, called 'The Academy of Fab Stuff', founded by Roy Lilley.[161] The idea is to continually highlight and celebrate the wonderful work going on in the NHS every day. It is quite a contrast to the negative headlines we often see in print.

Secondly, leaders need to be transparent, honest about what is going on and the kind of issues they are facing. It helps teams to understand why certain decisions are being made. It allows team members to feel included, important and honoured, and builds a real sense of trust with leadership. Brené Brown offers us a word of caution here.[162] Even though she champions vulnerability, openness, honesty and transparency in leadership, she says that vulnerability without boundaries is somewhat dangerous. There needs to be wisdom to accompany vulnerability about knowing how much to share and when. Leaders need to keep anxiety levels down and to keep trust strong but cannot afford to appear aloof – this can be a tricky balance.

Thirdly, leaders need to create a sense of psychological safety. Teams need to know that they will not be ridiculed for trying new things, asking questions, or coming up with new ideas. The worst thing a leader can do is belittle and humiliate members of their team. Team members need to know that it is OK to make mistakes and to learn from them, without shame. Joy is fostered by knowing that your voice and your ideas matter. When leaders ensure psychological safety, they find surprising members of their team can bring brilliant new initiatives forward, deepening a culture of respect and joy.

Fourthly, leaders need to make sure they are offering personal and career mentorship, encouraging team members to develop in their work roles and as human beings. Taking a coaching approach for individuals with one-to-one focus is an investment in their future, leading to a deeper sense of purpose and commitment for them, where the work they do aligns with a sense of their own destiny. Coaching the whole team enables all to play to their strengths and deepens the ability to collaborate on key areas of work.

Finally, if leaders want to create organisations with joy at their heart, they need to deliberately create inclusive teams. The Harvard Business Review has shown that the best and highest performing teams, have boards that are diverse facilitating a joint responsibility for equality, diversity and inclusivity across their organisation.[163] In my team, we further build inclusivity by investing time in building relationships, checking in together, at least once a week. We usually have a question which allows people to either have a bit of fun, or be a little bit vulnerable. Both laughter and vulnerability build trust and joy. Whether virtually, or sat in a physical circle, making sure we touch base as human beings is invaluable.

THE ROLE OF TEAM MEMBERS

Building joy is not only the responsibility of leaders though. Individual team members play an important part.

For each person there needs to be a sense of personal agency. In other words, each person needs to have a clear sense of responsibility for who they are, knowing that what they do matters. This is enabled by compassionate and empowering leadership. When each person turns up to work, or to an event, or takes part in a voluntary activity they need to know that their contribution is important. They are going to need to do it to the best of their ability.

Alongside this then, sits a sense of accountability and reliability. Each one of us is accountable for our own actions. We are accountable for how we show up, we have agency in the role that we play and the contribution that we make. A great example of this lies in the '15 seconds 30 minutes' (15s30m) movement within the NHS.[164] The premise is built around a simple question. What can I do in 15 seconds now that will save a colleague of mine 30 minutes tomorrow? There are countless times when we could act on something, but don't. But by not doing so, it causes someone else significant problems the next day. Individuals then, play a key part in building the wider team culture. Relationships with teams and ways of working together are also vital.

THE ROLE OF THE WHOLE TEAM

Firstly, teams need a sense of camaraderie. Teams need to carry that sense that we are all in this together, that we belong to each other, and each member is valued (or I prefer loved) for who they are.

Secondly, teams need a sense of shared purpose. The team must be clear about what their vision is; what they are there to do. They need to act together and play to each of their strengths. This means each team player is enabled to function at a high level.

Thirdly, because people are trusted to turn up and do their job well, to take personal responsibility and accountability because they have agency, the team learn to trust each other to do their work well. When someone is trusted to do their work, they feel a deep sense of contentment and joy, which fosters the culture even further.

These things are not beyond the reach of any person or team. They are straightforward principles of how to go about building such a culture. But I wonder how many of us feel like we work within a culture of joy. How much more enjoyable life would be if we did. For Tariq, it would have made all the difference. We must build a society in which we love and value all people. We must create a society that works for everyone. That includes the world of work. Our workplaces must become places that genuinely care, rather than treat people as fodder for the economic machine. This is especially true when it comes to issues of race equality and equity in the workplace. Tariq was a man who had significant injustice stacked against him before he set out to work each morning.

MIND THE (HEALTH) GAP

Men in our poorest communities in the North of England are expected to live 15 years less than those from our wealthier ones. Out of the poorest 20 neighbourhoods in England, 19 of them are in the North.[165] Overall life expectancy is as low as 73.5 years. But healthy life expectancy (life lived in good health) is considerably less at around 51 years.[166] However, in some neighbourhoods, this can be as low as 46.5 years. Tariq was around this age when his health was catastrophically changed for the worse. His life was going to become a much bigger struggle and he was going to require much more help from the state. Compare this to our wealthiest neighbourhoods, where people live well into their eighties and will often live a good sixty years before they expect to develop any ill health issues.

Every year, this same kind of thing is happening to thousands of men and women in our communities. They are not caught before it is too late. NHS health checks are available for all those over the age of forty. However, there are three reasons why Tariq wasn't picked up by one of these.

Firstly, he was rarely home. He was often away with his work, driving coaches. He didn't respond to text messages when abroad. He often left post unopened for months. And he wouldn't have responded to any invite, had there been one, as he would have struggled to find time to make an appointment before being on the road again.

Secondly, in our poorest communities, it is hard to recruit staff and the workload is utterly overwhelming. GP surgeries are struggling to even think about the possibility of doing extra things, like health checks on top of the busyness of every day. There are significantly less GPs per head of population in our economically poorer communities.[167] Bizarrely, to make matters worse, the funding formula works against GPs in these areas. They get less resources for dealing with populations with more complexity![168] So, when patients don't respond to invites, they are marked as 'non-responders' and considered 'difficult to reach'.

Thirdly, even if there had been an invite and the staff could have found the time to do one, Tariq is unlikely to have attended, due to a complex combination of factors. What we do know is that people from our Black and South Asian communities are at significantly higher risk of developing cardiovascular disease and diabetes.[169] The NHS has been slow in being proactive enough in a way that hits the mark in really involving communities in their own health and wellbeing. Unfortunately for Tariq, the first thing the health services knew about him was when the paramedics arrived on his doorstep. It is known that having a GP or health practitioner, who looks like you and understands your culture, makes it more likely for you to go and see them and receive the care you need.[170] In Liverpool, for example, which has the oldest Chinese (mainly Mandarin speaking) community in the UK, there are only a handful of Chinese GPs, and many of the community are not registered with a GP. This creates huge health inequalities for this community.[171]

As the teams I work with have listened to the Bengali community in Burnley, we have discovered a plethora of reasons why they have very low attendance rates at the National Diabetes Prevention Programme courses run locally. These include the courses being culturally insensitive, being in the wrong language, run in the wrong location and at an unhelpful time of day. Our teams are working much more proactively, co-designing courses with the communities they are aimed at, making a massive difference. Not only are our minority ethnic[172] British citizens generally living in greater poverty, but they are also experiencing significantly worse health outcomes.

We have witnessed this so cruelly during the Covid-19 pandemic. A combination of being in the kind of jobs which put them at more risk, having to work due to low incomes, and also living in poor quality and overcrowded housing has caused them to suffer far more than those in predominantly white-British areas.[173]

Across all our communities, those with the highest health risk factors also live in the areas of greatest economic disadvantage. These are the ones who end up with more frequent and longer hospital admissions,[174] creating more cost to the health and care system. Poverty leads to significantly worse health, which costs us far more socially and economically down the line than if we had tackled things further upstream. Yet, despite the excellent evidence supporting the need for good public health prevention of ill-health, there has been an overall public health budget cut of £13.20 per person in England. Overall, this amounts to a real-terms cut of £1 billion in public health spend since 2015, even though the evidence shows how cost-effective public health spending is.[175]

However, the cuts were higher in places of greater health inequality; £16.70 across the Midlands, £23.24 in the North East and £15.13 per person in the North West.[176] The implications for the North–South divide in health outcomes is profound[177] and maddening! It should be no surprise that this has led to greater health inequalities and a higher death rate due to Covid-19 in these areas. **It is especially affecting children,** with those **in the North** experiencing significantly **greater levels of poverty, inequality** and **deprivation.**[178]

UNPREPARED

At the time of writing, over 177,000 people have died from Covid-19 in the UK.[179] Professor Sir Michael Marmot and others have clearly highlighted in an important Covid-19 Review, four key reasons why the UK has one of the highest death rates in the world per million people of population from this pandemic.[180]

1. A poor culture within politics and governance – with a lack of social cohesion, a breakdown in trust and poor decision-making when it mattered.

2. Widening inequalities in power, money and resources – now even worse, particularly affecting our minority ethnic British communities.

3. Government policies of austerity – which left us without the necessary infrastructure within local communities to cope.

4. Health had stopped improving – leaving large numbers of people living with underlying health conditions which put them at greater risk.[181]

If Covid-19 has done anything, it has further exposed the vast inequalities and injustices at work in our society and our world. We can't go back to 'normal'.

We can't 'build back better' from such unsteady and uncertain foundations.

There are things which must be **undone, mindsets** and **ideologies** which must be **exposed** and **overthrown.** As we do this together then we can surely find the grace and the vision to build a more hopeful future.

THE COST OF ILL HEALTH

The truth is that sickness is costing the UK economy significantly. In 2021, 149.3 million working days were lost to sickness or injury. It was worst for women, older people with long-term conditions and for those living in greater disadvantage.[182] Inequality costs the economy tremendously. Data from 2020 show that poor mental health leads to time off work equating to between £42–£45 billion a year. The Department for Work & Pensions in the UK estimates that working age ill health costs the UK economy over £100 billion each year.[183] Unfortunately, post-pandemic, the picture is worse than it was beforehand. Ensuring we care for the wellbeing of workers is profoundly important if we are going to have a flourishing economy. The arguments for tackling inequality and inequity in our society are extremely strong.

ANCHOR INSTITUTIONS

Our workplaces have a key role in creating the kind of societal change we need. Businesses can be part of changing the tide in social inequalities and inequities. Anchor institutions are large employers in any given geography, which can take a sense of responsibility for the economic wellbeing of the citizens they employ and the area they are in.[184] The City of Preston, in Lancashire developed its own thinking about anchor institutions during the financial crisis of 2007–2008 and subsequent years of austerity. Councillor Matthew Brown did not believe, as leader of the city, that it was necessary to take an austerity approach for the economy to survive or be successful. It is a remarkable story documented in *Paint the Town Red*,[185] and has been followed closely by the Health Foundation.[186]

As a result, across the UK, the NHS is examining its own role as an anchor institution and how it can collaborate with other big employers to make a real difference. In Morecambe Bay, for example, having learnt from the Health Foundation about the work in the City of Preston, we are developing our own anchor institution network. Together, with our district councils, Lancaster University and large businesses, we have developed an anchor charter around six key themes.

Firstly, we are trying to ensure we widen access to good quality work. The NHS is one of the biggest employers in the world and the number one in the UK. We need to ensure that people who live in our most economically disadvantaged communities have great opportunities to join our team. This involves creating exciting apprenticeship schemes. It means that the work itself is done within a culture of joy, in which we care about worker wellbeing. We are a long way from getting this right, but we're moving in the right direction. A few years ago, our local hospital team in Morecambe Bay, started an award-winning campaign called 'Flourish' to help staff focus on their own health and wellbeing in a supported way.[187] Having good quality work also means ensuring that everyone is paid a real living wage and not having to use food banks on their way home after a long shift.

Secondly, we are trying to ensure that we purchase and commission for social value. What does this mean? It means that when we ask companies to do work for us, we want to make sure that they don't just do a good job. We want them to be aligned to our own values around, for example, how they pay and care for their own staff, or look after the environment. We also want to invest in local companies, wherever possible, because we care about the local economy and employment rates.

Thirdly, we want to use the assets (buildings/land etc) we have for the public good. For example, there are loads of empty NHS spaces at the weekends, which community groups could make use of. There are acres of green spaces where community groups could grow vegetables. NHS property that is sold and turned into flats can become social housing run by community land trusts, ensuring that those who most need help in getting housing are able to afford it.

Fourthly, we are looking to reduce our environmental impact. The NHS is not leading the way when it comes to the environment. This is criminal, given the impact of pollution on the health and wellbeing of the population. The NHS is one of the biggest sinners when it comes to plastic waste.[188] Our use of anaesthetic gases is a massive polluter[189] (though there are alternatives). Our travel plans for our staff are seriously lacking enough credibility. We have huge work to do. We are waking up, but not fast enough. We're beginning to realise the key role we have to play. Hospital Trusts, like the ones in Newcastle-Upon-Tyne, have developed whole new environmental strategies.[190] The importance of this cannot be underestimated.

Fifthly, we are looking to work with other local partners to maximise our collaborative impact. This includes our universities and further education colleges, our local councils, and big employers like EDF, BAE Systems and others.

Finally, we are looking at how we tackle the health inequalities affecting our communities. This means a deliberate and unapologetic focus on those living in our areas of greatest social injustice, no matter what their race or religion. We are proactively reaching out to them with an enhanced health check. We ensure a particular focus on our African, Asian, and Gypsy, Roma and Traveller communities due to their unmet health needs. We give special attention to those living with severe and enduring mental illness[191] and/or learning disabilities[192] because they are at much higher risk of dying significantly earlier. I am so grateful to Professor Bola Owolabi,[193] the National Lead on Health Inequalities for NHS England, for her superb Core20PLUS5.[194] This gives the NHS a razor-sharp focus on our 20% most disadvantaged communities. It ensures we are inclusive of people groups who experience particular health inequities.

Tariq's story reminds us that if we are to create a society that flourishes, our workplaces need to be healthy. Work must be meaningful, connected, joyful, pay sufficiently and enable space for life to be lived well.

This is a false economy...

- *So, what might it have meant for Tariq, had the NHS been even more proactive in working with his community and workplace to create health?*

- *What if the organisation which employed him had recognised the health risks which he was walking around with?*

- *What if he had worked in a team in which he was valued and not just a number?*

- *What kind of difference would it make across the UK if people were paid a real living wage and therefore didn't have to work gruelling, long hours, simply to make ends meet?*

- *If we know that the four-day week is better all round, why not adopt it more widely?*

- *What if employers across the UK took their role as agents of wellbeing more seriously?*

- *What might this mean for how we think about those who work oversees, but are unseen and are the recipients of the most brutal forms of injustice?*

- *Could our workplaces become institutions that help us build a kinder, fairer and more loving world?*

- *Could they become places of deep joy?*

- *If so, how are you going to be a part of that?*

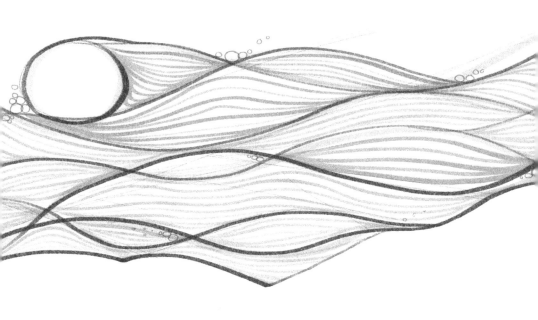

CHAPTER TEN
LOVE PARTICIPATION

NUMBERED

I was one of nine kids – my mum felt forced to drug deal, it was the only way she could feed us. The stress on her not knowing where the next meal was coming from – it all rubbed off on us kids. Kids absorb things like that, it's really hard living like that. The only thing that held us together was the community – the people on our estate. Everyone would chip in to buy food for a month for people like us who didn't have enough.

Nana was the heart of the estate, she took all the kids out, taking us on minibuses for days out. Out of her own pocket at first. So we had something to do cos we had nothing. And parents could have one day without worrying about feeding kids. Then she started running the community centre. The place was heaving with kids all the time. It was a tiny hut in the car park of our school. Everything happened there – it was all we had, all anyone had. We had parties there as kids; it was amazing, magical, a place of no worries. There was meals there too that was so important. If it wasn't for my nan and all she did for me and all the other kids, I would have killed myself.

Ten years ago the youth workers from the council came and did a project – a massive music gig with all the lads and girls from the local council estates. It was amazing – all us kids from same background, all in poverty, and without that project we'd just have ended up scrapping and gang wars cos it was the only way we had of releasing all the anger we had. The project brought everyone together. It stopped all the fighting, and gang crimes. It was the best thing I've ever done ever – it was amazing

*– everyone said that. Then the funding was
taken away from us, and we were left with nothing.*

*Our school was good – I had no bullying there. Many of the kids
had serious difficulties – ADHD, Asperger's – you weren't judged,
they treated you like family, they got to know your parents,
they went to appointments with you. You felt accepted there.
They've ... you've ... shut that now too.*

*Then when you have nowhere to go and nothing to do, you get
bullied – kids aged 13, 15 whatever, young kids, the main drug
dealers get you to sell heroin and crack – you're so afraid of what
will happen to you if you don't do it – and there's nothing else.
If all the youth stuff hadn't been taken away we wouldn't have
been pulled away to the streets ... to these men. A few of me
mates had to hide guns for them. They pay you – and when you
have younger brothers and sisters needing to be fed its stressful
trying to make the right decision. I thought my mum never knew
where we was getting the money from, I had a paper round,
and pretended it was that I gave her.*

*I hold the councillors who made these decisions responsible
for what happened to me. They don't understand what they
destroyed by taking those activities away. It was the only
freedom we had, and it was taken away.
We were just a number to them.*

*Then everything goes from worse to worse, my family gets
evicted, we are moved to another area where we don't know no
one. Then when your property needs work doing to it and the
landlord won't do it, it's condemned and you're moved on again
– same thing happened again, condemned, moved on.*

It didn't matter if my mum had to live in her mate's one bed flat and sleep on the floor with my brothers and sisters.

Nobody cares.

When you're in poverty you end up with nothing cos it's all taken away and nobody cares. I became homeless – but they said I was not a priority need as I was 24. Street homeless, the council tells me I am not a priority need. The council don't help you if you're homeless and young – it's all the charities and the churches. The council just tell you if you're sleeping at a charity shelter you're not sleeping rough. You have no hope. It feels like the government are trying to make a superior race – the rich get richer and the poor get poorer. That causes the poor to do crimes like robbing to feed their kids.

How can this be fair?

The government believes in money more than human beings. All they do is take, take, take. They worship money instead of heart. They give me a number – when you speak my name that means you want to talk to me. I am David John Roberts. When you give me a number – my national insurance number, my NHS number, my tax code – you just want to talk money. My name is David John Roberts. If I had one thing to say to the government, it would be treat me as you want to be treated. See me as a person, not a number.

See me as living.

I am flesh and blood.[195] *(emphasis added)*

You could have heard a pin drop and then spontaneously, everyone stood to their feet and applauded this young man on the stage, as tears rolled down their cheeks. A room full of local politicians, business people, civil servants, volunteers from various charities, chief executives of public sector organisations, medical and nursing leaders, teachers, religious leaders and two local MPs. They stood together and looked at David – a corporate recognition of his humanity and the hard-hitting truth he had spoken.[196]

It was the launch of the Poverty Truth Commission (PTC) for Morecambe Bay, when David shared his story. We must not lose the uncomfortable truth in David's words.

THERE IS SUCH A THING AS SOCIETY

Human beings do not exist in isolation. We belong in a body of families and communities of neighbourhoods, villages, towns, cities and nations within our ecology and global, political and economic systems. David lived with an incredible sense of community. It was the institutions that made things significantly difficult for him.

Beverley Skeggs, Distinguished Professor of Sociology at Lancaster University and Director of the Centre for Alternatives to Social and Economic Inequalities, talks about society as being a revelation of, and continual struggle for, our values and that which we value.[197]

So, if we're going to love and value people equally, then we must take a look at how society is set up, because clearly, our society does not apportion the same value to all people.

Skeggs challenges us to think about whose interest society is set up, and to do that we have to understand power and how it is maintained.

Our nation is held together by its institutions – law (and religion), the welfare state, politics, education (and media). Each of these parts form a whole and together they attribute economic value to people. But nations themselves are also parts of a global capitalist system, which shapes all our lives. So, the global capitalist set of values influences the World Bank and International Monetary Fund (IMF), which in turn influence and determine the economic value of nation states, which in turn apply measures to the citizens. In fact, both the IMF and the World Bank operate a definition of the 'subject of value'. This means they actually encourage a particular, ideal type of individualistic, competitive, self-interested, risk-taking, enterprising self. In other words, to these global financial institutions, people are valued and valuable if they are rational, self-interested individuals who continually accrue value to themselves in competition with others.

People are literally given a monetary value! This leads to 'people' being valued according to economic potential and output. But how is this decided? **This way of viewing**

people pits us against one another. But who are the people?

Historically, Skeggs tells us, people were basically divided into two main categories: 'individuals' and 'masses'. Individuals were property owning and had significant power. They were able to extract value (or take what they wanted) and were nearly always European, colonial, white men. The 'masses', on the other hand, related to everyone else. Labourers, enslaved people and peasants. They were portrayed as monstrous, ungovernable, degenerate, contagious, dangerous, dirty and often drunk. They were not considered as unique 'selves'. They didn't matter in and of themselves. The only value of the masses was to be found in exploiting them for the sake of the 'individuals'. Over time, the masses were recategorised into classes – namely the 'middle class' and the 'working class' (although further categorisations now exist). These were basically divided according to access to property and money, but further classified through perspectives on morality.

This is key. Society is shaped by both our politics and our economics. But as Skeggs demonstrates, we cannot understand our politics or economics unless we understand morality. She stated in a lecture delivered at an event entitled 'Love Society' that **'all economic choices are moral choices.'**[198]

So, we create a moral framework through the parts of our society which maintains the values we then apply to people. This is why we consider some people to be more deserving of love than others. It is how we justify in our heads the concept of the 'deserving' and the 'undeserving' poor. We value people according to their attributes and what they contribute to the economy. But this doesn't work for anyone except for the few who maintain the power and the money.

The middle classes can enjoy more privileges for sure. But they must constantly add value to themselves and their children in order to maintain their status and sense of value. Think about all the middle-class parents (especially mums – because it tends to fall to them) who are constantly running their kids to extra-curricular activities – violin lessons, horse riding, ballet and Brownies to make them more valuable in the exchange economy in the future. It's no wonder people are so stressed and burned out. Or what about the financial stretching that goes on to ensure that the children keep their nose ahead by attending the 'right school' in the 'right neighbourhood' or through paying for a private education? And why are those things only available to those who can afford to pay?

Think of the disadvantages this creates for the 'working class' who have little or no access to this kind of privilege or opportunity. Rather, when they fall on hard times (which for many is all the time) they have to defend their very right to help by proving themselves worthy of benefits.

It's fascinating to read the studies that show the 'middle class' make judgements about people who 'get something for nothing'. All the while they forget that the house they are living in is accruing significant value, simply whilst they live in it, further increasing the inequality in society. Margaret Thatcher once famously stated that there is no such thing as society.[199] She believed that in the end it's each person for themselves and we are each motivated by our own selfish wants and needs.

We have created an entire psychological narrative around this, replacing the role religion used to take about 'improving' ourselves. We have to make ourselves worthy of any help we may need. So, society has created a value set based around 'personal responsibility' and 'internal motivation' – blaming individuals for poor choices, rather than social explanations for staggering levels of inequality and inequity.

'It is your fault if you are poor.'

'You are living in bad circumstances because of your own choices.'

'You should just pull yourself up by your bootstraps.'

And we maintain this narrative through our plethora of reality TV shows, like *Benefits Street* and *Wife Swap*, in which we shame the poor/working class and judge their (im)moral choices. Even our comedy is used to laugh at the 'feckless wasters'. So, we stigmatise and ridicule the poor. How dare we suggest that society is stacked against people? It's all down to individual choice, isn't it?

Do you recognise the lenses of privilege here?

So much for loving people. We will love those who we consider worthy of our love. Our society is sick because **our values are sick.**

Love has to mean something. Margaret Thatcher was wrong. **There is such a thing as society,** and it doesn't belong to those who have the power and the privilege. It belongs to all of us, or rather, **we all belong together in our society and to each other.**

So, if we're going to say we love people and we love society then it must affect how society is set up. **A loving society must be a society of justice and care.**

IDEOLOGY HAS CONSEQUENCES

The last decade in the UK, prior to the pandemic, saw the deepest cuts in the British welfare state in its history.[200] It was a deliberate and orchestrated, political move, motivated by an ideology that believes in a small state and the benevolence of the free market. Behind it lay a slogan, which the then Prime Minster, David Cameron and now Lord Cameron, called the 'Big Society'. Really it involved cutting important local services, like libraries and children's centres, whilst expecting communities to pick up the tab. There was no real thinking about how society is built, or on which values.

George Osbourne promised the Conservative Party that he would introduce the 'most radical and reforming period of government this country has seen for a generation'[201] by providing the tough medicine necessary to drive people off benefits and into work. In 2015, he announced with great fervour that this economic approach would lead to,

The deficit down. Growth up. Jobs up.
Living standards on the rise. Britain on the rise.
... The Comeback Country.[202] (emphasis added)

He unleashed this package of austerity in 2010 when he became Chancellor and was in full swing by the time he made that speech. Unfortunately, as Tyler showed in her book, the political experiment failed. The tough medicine didn't make our society healthier. It left us more divided and with significantly wider inequalities and inequities.[203]

In 2018, the United Nations Special Rapporteur on Extreme Poverty and Human Rights came to the UK at the invitation of the British Government. His report is a **devastating account of the effects of the politics of austerity on the poorest and most vulnerable in our society.** Here is his overall summary.

> *Although the United Kingdom is the world's fifth largest economy, one fifth of its population (14 million people) live in poverty … Policies of austerity introduced in 2010 continue largely unabated, despite the tragic social consequences.*

> *… Food banks have proliferated; homelessness and rough sleeping have increased greatly; tens of thousands of poor families must live in accommodation far from their schools, jobs and community networks; life expectancy is falling for certain groups; and the legal aid system has been decimated.*

> *… The bottom line is that much of the glue that has held British society together since the Second World War has been deliberately removed and replaced with a harsh and uncaring ethos.*[204] *(emphasis added)*

During the decade 2010–2020, we saw deep and devastating cuts to local council budgets,[205] the greatest funding squeeze in NHS history,[206] and a growing gap in the life expectancy between the richest and poorest in our society.[207] The then Chancellor, Philip Hammond, rejected the report outright.[208] Yet in 2022, there were more branches of food banks across the UK than McDonald's restaurants;[209] food banks which barely existed before the politics of austerity were introduced.

Austerity has particularly affected working class children, working class women – especially women of colour – disabled people, migrant workers and asylum seekers.[210]

Our values base shifted against welfare, choosing to believe instead that only certain people were truly deserving of it. I can't tell you how many patients of mine, severely disabled or living with severe life-limiting conditions, were assessed by clinically unqualified professionals as being 'fit for work'. I wrote countless reports to appeal on behalf of them, staying late and missing bedtime stories with my children to do so. Although the appeals were and still are, often successful (as this work is ongoing), the process had a profoundly negative mental health effect on many of the people I was supporting. And all the while, the super-rich, who we laud and seemingly adore were hoarding their wealth in offshore tax havens, many of which are British territories.[211] The number of billionaires and their combined wealth soared during the pandemic,[212] whilst many fell deeper into poverty.[213] Britain is a vastly unequal country[214] – one of the worst.

FINDING HOPE FOR A MORE LOVING SOCIETY

In Morecambe Bay, we are discovering three key ingredients to building a new society with love at its core.

The first is to humanise and learn to love the 'other'.

The second is to focus on the real issues being experienced by the 'other', through deep listening, allowing new perspectives through humility.

Thirdly, creating space for reimagining what a more integrated and reciprocal life might be like together.

We've begun to develop a practice of hospitality as leadership, discovering uncomfortable and inconvenient truths through initiatives like the PTC and creating space to imagine together how we might do things differently. In turn, these lead to the mobilisation of a social movement, infiltrating our systems and structures with a new set of values, to shape a new culture.

THE POVERTY TRUTH COMMISSION

Over the last few years, I've had the privilege of being involved in the PTC. Perhaps, more than anything it has shown me just how fragmented, fractured and dislocated our life together in society is. The principles of the PTC[215] were drawn from the rebuilding of South Africa, post-apartheid. The PTC's phrase, **'nothing about us, without us, is for us'** shaped the way in which communities were involved in the process of reconciliation, reimagining the future of that nation.

The principles were taken up in Scotland and the PTC began there. It was then adopted by various cities and regions across the UK. The basic premise is that people who live in, or have significant experience of poverty, are often 'done to' by people in positions of influence or power. They are recipients of, rather than involved in, the decisions that most affect them. It gives people who live with the reality of poverty the opportunity to tell their stories to those with 'power and influence'. These 'testifiers' then invite those who usually wear the important lanyards to become co-commissioners with them. **Relationships are built. Suspicions are dissipated. Understanding grows. Injustices begin to be seen from new perspectives and so can start to be broken down.**

In Morecambe Bay, we brought together a group of leaders who believed that such an approach was worthwhile.[216] We raised some finances and appointed a 'key worker', who then spent time building relationships with people in our communities experiencing poverty in their day to day lives. This group of people, who we call the 'testifiers' or 'community commissioners', spent time together over several months. They learned to trust each other through telling one another their own stories. After a period of time, they then invited leaders and people of influence to an event which they designed themselves. This was in a location of their own choosing.

The testifiers of our first commission held their event at the Ashton Hall in Lancaster and invited 150 guests. The stories they told were so powerful that there was not a dry eye in the audience by the end of the presentations. I opened this chapter with David's testimony. The testifiers then invited a selection of the people present to form a commission with them. Over the course of a year, this newly formed group of people became good friends and began to understand the issues being experienced, with a great deal more depth and insight. This led to real empathy and changes of practice, particularly within the district council and NHS.

The PTC in our area divided into three subsections, as determined by our community commissioners. This was based on their experiences of poverty and its associated barriers: health and mental health, community issues, and benefits. The whole point of a PTC is to learn to be together, and in particular, for the civic commissioners to stop trying to fix things on behalf of people. It's about learning to be with people in their pain and together finding a way forward. This involves humility and deep listening. How can we hear people we have never met?

I was more directly involved in the health and mental health group. Along with our community commissioners, there were other GPs, a chief executive and a senior commissioner involved from the civic side. We spent several months building relationships, hearing one another's stories. We gained insight into the complexities of the health and care system from several perspectives. Two things struck me about the stories I heard from my new friends.

Firstly, I was humbled by how varied each of their journeys into poverty had been. Sarah had suffered an accidental injury, a job loss and marriage breakdown. Ruth had a severe mental health crisis and had also lost a highly successful job. Sheila had a life-long and debilitating illness. Angela was experiencing generational poverty, which is altogether very hard to escape from.

Secondly, the health and care system is horrifically dehumanising and uncaring at times. I heard about the utterly humiliating and quite frankly barbaric treatment of Ruth, whilst detained under the Mental Health Act. I listened to the most shocking and unkind 'computer says no' lack of care for Sarah when attending late to sign on at the Jobs and Benefits office during a mental health crisis. I saw the pain in Sheila's eyes as she told me about how she had spent years being part of patient groups to improve the care of people living with disabilities, only to see everything she had fought for dismantled within a couple of years of austerity. 'Like we never really mattered at all.'

The thing was, although it was heart-breaking and we shed many tears together in our meetings, none of it surprised me. I know the stipulations staff are under and the pressures they face. I know what compassion fatigue can do to the human spirit and the sense of powerlessness of working 'for the system'. After months of listening and trying to understand the issues involved, we began to ask how our relationships together might enable some change.

Our friends Sarah, Ruth, Sheila and Angela came up with a brilliant idea of a 'citizen representative/advocate'. This person would be a friend to a person caught in poverty and having to negotiate the complexities of the health, care and benefits systems. This person would also be able to help them write out their story, so they don't have to retell it over and over, which can be retraumatising.

They can also go with them to appointments and advocate for them when they are having a tough day or being spoken down to by a health or care professional.

After months of designing the job, working out the best vehicle of employment and getting through the commissioning hoops, we finally reached the stage at which this has become a reality. The person is employed through Citizens Advice. Early indicators show this work is having a positive impact. The work is being researched as part of a PhD programme.

We were changed because of relationship and could no longer see things the same way anymore.

WHY?

We recently had a series of conversations in Morecambe Bay, in which we were exploring what it might be like if love and kindness formed the basis of our society, politics and economics.[217] During a panel discussion, Mike Love, a thought leader and peace builder in the City of Leeds was asked, **'How do you see poverty?'** He responded by saying that we need to get to a deeper question.

We can't answer how we see poverty until we understand why we see poverty.

Why do we see such staggering inequality and poverty in our society? Globally, nationally and locally, we see it and we tolerate it. In a world of bountiful plenty, as we sit round the table of humanity, we have a picture of mass surplus and mass starvation – mega portions and meagre ones, huge waste and massive want.

How is this good economics?

Why is it this way?

The truth about poverty is that it exposes our values.

It doesn't have to be this way. We can change policy. We can re-evaluate our values. We can transfer meaningful power to people with lived experience of it. We can change hearts, mindsets and attitudes through compassionate leadership and the refusal to 'other' our human brothers and sisters.

PROXIMITY AND PARTICIPATION

Perhaps what the PTC has revealed to me more than anything is just how important proximity is. It has also shown to the contrary how utterly dislocated our communities are from those in power. Very few people in senior leadership positions ever step out of the safety of the boardroom to put themselves in uncomfortable, real contexts. Our politicians and civil servants make decisions on behalf of people whom they have never met based on inaccurate assumptions and flawed ideologies.

One of the results of our PTC in Morecambe Bay and the sterling work of the Morecambe Bay Food Bank was that on 12 February 2019, Frank Field (then) MP and Heidi Allen, who is also no longer an MP, decided to come and meet with members of our community. They were doing a national tour of the UK, on behalf of the Department of Work and Pensions Select Committee, to better understand the effects of the roll out of Universal Credit. Many members of the PTC and others from the community stood up, bravely, to bear witness to the effects of austerity and poverty in their everyday lives. They gave evidence about how government schemes were failing to address the issues they face.

My friend David spoke again about his experiences growing up and how the decisions made by those in power had such detrimental effects on his own health and that of his family. Things that were done to him without compassion or understanding. Callous decisions made by looking at numbers on a page, and with the stroke of a pen, without thought to the human cost and consequences. 'See me as a person, not a number. See me as living. I am flesh and blood.'[218]

It was moving to watch Heidi Allen, in particular, sit and listen to story after story with tears streaming down her face. She reflected to us that she hadn't realised the layers of poverty; the hiddenness and pervasiveness of it. She was especially shocked when she heard about a local mum who was feeding several families on her street from a freezer she kept in her front room. Extraordinary acts of kindness in the face of such a grim economic reality. We need an altogether more connected and compassionate politics. We need a politics which isn't about braying across the aisles of the House of Commons (how common is it when we examine the backgrounds and educational institutions attended by the members?). We need a politics which enables us to recover a relational basis for how we do life together.

Professor Sir Michael Marmot argues that tackling disempowerment is crucial for improving health and improving health equity.[219] However, proximity, relocation and reconnection will not be enough. Government itself requires significant reimagining and transformation. Professor Mariana Mazzucato demonstrates this, so eloquently in *Mission Economy*. 'The problem,' she argues, 'is not "big government" or "small government". The problem is the type of government: what it does and how.'[220] Mazzucato continues, 'The case for radical change is overwhelming ... The reason is simple: only government has the capacity to steer the transformation on the scale needed – to recast the way in which economic organisations are governed, how their relationships are structured and how economic actors and civil society relate to each other.'[221]

The task is huge! But a time of crisis is exactly the moment to reimagine what type of society we want to build, and the capabilities and capacities we need to get us there.

We find ourselves in that critical epoch.

- *Why do we see poverty?*

- *How do you view poverty?*

- *Where do you see people being stigmatised because of poverty?*

- *What damage has the narrative of the 'deserving' and 'undeserving' poor done to our society?*

- *What might an economy built on love be like?*

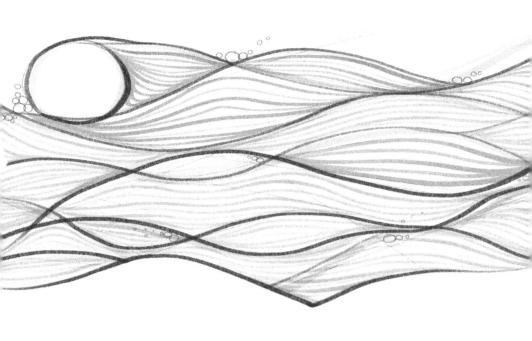

CHAPTER ELEVEN
LOVE FOOD

STUCK

Cameron and his mum, Julie, sat down together and I asked them how I could help.

'It's a bit embarrassing,' started his mum, 'but we've been told to come and see you because we got a letter from school about his weight.'

The school nurses had been into Year 6 in all the local primary schools to weigh and measure all the children. This happens twice in primary schools in England – once when the children join their school, aged four or five, and once when they are soon to leave at ten or eleven years. Any concerns are dealt with in a letter to their parents or carers and sometimes a visit to the GP will ensue.

I looked at Cameron and smiled kindly. He was overweight for his age and height, for sure, and I wondered how he felt about getting that letter. So, I asked him. He shrugged, his freckly face flushing red, his eyes filling with tears, before he quickly wiped them away.

'I dunno. I feel sad. But I don't want to be fat. It's just hard, isn't it, Mum?'

'The thing is,' Julie continued, 'people judge you, like you don't care. But I'm a single mum. I work two jobs. I never know when the work will be coming in. By the time I've paid the bills and tried to sort out some of the debts I owe, I can't afford all these things the government tell us will lead to a balanced diet. You know what it's been like since his dad left (and thank God he did, cos you know what he was like). To top it off, I have to care for my gran who's got dementia as well. He doesn't like exercising, cos he just gets laughed at and called all kinds of names, and I guess we've just got a bit stuck.'

What was I supposed to do? Wag my finger and heap shame onto this mother? Put them forward for some cookery classes and try and find some kind of sports activity that Cameron might enjoy? There were layers of complexity to Cameron's weight issues, most of which could not be fixed by simply offering guidance or signposting for some help. It's not as simple as 'you are what you eat'. Cameron and his mum live on an estate with no easy access to healthy food and poor transport links to any supermarkets. They are surrounded by junk food cafes (five times higher than you find in a more affluent neighbourhood[222]). What are they supposed to eat? Cheap and easily available food sources are now more sugar-filled[223] and calorific[224] than they used to be. Advertising is also playing a huge role in affecting what children are eating.[225] The reality is that childhood obesity in the UK is found mostly in our areas of greatest economic poverty.

As Professor Sandro Galea (Dean and Knox Professor at Boston University School of Public Health) has shown, it is a phenomenally complex issue.[226] Genetic factors play a part, but the ubiquitous factor is the kind of environment the child grows up in. Most childhood obesity is linked to having a poor nutritional state. So, it's important that as a society we think about how we create healthy environments for our children. But the notion that people should just exercise more and eat a more balanced diet is over simplistic at best, and could be considered both patronising and cruel.

Public Health England (before they were dismantled) published what is supposed to be a helpful healthy eating guide.[227] A 2018 report by independent think tank the Food Foundation found that it's not that helpful after all. More than one in four households would need to spend over a quarter of their disposable income after housing costs to meet the guide's recommendations.

For parents in the bottom 20% of earners, the cost would be 42% of their income. It's completely unaffordable. **In the UK, 3.7 million children are living in these households, earning less than £15,860,** and are likely to be unable to afford a healthy diet as defined by the government.[228] It is not a question of people just taking more personal responsibility for themselves. **Social injustice is ingrained in our society,** and it is making children in our areas of greatest disadvantage more unwell. Our society is sick because our economy is sick. It is love sick.

Following my encounter with Cameron and his mum, I asked if I could sneak into one of our local head teachers' forums to talk to them about the issue. I shared with them some of the data we were collecting on childhood obesity in the area. I discussed some of the complexities involved and some of the long-term consequences on the health of future generations. Recent studies have shown that maternal obesity can have profound effects on the health of the children in their womb, decades later.[229] Having a mum who is overweight during pregnancy increases your chance of getting heart disease under the age of sixty, significantly.

This particular fact seemed to light a fire in the belly of one of the school leaders present, Mrs Simmons. She invited me for a cup of tea at her school the following day. She realised that what she did in her school might have an impact on the future health of the girls and boys in her care. She wondered what we could do. So, I shared some evidence with her about The Daily Mile initiative,[230] and we talked about what might be done around school meals and helping families who were struggling. In line with the best evidence, she instigated an extra exercise break in the mid-afternoon, shortly after lunch. During this extra window in the day, the whole school would run their mile. Big kids would help the little ones and all the staff joined in too. School meals were given a health overhaul and a breakfast club was started.

Although initially it cost the school, Mrs Simmons thought it worthwhile. I went back regularly to see how it was going. After six months, the results were staggering. The boys, in particular, were concentrating better and improving in their maths. Parents reported that their children were sleeping better. The head teacher herself, had lost over three stone in weight and is still running five kilometres every day. The school have reduced hiring transport to take them to local sports matches and often walk instead. Better still, they were now winning on a regular basis. This was a big cost saving and helped to fund other activities. A cooking class had started for parents or carers after school, with childcare provided for families who were invited along.

I even had a letter from a father of a child in the school, who told me that his kids were misbehaving and bouncing off the walls during the weekend. So, at their request, he'd started to do the weekend mile with them. It had great results. Their behaviour improved and they slept better, giving him and their mum more time in the evening. We had a new evangelist in Mrs Simmons and soon whole clusters of schools around Morecambe Bay had picked up the baton. Cameron's school was one of those to take it up. When I visited, his teacher told me he was now regularly playing football in the playground every break time, instead of sitting on the edge, feeling left out. He was in a much healthier physical state as well. These kinds of interventions do have some merit and do work, to some extent. I was hugely encouraged, at least to begin with.

HUMBLE PIE

As news spread about The Daily Mile, I found myself visiting several other schools in the area. In one school in Morecambe, I was sat in a circle with a set of parents, carers and the head teacher. We had a conversation about how we could work together to improve the health and wellbeing of the children in the school. One of the mums, Trina, a truly amazing human being, looked me in the eyes and said, 'I don't think you get it, do you?' She continued, explaining in detail her personal experience, which she later posted on a thread on X (previously known as Twitter):

Ending up on benefits isn't always as simple as
losing your job. It can be the result of bereavement,
illness, injury, or a breakdown in a relationship.
It's a culture shock. For me, one day I had a grand
a week coming in. The next day I was applying for IS.

It took 14 weeks for my payments to come in. 14 weeks
where I still had to pay the rent, pay bills, feed my child.
You default on anything on a contract. Worry about it later.
And you sell all your 'nice things' for pence,
to keep a roof over your head.

Then the fridge breaks - or the cooker, or the washer
- but you're still only getting your IS payment,
not housing benefit or tax credits.
It's different now, it's all UC - but that's harder,
coz it's all rolled into one so you don't
even get that small amount of IS.

With no other option (you can't get normal credit)
you go to Brighthouse (or the current equivalent)
or you get a loan from Deebank/Provident/Greenwoods.
You pay 4x as much back in total, but it's only £5 per week.

Your credit rating gets worse because you've defaulted
on all your 'luxuries' - contract phone, sky tv, landline phone.
Debts become bailiffs knocking on your door, and if you
hide from them long enough... county court judgements.

You're still trying to learn to rebudget
on less than 30% of what you used to have. All whilst dealing with
illness, bereavement, disability, or social workers on your case
because you were a DV victim and the police involved them. You
move house because you can't afford the rent

Then you're sanctioned. Because despite telling
the job centre three times that you've moved,
they sent your appointment letter to the wrong house.
Or you were in hospital. Or your child was sick.
You appeal, but they uphold the sanction.
You try to rebudget again.

Your ex-partner decides they don't want to bother
with the kids anymore. So they stop paying child support

and disappear. The CSA/CMS 'can't find them'
despite you providing their address and phone number.
You try to rebudget it again.

If that doesn't make you think twice about judging people
in poverty, consider going through that - which was my
experience in 2009 - in the midst of a global pandemic,
when there's no jobs, food has gone up 60%
you're frightened to leave the house in case you get sick....

And the world and his wife are taking to social media
to espouse how you're a shit parent and need your kids
taken off you, because no matter how hard you try to explain
that you're not a scrounger, they tell you that you should
use your non-existant money to just make soup.[231] *(emphasis added)*

She was right. I didn't get it. I felt deeply humbled, horribly naive and embarrassed by my do-gooding and overly simplistic ideas. Of course, getting kids to run a mile a day at school isn't going to fix the deeper societal economic cesspit that means many of them can't afford to eat. That doesn't mean that we don't go ahead with such initiatives. But we do need to recognise their significant limitations. We need humility to listen to the testimonies which make us uncomfortable.

The Trussell Trust is clear. **The problem of food poverty and hunger in the UK is getting worse.** Outside London, the North West of England is facing the most significant problem. In the year leading up to 31 March 2021, the Trussell Trust handed out 2.5 million food parcels. This was a 33% increase on the year before. It is affecting children more than adults. Nearly one million children were given food parcels by the Trussell Trust alone during the Covid-19 pandemic. The Trussell Trust doesn't see this as a good thing; it would rather not exist. It's become an all too easy way for members of the public to feel like they are helping out. People are donating food, tapping themselves on the back whilst propping up a political and economic ideology that have made this possible in the first place. This is only the tip of the iceberg. There are many independent food banks and food clubs also providing help. In this same time frame the number of people claiming Universal Credit has risen from three million to six million people.[232]

ECONOMICS AND SOCIAL JUSTICE

Our economic values and principles sit at the root of social injustice.

For all those who lost the £20 a week uplift to their Universal Credit there is little sense of justice.[233] The government argue that losing it will get people back into work, but this shows a lack of understanding around the cost of living and the realities of endemic poverty in our communities experiencing daily social injustice.

For those who are living in utter squalor, or the eight million people in housing that is unfit for human habitation, **there is no justice.**[234]

For those who have disabled children but are forced to live in accommodation that is unsafe, **there is no justice.**[235]

For communities in the North of England, when it comes to affordable and connected transport infrastructure, or funding that truly levels up, **there is no justice.**[236]

For those fleeing war-torn countries and crammed into old army barracks whilst being treated as less than human, **there is no justice.**[237]

For those queuing round the corner to receive food from the food banks, in ever-growing numbers, **there is no justice.**[238]

For the rising generation who will have to pick up the economic tab of climate change,[239] **there is no justice.**

For the rising numbers of children stuck in poverty across the UK,[240] and the millions of pensioners who cannot keep warm,[241] **there is no justice.**

For the billions of people worldwide trapped in poverty, whilst the obscene wealth of billionaires continues to grow, **there is no justice.**[242]

For the millions of lives displaced by the western war machines, forced to flee their homes, having lost many loved ones as part of what we barbarically called 'collateral damage', **there is no justice.**[243]

If we put love at the heart of our economic decision-making, we would have to **ask ourselves some much more**

fundamental questions about what shapes our economy and whether or not it is a model we should continue with. Our society is sick because our economy is sick. **It is love sick.**

WAS BLIND, BUT NOW I SEE

I recently hosted an online discussion following a TEDxNHS talk by Nadeen Haidar about food poverty in the UK.[244] It involved a panel with Emma Revie, CEO of the Trussell Trust, which oversees more than 1,200 food banks in the UK; Jack Monroe, British food writer, journalist and activist; and Jemma Gilbert, Director of Transformation at the Healthy London Partnership. I asked them why we are seeing such staggering poverty across the UK and what the state of hunger is like, currently. They agreed together that Covid-19 has been a wake-up call to us all about how easy it is to fall into poverty. Very few people are immune from this. The safety net is lacking and the journey into poverty is a slippery slope with multiple possible triggers and factors. These include for example, adverse childhood experiences (ACEs), learning difficulties, severe and enduring mental illness, the loss of a job or the death of a family member. Our entire societal experience has become more insecure.

No longer does poverty and hunger happen to 'them over there'. Now it happens to us.

We have been willing to tolerate the intolerable because until now it hasn't touched us.

Poverty exists and is pervasive because we judge people struggling in it, and together we tolerate it. There was staggering poverty and food hunger across the UK before Covid-19. This virus has simply taken the corporate blinkers off our eyes and caused us to see that which we had previously blinded ourselves to. Suddenly, the invisible people have become visible. We are awake to the fact that poverty is a more pervasive virus than Covid-19 and this pandemic has thrived on it. Not only do the poor live shorter lives with longer periods of ill health, but they also have less care available to them at times of need. It's not because there isn't enough to go round. Rather, as Professor Beverley Skeggs argues, from a sociological perspective, it is a question of our values and what or whom we value.[245] How much value do we give to Cameron, whom we met at the beginning of the chapter?

MIND THE GAP

Let's get back to the question about why we see poverty. **For too long, poverty has been weaponised and maintained through the practice of shaming the poor.** We cannot talk about what it means to be well when there is this level of inequality and injustice in our society. Our society is sick because our economy is sick. **It is love sick.**

We are allowing poverty. Poverty exists when people have insufficient income. They therefore have an inability to take care of their most basic needs, having to choose between eating and heating. It exists because labour is exploited, because people are not paid enough for the work they do. It happens because when people are struggling with physical or mental health issues, sadly they find that the benefits available are insufficient to see them through. This is the result of policy. Policy decisions made by people. For example, between 2016 and 2020, the benefit freeze affected more than 27 million people and swept 400,000 into poverty.[246]

Ten years ago, food banks barely existed; in the five years leading up to Covid-19 there was a 74% increase in the use of them across the UK. In the year leading up to March 2020, 1.9 million people accessed the support of the Trussell Trust.[247] In the second two weeks of March 2020, there was a 100% increase compared to the first two weeks. Covid-19 hasn't caused poverty, but it has significantly compounded it. Consider this: in 2020, 20% of those accessing help were single parents and a staggering 63% of clients were living with a disability or supporting someone who has one. By 2021, 94% of people accessing food banks were facing destitution.

DESTITUTION

Destitution denotes the circumstances facing people who cannot afford to buy the absolute essentials that we all need to eat, stay warm and dry, and keep clean. The Joseph Rowntree Foundation UK Poverty 2020 report into destitution in the UK makes stark reading.[248] The data show that in the two years between 2017 and 2019 there was a 35% increase in the number of people experiencing destitution in the UK, a total of 2.4 million people which includes 555,000 children. Of these 2.4 million destitute people, 57% lacked basic food, 49% lacked the clothing they needed, 43% went without toiletries – particularly affecting women on their menstrual cycle – and 32% had no income at all. This is getting worse as a result of rising inflation and the cost of living crisis.

It took the Manchester United football player, Marcus Rashford, to force the government to pay attention to the reality of child hunger across the UK.[249] These extremes of poverty in the UK are disproportionately impacting on women and young people under the age of twenty-five, with very few over the age of sixty-five affected. Of those in destitution, 72% were born in the UK and 54% are limited by health conditions or disabilities. The use of food banks is 81% higher than five years ago. In 2022–2023, there were over 2.9 million food parcels given to people in the UK, including 1 million children.[250]

When you add into this picture of social injustice in the UK the layers of complexity associated with crippling debt, precarious or limited employment, poor and unaffordable housing, over-crowded hostels and the associated increase in psychological strain, we have a real problem.[251] The economic forecast remains bleak due to the combined effects of Covid-19, the war in Ukraine with its associated rise in fuel and food prices, and Brexit. Even more heart-breaking and maddening is the reality, highlighted by the Institute for Public Policy Research (IPPR) 'Levelling Up Health for Prosperity', that our poorest areas are the ones which have had the deepest cuts to their public health budgets.[252] This is making it far harder for health and social care professionals to reach and work with those people who are most in need of support.

This is outrageous. Are you outraged?

It certainly makes no sense economically.

We have known about the reality of health inequalities in our communities for a very long time. It has also been clear that only a whole-societal approach will bring about meaningful change.

Health is political, economic, ecological and sociological.

All parts of government and public services need to ensure that reducing health inequality is a priority and act accordingly.[253] This joined up or integrated approach to population health can only work with sustained energy and commitment. We need political will and public buy-in. This is beginning to happen. But there remain too many slogans and not enough resource or real action.

Our society is sick because our economy is sick. **It is love sick.**

We cannot tolerate the injustice of unequal health for our communities. We will not accept the reality that life expectancy is falling for people, especially women, in our most economically deprived communities.[254] We will no longer turn a blind eye to those who are street homeless with an average life expectancy of less than 45 years. We own up to the fact that the experiences of hunger and malnutrition for children growing up in poverty is a national shame.

We must act now.

Our previously ineffective top-down strategies are inadequate. Our national funding allocations and centrally driven targets are stopping us from doing the transformational work required. We must take an entirely different, collaborative approach to health and wellbeing in society. We must build our society and level up, motivated by love. We are learning to work differently.

'ECO'-'NOMY'

The word 'economy' comes from two Greek works, *oikos* and *nomos*. It literally means the values or principles on which we shape the household. It is true that we fall into trouble if we think of the economy too simply as a 'household'. Economies are dynamic, living systems. However, the truth is that our economies need to be underpinned with values that are life-giving and full of hope. Otherwise, they lead to the kind of injustices and climate breakdown we are witnessing all over the globe. In the last chapter I explored Skeggs' work on how we apply value to people, based on our moral choices. This then shapes the values of our society.[255] Professor Mariana Mazzucato, as an economist at University College London, implores us to think about how our economy is shaped by these same values.[256]

A QUESTION OF VALUES

In *The Value of Everything*, Mazzucato challenges us to reimagine the economy based on more compassionate values and what we value. She goes on to demonstrate how political choices can significantly affect economic policies, as for example, with austerity. In this case, an under valuing of the public sector led to communities paying the price of a global, economic crisis caused by a combination of high private debt and reckless financial sector investment. It was easier to blame governments and cut public services to the bone, in response to the financial crash, than to take stock of just how broken and morally rudderless our global economy has become.[257]

When governments want to do something, like go to war, they seem to be able to find however much money is needed. But when it comes to ensuring citizens all have a good quality home to live in or are properly cared for when living with a disability, the money is harder to find.

Cutting services which actually enable a population to flourish will only damage the economy in the long run.

We need to think of our public services, not as a cost to the economy, but as an investment in our future. Our discussion should not be about how much money we can save from the NHS, to invest further upstream. Rather, we need to ask ourselves how we can create an economy which builds overall wellbeing, based on an ethic of love and kindness. This is fundamentally different to the broken framework of Utilitarianism, on which we have placed far too much emphasis. This notion of 'the greatest good for the greatest number' is woefully lacking. It excludes those who need the most care.

A BROKEN SYSTEM?

For years I have thought the economic system is broken. It doesn't seem to generate resources in a way which is sustainable for the planet. Nor does it distribute them in a way which ensures everybody has enough. Then I met the brilliant economist, Professor Katherine Trebeck, when she came to speak at our 'Love Economics' event in Morecambe Bay.[258] She advises the Scottish Government and helps facilitate the Wellbeing Economy Alliance (WEAll).[259] According to Trebeck, the economy is not broken – not at all. It is doing exactly what it was designed to do. In shape, it is like a champagne glass, siphoning off riches to the wealthy and powerful. The system is not broken. But it is entirely dysfunctional if we want an economic model which will lead to social justice and environmental recovery.

Our society is sick because our economy is sick. **It is love sick.**

Trebeck describes the shift in values at the foundation of our economy to be about building an economy of wellbeing.[260] Her influence is beginning to have an impact, as countries like Scotland, Iceland and New Zealand are beginning to talk this new language.[261]

Providing overall wellbeing, through the tackling of inequality, is at the heart of what it means to create a loving civilisation. **There is a massive mismatch between what the economy is set up to do and what people and the planet need.** We need different measurements and different tools to build an altogether different kind of economy.

The purpose of economics is not infinitive growth but rather to ensure the appropriate stewardship of our resources to serve the needs of the environment, humanity and our fellow species. In a loving economy, Cameron and his family would not be going hungry. Rather, they would be well nourished, able to access healthy food and flourishing in a connected community in which everyone has enough.

- *What does our economy tell us about whom and what we value?*

- *What emotions are stirred in you when you consider the reality of food poverty in the UK?*

- *What are the values that you would like to see underpinning our economy?*

- *What might an economy of wellbeing be like?*

- *What would an economy of wellbeing mean for Cameron (whom we met at the beginning of the chapter)?*

- *What might it mean for his family?*

- *What might it mean for you and your own family and community?*

CHAPTER TWELVE
LOVE FREEDOM

TRAPPED

Let us return to Julie, whom we met with her son, Cameron, in the last chapter. Julie is disabled. She has a neurological condition which affects her mobility. This means that she finds it difficult to walk. She mostly gets around on crutches. At thirty-six, Julie works two jobs, both on zero-hour contracts because her Personal Independence Payment (PIP) doesn't allow her to live well. Her income is erratic and insecure. She is the main carer for her gran, Angela, who has dementia, and she looks after Cameron and her older daughter, Sara. Sara is fifteen, and although heading towards GCSEs, also works around 12 hours a week, trying to support her mum with the family finances. They live on a housing estate, with very poor transport links and Julie is in the early stages of developing diabetes. They often rely on food banks.

I had first met Julie about four years after Cameron was born. She came to see me at the time, as she found herself in a pickle.

'I'm pregnant,' she told me.

I have learned, through my career, that it's not always a good idea to follow this statement with 'Congratulations!' Some women are not happy to be pregnant.

'OK, how are you feeling?' I responded.

Julie started to sob. 'I don't know what to do,' she continued. 'Darren is furious. He said that I'm stupid. That it must be my fault. That I've ruined everything. He says I've got to get rid of the baby. He's probably right. It is terrible timing. And we can't afford to have another one – not now. He says that if I carry on with it, he's going to leave me. I can't have him leave me. I can't get good work. But I don't want to have an abortion. I feel trapped. I'm dammed if I do, and I'm dammed if I don't.'

'Oh Julie! This is so tough. How can I help best?' I asked.

'I don't know; I just needed to come and tell you,' she answered. 'I need some thinking time.'

'OK, well, whatever you decide, we will help you,' I assured her.

'You won't judge me?' she asked.

'Julie, I'm your doctor, not your judge.'

She came to see me a week later. 'OK,' she said, 'I've made up my mind. I'm going to have an abortion. My head has won over my heart. I've got to be practical.'

We talked this through. She decided to give it a few more days as she was still slightly unsure. She saw one of my colleagues after the weekend. She was referred to our local gynaecology unit and had a surgical termination of her pregnancy. Four weeks later, she was back to see me again.

'He's left me! The fucking sod has left me! After all of that. After making me go through with it and threatening to leave me. He's just fucking done it anyway.'

She was incandescent with rage. It turns out that he had shacked up with someone from work, whom he'd also managed to get pregnant. And so here she was, sat in my consulting room, angry and now alone. Left to pick up the pieces of her life and carry on. She was as trapped as ever. But now with less support. I wondered how she would find a way through. But her son and daughter needed her. So, she would have to find a way.

A few months later, I was watching BBC *Question Time*. Rosie Jones, who is a comedian with cerebral palsy gave an impassioned plea that disabled people should receive extra support. She talked about how revolutionary the Disability Discrimination Act 1995 was for so many people, who live with disabilities. However, she went on to detail how when the Disability Living Allowance was replaced by the Personal Independence Payment during the Conservative-led revision of the welfare state, 650,000 people (those over the age of sixteen) had their benefits cut.[262] The effect of this is that the rights of disabled people are not just being overlooked, they are being ignored. They are no longer able to get the support they need, and this is driving them into poverty. During the Covid-19 pandemic, people living with disabilities have had to access food banks at alarmingly high rates. As a result of these kind of policies, Julie must regularly use food banks. Over the last five years there has been a 128% rise in the need for them nationally.[263] People living in poverty are trapped. There is nothing that Julie can do to 'take more responsibility'. Her 'choices' are actually very limited. This is worth exploring more.

FREEDOM FOR WOMEN?

Statistics clearly show that out of the 207,384 terminations which happened in England and Wales in 2019, the vast majority were for women in the most economically disadvantaged areas.[264] We say abortion is about a woman's right to choose. But how much choice do women in our poorest communities have? Given the way society is stacked against them, there is often no choice available to them except abortion.

Recently, the row over this issue has intensified in the USA, with the overturning of the landmark Roe v Wade case.[265] It is only in very recent times that abortion has been legalised in Northern Ireland[266] and the Republic of Ireland.[267]

The 'pro-life' versus 'pro-choice' arguments are so entrenched. Neither side can listen well to the other. Both sides caricature the other. For example, the 'pro-lifers' are seen as religious weirdos and total hypocrites, because they will not support societal measures to support women once they have their children; while the 'pro-choicers' are seen as baby-killers and are destroying traditional values.

I know people who are pro-life; not because they are anti-choice but because they feel deeply uncomfortable about ending the life of a developing human being, especially after the first 12 weeks of pregnancy. I also know people who are deeply religious and still compassionately pro-choice, given the complexities often involved.

The problem, as I see it is this: even if you are ideologically pro-life (and I have to confess, I have deep sympathy with this position, because I believe that life is sacred), pragmatically, given the societal injustice meted out to women, it is hard not to be pro-choice also. Why? Well, because in order to be pro-life you have to be pro the life of the child *and* the mother. You also have to care about the kind of life the child will have after they are born. It's not just the point of being born that matters.

Rachel Cunliffe, senior associate editor of the *New Statesman*, argued in a thread on X (previously known as Twitter), what a truly pro-life perspective must also strongly advocate for.[268] Her list includes more holistic sex education, widely available free contraception, free and excellent prenatal and postnatal care, accessible childcare, improved parental leave policies, better schools, welfare for families growing up in poverty and higher prosecution rates for rape and domestic abuse.

I would add that we also need equal pay for women in the workplace, including a universal basic income for those who must take on the role of carers in a society where this invariably falls to women.

On top of this, the pro-life argument must also be honest about what kind of lives it is 'pro'. If you are pro the life of an unborn child, you should also be pro the life of the people being killed unnecessarily by guns. Being pro-life means you should be anti-killing people, including on death row or in the machines of war. There is just so much hypocrisy about this, as we see in the USA around the gun lobby. People want the politics of freedom for those who want to buy guns, despite the killing of innocent children, but want women to be slaves when it comes to their own bodies to protect the lives of innocent children.[269]

If we are to be a pro-life society, then we should care deeply about the lives of the refugees drowning in our seas. In a loving, pro-life society, we would not see them shipped off to somewhere far away, like Rwanda, where we no longer have to think about them.

Compassion is not just for one pet cause. It is for everyone, everywhere.

Until women gain true equality in society – with an end of misogyny and male sexual violence, and a far more equal sense of male responsibility in child rearing – there isn't really a conversation to be had. This is an example of where the law kills but love creates both hope and life. The reality is that pro-choice governments see less abortions taking place, because they also improve the lives of women and therefore make abortion more safe, less common and less necessary.[270] In a loving society, we do not use the law to create slavery. Rather, we create a culture of love in which life is perpetuated.

Women are recipients of massive social injustice. In our poorest areas they are living in poorer health for longer periods of time.[271] Not only so, the life expectancy gap between rich and poor women in the UK is widening.[272]

INVISIBLE WOMEN

In her vital book, *Invisible Women: Exposing Data Bias in a World Designed for Men*, Caroline Criado Perez reveals the vast injustice being meted out to women.[273] She details how – following the 2008 financial crash and the introduction of austerity economics – children's services, children's centres, social care budgets, social security payments and carers' allowances were all cut drastically. On paper, this looked like lots of lovely money savings for the government. In reality it meant a massive shift of costs from the public sector onto women, who were left to pick up the bill. This led to a huge rise in female unemployment (a rise of over 20% by March 2012 alone – the highest figure in 25 years), whilst male unemployment stood still. By 2014, this had risen to 74% underemployment for women. Between 2010 and 2020, *86% of all budget cuts fell on women* and hit their incomes twice as much as men's. The changes made life considerably more difficult for women in our poorest communities, especially for single mothers and British Asian women, in particular, whilst men in the richest 50% of households actually gained from tax and benefit changes.

This model of economy is morally and ethically defunct.

It leaves women in our most economically deprived communities utterly trapped. Especially if they are living with a disability. Period poverty is also causing significant stigmatisation and shame. The Scottish Government have made massive strides to end this injustice,[274] but England lags woefully behind.

Philip Alston, the United Nations Special Rapporteur, wrote in his report on extreme poverty and human rights in the UK[275] that the situation is both systemic and tragic.[276] The removal of £26 billion from the UK welfare system, with punishing regimes like the two-child limit[277] (introduced by a chancellor who grew up with significant wealth) was, according to Alston, both harsh and uncaring. His investigation involved deep listening to those living with the experience of poverty in the UK. But when his report was presented to the then Chancellor, now Rt Hon Lord Phillip Hammond, his response was genuinely shocking to me. He said that he did not see people living in poverty across the UK.[278] Other politicians described Alston's report as being 'barely believable'.[279] But now Covid-19 has forced us all to see the staggering levels of poverty and disconnection in our society. We cannot unsee it. **We cannot unsee Julie.**

Our society is sick because our economy is sick. **It is love sick.** It is trapping people, especially women, and reducing their freedom.

Sara, Julie's daughter, is a hidden character in this story. She is growing up in poverty. Given her working hours, she is likely to perform poorly in her school exams. This will make it harder to escape the 'poverty trap'. Angela, Julie's gran, is also hidden, along with many elderly citizens in our most economically disadvantaged areas. We now have over two million pensioners in this country living in poverty,[280] the worst rate in Western Europe,[281] thanks to policies which have failed on pensions, coupled with the cost of living. Many families can't even think about affording the care they need, and our social services are too stretched to provide what is needed. So, it falls on women, like Julie, to do all she can. Women like Julie are abused by an economic system which simply does not value them.

THE POLITICS AND ECONOMICS OF FREEDOM

Mioslav Volf, Founder and Director of the Yale Center for Faith and Culture, talks about the concept of 'freedom' in politics as being two-fold.[282] Firstly, it relates to the freedom won hard from slavery or emancipation of any kind. This is a good thing!

Secondly, the concept of 'freedom' is what modern liberal democracies are built on. The pillar of 'freedom' with its 'free' market. The idea is that people should be free to make their own choices, live life the way they want to and express themselves however they so choose, as long as it doesn't hurt anyone else. In fact, we consider people to be oppressed when they are restrained from their own personal freedom by the state or a dominant culture.

But what of the motivations that sit behind our notion of freedom? Or what of its consequences? Sure, we are free to live exactly how we want (if we are privileged enough). But at what cost? The USA calls itself 'the land of the free' with its bill of rights. So, it is every person's right to own a gun, but what are the consequences? In the politics of freedom, everything is permissible, but not everything is beneficial.

The reality is, that this kind of freedom is both relative and a luxury for the few. This kind of freedom is often used to protect the rights of the 'elite', who do not want other people poking their noses into their business. This kind of freedom gives rise to toxic consumerist individualism and enslaves many people.

Freedom is the power to live with dignity. What does freedom mean for Julie? How do the politics and economics of freedom work for those who live with little choice about what happens to them? How many choices do people in our most economically disadvantaged communities have? Or how do we love best those who have no ability to make choices? Our economy has to mean something radically different for women in our society. There is much work for us to do if we're serious about living free and fully.

FREEDOM AND OPPRESSION

Freedom is, as Volf argues, caught in a cycle of freedom and oppression. The people who are freed so easily become the oppressors. They either oppress those who have previously subjugated them, or another group suffers, whom they must suppress to maintain their own freedom. So, although freedom is patently a good thing, it is clearly not creating equality or equity and is certainly not a good thing for those who are oppressed by it!

We ourselves live free but imprison the traumatised. We are free to bomb the countries whose political ideas we oppose, but we allow those who flee from that nightmare to drown in our seas. We are free to fly around the world, drive our cars and heat our homes with fossil fuels, but what of the climate crisis we are causing? How can we live free and fully without it being at the expense of those around us or indeed at a cost to the wider environment?

Does love demand of us that we limit our freedoms in order to build a society that works for everyone? What if we used our 'political' freedom to love? Or what if we used our economic freedom to ensure that everyone has enough? Isn't that what compassion does? Isn't that love in action? **Our disconnect from each other and**

the world we co-habit demonstrates to us just how unwell we have become.

We have known about the realities of climate change, social, and economic injustice for years. For so many of us though, we are just trying to make our own ends meet and thinking about these issues can feel too overwhelming. Or maybe, we have had our heads buried in the sand, or felt too powerless to do much about it. However, something has shifted. These huge issues have found their way into public consciousness. We see with utter clarity; the status quo is broken. Levelling up has to mean something in this country, especially for women.

We need an economic system based on love.

There is, for example, a world of difference between the notion of the American Dream, on the one hand, which hugely influences our current economic values, and Martin Luther King's 'dream speech' on the other.[283] One is true emancipation for all people, the other is about freedom for a few, based on the slavery of many. This is a dream for some, maybe, but an utter nightmare for the majority.[284] We cannot talk about population or planetary health if we do not radically shift our values base and therefore our model of economics. We need to open up our imaginations to a much more socially just and environmentally sustainable way of stewarding our resources together. In time, this will lead to many more healthy and well communities.

Julie's story calls us to wake up and pay attention. It should make us feel deeply uncomfortable about the values on which we have built our disconnected economy. Now we see Julie. Julie belongs to us. She reminds us that not all people are currently valued equally. And some people, especially women in our most disadvantaged communities, are far less free than others.

Freedom
Isn't
Equal

- *Do you recognise the cycle of freedom and oppression?*

- *How might some of your own freedoms lead to the slavery of others?*

- *After reading about Julie, Sara and Angela in this chapter, how do you feel?*

- *Do you see that it doesn't need to be this way?*

- *Are we able to turn the tide of injustice against women?*

- *Are we able to use our freedom to build an economy of wellbeing?*

- *What might this look like in your own home, family, neighbourhood and district?*

- *How will it affect how you vote?*

- *What values are important to you when you think about the politics and economics of freedom? How will embracing compassion effect your actions?*

CHAPTER THIRTEEN
LOVE MONEY

TRICKLED

When I was a medical student, I came across a chap called Theo. Theo was also a student at the time and a keen rugby player. He was troubled by severe muscle fatigue in his legs, which were rather scrawny compared to his well-muscled shoulders and chest. He was also getting headaches and nose bleeds. After a visit to his GP, who found he had high blood pressure, he was referred to a cardiologist. The cardiologist took his medical history and then lay him on the couch to examine him. Having done so, he summoned us, as his students to see if we could also try and reach a diagnosis. None of us could.

'Have a feel of his femoral arteries,' we were instructed. The femoral arteries are the largest arteries to supply the legs with blood and the pulse can be felt in the groin. Not one of us could find Theo's.

'This is fascinating,' we were told. 'I have never seen this before in my career as a cardiologist. Do you know why?' We collectively shook our heads, having only recently started our clinical placements in the 'heart, lungs and blood' module.

'I'll give you a clue. This is usually picked up at the six-week baby check and should have been spotted a long time ago. You're actually rather lucky to be alive,' he informed our increasingly alarmed looking patient. He continued, 'This is the very reason you are asked to check for femoral pulses in newborn infants. Anyone got any ideas?'

We scuffed our feet and looked at our shoes.

One of the junior doctors hazarded a guess. 'Is it a coarctation, Sir?' she asked.

'BINGO! Gold star for Dr Hassan!'

A coarctation of the aorta is a rare condition, especially in adulthood. As the blood flows out of the left side of the heart and to the body, it flows through the largest blood vessel in the body – the aorta. This forms an arch. At the top of the arch are the three main arteries which carry blood to the upper half of the body. Just after this point, at the downturn of the arch, Theo had developed a severe narrowing of his aorta. It was, essentially, a human dam. So, rather than a great gushing river of blood flowing to the lower half of his body, Theo had merely a trickle. This was creating high blood pressure and higher resource distribution to his chest, shoulders and head. This was giving him bulky upper body muscles, headaches and nose bleeds, and somewhat under-developed legs. He required urgent surgery, to remove this fibrous band of tissue, causing the blockage. This was necessary to prevent him from developing heart failure or having a haemorrhagic stroke (bleed on his brain), and to alleviate his other symptoms.

There were no adult cardiothoracic surgeons in the North West, who had ever operated on one. So, an eminent Paediatric Heart Surgeon from Alder Hey in Liverpool, was called upon to carry out the procedure. I was given the amazing opportunity to watch Theo go under the anaesthetic and have this high-risk procedure performed on his thorax. A cut was made between his ribs on the left side, and they were cranked open. His blood flowed out of his body into a mechanical heart, which was used to keep him alive, whilst the fibrous tissue causing the coarctation was removed.

In its place a small sock was carefully sewn. This would become part of the aorta and new cells would form over it. Once done, the blood was allowed to flow back to the cardiac tissue and a small shock to the heart kick-started it back to life. Theo was on his journey to recovery. For me, it is the starkest picture I have ever seen that trickle-down economics simply doesn't work. It over resources the 'higher' parts of the body (society) and leaves the rest starving of the resources needed to develop properly. Simply by removing this unseen blockage, the whole body could thrive.

GROWTH OBSESSED

My first lecture in medical school at the University of Manchester in September 1999 was delivered by Dr Stoddard. It was about mastication (chewing our food). Mastication is the first important step of digestion in which we break down the food we are eating, so that we can absorb the goodness and distribute the resources around the body via the cardiovascular system (heart and blood vessels). The way in which the human body ingests and utilises various forms of energy and resources, and then excretes what it doesn't need, can form a basis for us to think about economy.

Our current economic theories and systems seem to be utterly obsessed with growth, especially growth in gross domestic product (GDP).

Growth is important, for sure, but only to a point.

The right kind of nutrition is vital if the human body is to grow and develop normally. However, there comes a point at which the body reaches a state of balance or what we call homeostasis. If we continue to grow, either upwards or outwards, indefinitely, then we will either fall over or pop! It's also vital that as we grow, there is good distribution of those resources around all our tissues, otherwise we can have highly over developed areas and other parts which remain essentially emaciated. Indeed, the body can store excess food in the liver and in our fat tissue, but if that resource just sits there, then it works against us being healthy, leading to diabetes and heart disease.

A BROKEN IDEOLOGY

The problem lies in the ideology of unbridled, free-market capitalism.

In their brilliant book, *The Economics of Arrival*, Professor Katherine Trebeck and her co-author, Jeremy Williams, illustrate for us three ways in which our addiction to the growth of GDP is no longer delivering what matters to us. It is incapable of fixing the issues we are facing. Here I summarise the three main ways it is failing us:

1. It is delivering diminished margins of return. In fact, since 1978, genuine social progress has effectively flat lined in most western economies, whilst GDP has continued to grow.

In other words, our economies have continued to grow, but we are no happier. There is no increased equality and key societal indicators haven't changed. So, we're working harder and longer simply to maintain things as they are, but we are less able to enjoy the fruit of our labour. We are getting burnt out and stressed simply to drive the economy forward, but without reaping the benefits. Why do we keep doing this?

2. We are experiencing significant failure demand. It is estimated that 40% of the local authority expenditure in Scotland is given over to responding to things which could have been prevented in the first place. We see this, for example, through the thoughtless use of inappropriate cladding on the outside of buildings, leading to the devastating fire in Grenfell.[285] We see it in trying to 'fix' childhood obesity after filling our most disadvantaged neighbourhoods full of takeaways, with little space for exercise, and lots of adverts on TV for sugary foods at peak times, and high usage of food banks.

3. We have created a whole economy around pseudo-satisfiers. This means we are spending money on extrinsic goods to compensate for the reality that our intrinsic needs are not being met.[286] This is seeing the rise in what are called consolation goods. Our obsession with growth is having a direct impact on our happiness. Just witness the huge rise in anti-depressant prescriptions in the UK over the last five years.[287] Now, don't mishear me. I'm a huge fan of anti-depressants and see the real benefit of them in many of my patients' lives. However, the rise in these prescriptions is not only because mental health has become destigmatised. Rather, the way we are living is making us less happy. We feel used and abused by the economy, instead of being resourced by it for life.

So, what if GDP is growing, but people are less happy and we're wrecking the climate in the process? **We get what we measure. So maybe we need to measure some different things?** If we are to recover and reset our economy towards one of wellbeing, we must dive a bit deeper to diagnose the wider issues before we can turn towards solutions.

CAPITALISM IN CRISIS

Professor Mariana Mazzucato is perhaps the most influential economist in the world right now. She highlights in her latest book *Mission Economy*, that capitalism is in total crisis.[288] She diagnoses the problem with the current set-up with pin-point accuracy.

The finance sector isn't doing its job properly. Instead, it is funding itself! So, rather than actually tackling inequalities in society, which the financial sector could choose to do, it is making things worse – deliberately! That means resources are not getting to where they need to get to. In the UK, only 10% of all bank lending helps non-financial firms; 90% goes to fund property and financial assets. This leads to ever more debt, which people get trapped in and struggle to pay back. The financiers basically bet on certain things growing or working out. This leads to the growth of what economists call 'speculative bubbles'. When things don't go as predicted, these bubbles then burst.

So, the sector then has to go on bended knee to governments, begging for bailouts. This is exactly what happened in the 2008 financial crash. Incredibly, it means that profits stay in the hands of private companies. But all the risk remains with the public and the taxpayers, who have to pick up the bill when things inevitably go wrong. All the benefits sit in the private sector and none of the consequences. The pockets of the 1% are lined even further, whilst the planet is destroyed, and the poor suffer what they must. Does this make you outraged?

Business doesn't act for the long term. Rather, it focuses on quarterly returns. In other words, there is no long-term investment in the kind of things which could bring genuine transformation to society. So, when we talk about 'health creation' or a genuine transformation of our social care system, our transport infrastructure or education systems, there is no real commitment. The Institute for Public Policy estimates that between 2012 and 2017, 130,000 people died unnecessarily due to a failure to take a positive prevention approach to ill health.[289] The vision in government to fund such initiatives is lacking. The focus has become all about 'shareholder value' with no thoughts about what is good for society. Short-term gains for a few, but long-term disasters for the rest.

Alongside all of this, the planet is warming. We have until 2029 before climate breakdown becomes irreversible, with catastrophic results.

STOP.

Pause.

Take a breath and let that sink in.

Read it again.

We have until 2029 before climate breakdown becomes irreversible, with catastrophic results.

The way we are currently living is causing devastating loss. And rather than invest in that which would stay the rising tide and instead seed life for future generations, the financial sector is still massively investing in fossil fuels, for example. This is not only harming the planet, but also making us more unwell. In 2019, the USA gave $20 billion in subsidies to this industry, whilst the EU dwarfed this with €55 billion![290] Fossil fuels are bad for health and bad for the environment. This should be enough for us to sit up and realise that we must reimagine the world together. The war in Ukraine is showing us not only how reliant we are on fossil fuels, but how much we are willing to compromise in the process of retaining them.

This model of economy is no longer fit for purpose. Yet the malaise of the disconnection and the sense of disempowerment that we could ever change much paralyses us. Or maybe, we join a march or two and feel sympathy or even participate with the Extinction Rebellion, until it delays our commute to work, that is. We will see if the promises made at COP26 make any difference at all.

Mazzucato chastises governments for having lost the habit of leading. She criticises them for tinkering around the edges, whilst global corporations, many of which have larger economies than entire nation states, call the shots. The lack of accountability in this is startling. Governments are in the pockets of billionaires rather than serving the needs of those who elected them.

Our society is sick because our economy is sick. **It is love sick.**

HOW DID IT GET TO THIS?

Mazzucato tells us it is because we have believed some false myths about economics. We have believed that businesses create value and take risks, whereas governments should only de-risk and facilitate. We have conned ourselves that the purpose of government is to fix market failures, rather than to set the agenda. We've swallowed a lie that governments should behave like business, rather than hold them to account. Finally, we've accepted the false narrative that governments shouldn't try and pick winners, when of course they should. We're not talking about individual companies, but sectors of the economy that really need to be enabled to thrive. For example, right now, if governments are serious about tackling climate change, they should be massively disinvesting in fossil fuels and igniting the green economy.[291]

Somehow, we have taken as truth that the private sector is more efficient, when in reality its aim is profit. We have seen this again and again in the NHS. **It's why privatisation of healthcare is an oxymoron. Those who care most about profit margins do not care about those who cost the most money and make the least economic sense.** Shareholders in private healthcare companies, who live halfway around the world, do not care about people in our poorest communities who are suffering the worst health inequities. They care about a return on their investment. So, in an economy driven by this motive, the inequality gap widens and health outcomes for the poorest in society get worse. We see this in the USA, most starkly, which despite having one of the highest GDP spends per head of population on health care, has the widest inequality gaps.[292] It is failing.

The truth is that governments *are* able to make long-term investments. Therefore, rather than being left to simply hold the risk if things fail, they should also be able to reap the rewards and return those benefits to society at large. For example, if governments invest in a company to start with and that company goes on to huge success, then the government and taxpayers should reap a fair share of the rewards. That sounds like justice, rather than government interference – true partnership, rather than being taken for mugs. Yet, there are many examples, like with Tesla and Apple, where the US government made a huge initial investment but has reaped very few benefits at all from companies that many would say don't even pay their fair share of taxes.[293] The role of government at every level of society has been diminished. This has left us with an economy that lacks accountability. In turn this leads to growing inequality, inequity and damage to the environment.

BREAKING THE LIE

We have been sold a lie. We have been told again and again by politicians and the press that this economic ideology is fiscally responsible. **In truth it is irresponsible, unkind and immoral.**

We have been convinced that outsourcing saves taxpayer money and lowers taxes when the opposite is in fact the reality. This has been seen in the outrageous Private Finance Initiatives (PFI) contracts, consultancy bills and bailouts across the UK public sector in recent years. Worse still, secrecy clauses are hiding the truth from the public. In 2018, the UK Government outsourced £9.2 billion worth of health contracts,[294] whilst significantly shrinking the amount of money given to local preventative services.

The UK Government has been wedded to the notion of outsourcing. Between 1980 and 1996, the UK accounted for 40% of the total of all assets privatised across the Organisation for Economic Co-operation and Development (OECD)! This is having profoundly negative effects. Since 1998 (under both) New Labour and Tory governments 700 projects have been financed through PFI in the UK with a capital value of £60 billion. The maddening truth is that in total, these will end up costing £310 billion – five times the original capital outlay.[295] To make matters even worse, the National Audit Office estimates that the cost of a PFI project is typically around 40% higher than an *identical* project financed by government borrowing.[296]

The Test and Trace system, which was outsourced to private companies[297] during Covid-19, was an unmitigated financial disaster.[298] Along with the government's failure to close the borders, protect care homes,[299] and lock down fast enough, this led to the UK having one of the highest death tolls in Europe from Covid-19. The government has been burning a wasted £8.7 *billion* worth of unusable PPE at the rate of 15,000 pallets worth per month.[300] What a waste!

It is, of course, the human cost that is far harder to bear. **Our economic system and the ideology behind it are costing too many lives. It is making us sick.**

Had Theo been left with blood trickling down into the lower half of his body, he would have died from a devastating stroke at a young age. Nearly 25 years later, he is still going strong, running and enjoying life. Our economy is currently stifling the flow of resources to the parts of our societal body that need it most. It requires radical change.

A ROLE FOR EVERYONE

Prior to the 2019 UK election, the Rt Hon Priti Patel, MP, came to Morecambe Bay to visit Barrow-in-Furness. Barrow-in-Furness is a traditional ship-building port. The town has a great community spirit and a deep sense of pride in its history. Like many coastal areas, over a quarter of the children live in poverty. It was a hotly contested seat and one of great political importance. This is where the nuclear submarines of the British Navy are constructed.

The Conservatives won the seat successfully, taking it from the Labour Party. During her visit, Ms Patel, gave an interview to the news, whilst visiting 'The Well Communities', the LERO working with recovering drug addicts. She was asked about whether or not the government was to blame for the fact that in parts of the town 40% of the children were growing up in poverty. Her response was that it was not the fault of central government but that every sector of society has a role to play.[301]

There is no doubt that a truly vision-led and values-driven central government can make a huge difference to poverty. The importance of this cannot be underestimated. So, government can't be let off the hook. However, Ms Patel is not wrong. If we want to turn the tide on poverty, or any of the United Nation's Sustainable Development Goals, we *all* have a part to play. Our approach to economics needs to be far more participatory and 'owned' by the people.

We need to change the rules by which local governments are allowed to function. This is difficult since they rely totally on central government for their funding, apart from council tax, which is unjust because northern councils cannot raise as much revenue in this way, compared to more wealthy areas in the South East, due to cheaper housing and lower income rates.

Also, local governments have a legal duty to balance their books every year, which makes investment in the future an impossibility. But they are far better placed than central government to listen to their communities and act accordingly. The allocation of resources to regions around the UK also needs a new and fairer formula. It must give more emphasis to the index of multiple deprivation and ethnicity. Local commissioners, civil servants and providers of services need to be braver at choosing to get up stream with how they are investing tax-payer resources. Local government can only work well with devolution to the various regions.

Businesses have a huge role to play in how they invest in communities, who they recruit and from where they procure, ensuring they pay a true living wage and caring for those they employ, as we explored with Tariq's story in Chapter 9.

We need to let go of our own need for personal sovereignty and our desire for our own power. Instead, each of us must embrace the way of love, thinking about how we can live more generously.

The problem for us is that we are swimming in a sea of ubiquitous greed.

It is so normalised in our society that learning to think about the needs of others, to limit our own freedom for the sake of the whole, is extremely countercultural. If we put love at the core of how we think about our economy, I wonder how that would cause us to live more simply. I also wonder how we might choose to vote and hold government to account differently. Less self-protectionism, more together for the good of all. Choosing to participate in the process of economic decision-making through initiatives like Citizens' Assemblies allows us to involve ourselves and be active, rather than passive, powerless to affect much change.

Mazzucato calls us to aim higher. We have some enormous challenges in front of us. We need to build our economy around the mission that will enable us to meet them. We must break down our silos and join up our sectors and departments in collaboration. Let's use the best of our imaginings and experiments to share our resources and solve the wicked problems in front of us. Projects must be designed so that we learn from each other and are focused on our corporately owned mission.[302]

HEALTHY DOUGHNUTS

I never thought that economics could be such an interesting and passionate subject! To be honest, I thought it was the remit of dull men in dull grey suits. Perhaps I can be forgiven if we examine the UK Chancellors of the Exchequer over the last few centuries! That was until I read the profoundly beautiful work of Professor Kate Raworth, in *Doughnut Economics* a few years ago, with tears streaming down my face. What a book! Raworth is Professor of Practice at Amsterdam University of Applied Sciences, and her doughnut model takes the economic textbooks of the last 150 years and declares them no longer fit for the future.[303]

She demonstrates how our economic models, built on the premise of the self-made man, fail to take into consideration not only women, but our relationality as human beings in community. She exposes our addiction to growth and the fallacy of such dogmatic beliefs. She illustrates how they are causing severe destruction of the environment and huge social inequality. **Yet we remain committed to the model of unbridled free-market capitalism, decoupled from any sense of values, as though it were self-evidently true. It doesn't work for the majority,** and it is being maintained by the powerful and the rich for their own benefit. But it is leading to the detriment of us all and we can no longer tolerate it. Rather than focusing on graphs of growth, Raworth invites us to redraw how we think about and measure our economy.

She replaces the traditional graph with two circles – one inside the other, like a doughnut.[304] The outer circle represents environmental sustainability. The inner one pertains to human flourishing and social justice. Our invitation is to learn to live in the 'sweet spot' or the doughnut, between the two lines. To create a way of **'doing economy' in which we respect our planet's boundaries and ensure the wellbeing of all people and our fellow inhabitants.**

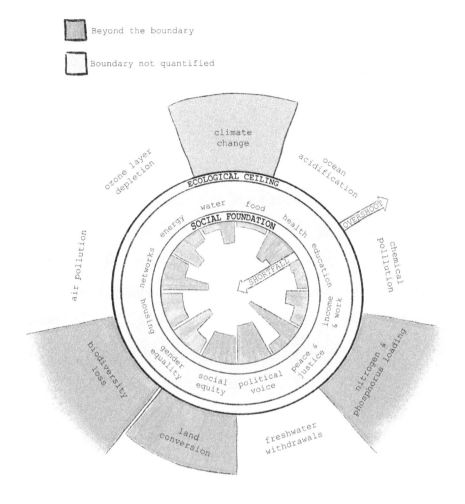

Figure 3: The Doughnut of social and planetary boundaries[305]

Raworth's principles for a reimagined economy are straightforward and are catching the attention of many global cities and indeed nations. It is exciting to see Amsterdam,[306] Copenhagen,[307] Philadelphia and Portland (Oregon),[308] Leeds,[309] Birmingham[310] and Preston[311] exploring what it means to be 'Doughnut Cities'.

Raworth isn't saying that growth is bad. She's asking us to recognise that sometimes it is vital and sometimes it is harmful.

Some parts of our economy need to grow, whilst others must shrink, or remain steady. A growing economy does not necessarily equal a sound or good economy, in fact it could represent a deeply damaging one. The balance has shifted. Our planet's wellbeing and that of billions of people, particularly living in the global south are suffering so significantly that we can no longer tolerate things as they are. Stewardship is everything when it comes to economy. It's why a radical politics and economics of love focuses on debt cancellation. Love sets us free from the slavery of debt so that we can all flourish.

In a Doughnut Economy, children like Cameron, whom we met in Chapter 11, are prioritised. More than ever, we need an economy of wellbeing for our people and our planet. We must free ourselves from ideologies and practices which are unable to meet these needs.

What good is a growing economy to people like Cameron, Julie or Tariq? What material benefits does it bring to them? They are at the mercy of a system which fundamentally doesn't value them.

It can feel unsettling to recognise and own the brokenness of our economic system. But it's far worse to try and maintain something which is destroying the planet and creating such staggering social injustice. The global system of capitalism is built on the privatisation of land, the enslavement of people and the protection of borders by all means necessary. The surgery Theo had to go through was life threatening and yet he would not be thriving today, had he remained as he was.

The diagnosis is clear. **Without a complete realignment of values, unbridled, free-market capitalism will**

destroy us all. We must embrace an economy of wellbeing and learn to live in the healthy doughnut together!

The 2008 financial crash was both a wake-up call and an invitation for us to recognise that we need to embrace a much more relational and connected way of thinking about our economy. The free market is not benevolent and does not hold the answers. But that does not mean that we need big centralised state power to rescue us. This is not liberalism versus socialism. It is an entirely different kind of conversation. We're talking about the renewal of a more ancient way of thinking about politics and power.

Our economies grow
but we're no happier

- *Did you find yourself outraged as you read about how our economic model is causing such injustice?*

- *Can you allow yourself to believe that this is not the only model available? Are you willing to challenge the sense of inevitability that it's always going to be this way?*

- *Are you willing to explore in your locality/city/region what some alternative ways might be? What is already happening that you could join in with?*

- *What might it be like to host a conversation about this where you are? Who would you invite? What questions would you ask? How would you harness the passion for change?*

- *What if we put love and kindness at the heart of our economic systems? What and who would we choose to prioritise?*

- *What if the vision shaping our economy was to leave the world in a better place than we found it?*

CHAPTER FOURTEEN
LOVE POWER

OVERWHELMED

Mark walked timidly into my room. Dressed in blue jeans and an orange T-shirt, he was a bit dishevelled. He was visibly shaking and looked frightened. This was such a change to his usual demeanor, and I was concerned. I watched this highly intelligent and usually confident man settle himself into the chair next to me.

'Goodness me, Mark. What's going on? How may I help?' I began.

'I don't know, Andy. I just don't think I can do it anymore. It's all too much.'

He began to cry. And not just small tears. He was beside himself with grief. It was incredibly moving to sit and watch him falling apart. We simply sat for a while, I passed him some tissues and waited until he felt he could speak.

Mark was 'acting up' into the role of senior manager of the social care team, after his boss retired. He had found members of his team sitting under their desks, rocking themselves back and forward, weeping. Their team had suffered significant cuts. They were dealing with a highly demanding caseload. They were managing levels of risk with children and young people which felt completely unsafe. The day before he saw me, Mark had been reviewing one particularly difficult case. He had found himself spontaneously vomiting into a bin next to his desk. He was having panic attacks each day before going into the office. Worse still, he felt exhausted. He was travelling miles every day into another county, and was in danger of falling asleep at the wheel. He was desperate for some time off, to get his head together, maybe even to quit his job altogether. Yet he was utterly guilt ridden for even considering this as an option. He knew what it would mean for his already overstretched team. He also had the reality of a mortgage to pay and his kids to support at university. Mark felt trapped.

This story is not unique to Mark, nor the council he was working in. Across England, social care teams – particularly those working with children – feel unsupported, unsafe and under resourced, made worse during Covid-19.[312] It isn't because they or their senior managers don't care. The cuts to local governments over the last ten years have been utterly devastating. In 2018–2019, there were 102,000 children in care across the UK. In England, there has been a 28% rise in a decade.[313] There is a complete mismatch between the level of support needed and the level of care which councils can provide. Unfortunately, this has led to thousands of children being placed in unsafe and unregulated settings.[314] It places our most vulnerable children at even higher risk of sexual exploitation, physical and verbal abuse, being groomed by gangs, or used as runners across county lines for drugs.[315] This is unacceptable in any society. It is also a completely false economy.

The cost of austerity politics and economics as an ideology has been nothing short of horrific and its impact on society has been criminal.

Yes, post 2008, the economy was in a mess following the global financial crash. But austerity was a political choice, not a necessity. Even if change was necessary, the cuts did not need to be as deep and vicious as they were. Those who decided to enact them on the British people have faced no consequences. Yet there has been a direct link between this economic policy enacted on our most vulnerable families and the deaths of children through abuse.[316] Despite a rising level of children needing help,[317] a 50% cut in children's services over a decade left our social services floundering,[318] unable to prevent real harm.

I am not saying that social work teams don't make mistakes or suffer from compassion fatigue, in response to the huge pressures they work under. Sometimes they are chaotic and poorly managed.[319] Some manage to turn themselves around by putting whole families at the centre of how they design care.[320] But whenever something goes wrong, the blame is always laid at the feet of the social workers and managers, like Mark, and they often lose their jobs in the process. Yet those who design the policies and cut the funding, refuse to listen, and then seem to get directorships and highly paid jobs, once out of office. Where is the love or justice in that?

There is such a lack of understanding between centrally driven financial decisions and the realities involved for local communities. It applies to adult social care also. When then Prime Minister, David Cameron and now Lord Cameron was dismayed by the lack of care available for his elderly mother in Oxfordshire, he wrote to the Conservative leader of the council to complain. The response he received from Councillor Ian Hudspeth, was played with a straight bat. How could Lord Cameron possibly expect services to be able to run, when the budget cuts to local governments by his own national government had been so devastating?[321] It exposed the dislocation and disconnect between those making decisions and those who experience and suffer the consequences. Our politics is broken.

Our society is sick because our politics is sick. **It is love sick.**

It fails to listen, and it fails to include. If we are going to create a politics, which has love at its core, then we need something that is far more participatory and engaging.

THE POLITICS OF SOVEREIGNTY

I love the thought leader Simon Sinek's simple analogy about the key question for leaders.[322] Sinek says we perpetuate so much of the way we go about life together through 'What?' and 'How?' questions. What are we going to do about the crisis in social care? How are we going to fix it? If we're going to reimagine our life together and build a society that is truly healthy then we must, as Sinek implores us, get to the 'Why?' Why do we perpetuate such staggering inequality? Why is it that despite 'democracy' there is such dislocation between those in power and those who suffer the experience of that power? To find some answers, I think we must go back to discover how the myth of sovereignty gained such a place of prominence in our thinking. This will help us to understand why it needs dismantling and reconfiguring if we're going to reimagine the future.

In Morecambe Bay, where I live, we've been having some conversations together about what it might be like if we developed a politics based on love and kindness. Some of the inspiration for these conversations has flowed from the inceptive work of political theologian, Dr Roger Mitchell. Mitchell peels back the layers of our political philosophies to reveal how (misconstrued) theology has shaped the politics of the West, particularly through Christendom.

Like it or not, the politics of the West is inextricably linked with theology – that is, how we understand God. If you'll bear with me, I will unpack a little of how a particular reading of the Christian Scriptures has legitimated empire and the politics of sovereignty in its various forms. In doing so I want to be authentic to my own faith journey and perspective, and I hope this is not offensive to you. I completely understand that for some readers even approaching the subject of theology may feel either completely irrelevant, deeply troubling or utterly delusional. I know that for some others, it will feel very clumsy for me to try and deal with huge issues in such a short space. But I do not come at this lightly. I have taken time to examine this in depth, including postgraduate study, for well over a decade.

My contention is this: if we do not understand what has shaped us thus far, it will continue to do so. Therefore, we will remain unable to reposition ourselves into a more loving, kind and fulfilling future.

I'm trying to get to the deeper roots with humility, without butchering deep theological concepts. I want to uncover how we've ended up in such a mess and how we might discover an alternative way together for society.

AN UNHOLY ALLIANCE

Mitchell demonstrates how the partnership of church and empire became manifest. It's important to understand because this unholy alliance continues to underpin the substance of our corporate life. Follow this through carefully and see how it developed to shape much of how our society holds together now. I have summarised Mitchell's thinking into four main stages.

- Jesus of Nazareth came of age at around the same time that Tiberius Caesar was denoted 'the son of God', as Emperor of Rome. When Jesus called himself the Son of God, it often astonished or offended his hearers. In doing so, he was deliberately pitting himself and his way of love as a counter-political reality to empire. He was emphasising that the way of God has nothing to do with empire. In fact, it is its antithesis, the antidote to top-down, centralised, hierarchical power. This was demonstrated through humble, servant-hearted and life-poured-out, sacrificial love, particularly of the poor and outcasts. The early community of people who followed in this way of life, was a radically alternative social movement. To begin with, it maintained a counter-political distinctiveness to the dominant expression of imperial political and religious power.

- The cult of Caesar worship, which was widely practised throughout the Roman Empire, involved believing that hierarchical power and divinity are combined in the 'supreme Lord'. Ever so slowly, this began to affect the early church leaders' thinking. By the fourth century the clear line of distinction between God's power and the power of empire was lost. Mitchell argues that the early church leaders/bishops began to develop a theology of God as the ultimate, hierarchical ruling power of the universe, who operated just like an Emperor. This allowed the bishops to develop a certain style of leadership as power over rather than leadership among. This was contrary to what Jesus revealed God to be like – sovereign but not like a Sovereign, Lord but not lording over.[323]

- In 314 CE, a chap called Eusebius became the Bishop of Caesarea. He was close friends with and the biographer of the Emperor Constantine. According to Mitchell, Eusebius believed that the whole purpose of Jesus' incarnation, death and resurrection, was for the Emperor of Rome to convert to Christianity. This would ultimately enable worldwide peace through mass adoption of the faith and obedience to God. Having equated the idea of God with imperial rulership, the story of Jesus began to be interpreted in a very different way from how the early church would have understood it.

An earlier, more orthodox interpretation of the story of Jesus is that he is *the* Good Samaritan. That he came as God, to reveal what God is like, through his life and teachings. He preached about the 'Kingdom of God'. This Kingdom was a political counterpoint to the domination of empire and the control of religion. The imperial and religious powers of the day were threatened by this. So, to silence his criticism and maintain a system of greed and exploitation, they had him crucified.[324]

They killed God.

The early disciples believed (and many Christians still believe) that through his death, Jesus refused to condemn the world to the endless repercussions of individual and corporate domination.[325] Instead he soaked up into his own body, all the toxicity of 'sin' (which I think of as all that is contrary to the way of love which flows from God). He did this to save humanity from our own ego-driven, destructive behaviours, and to reorientate us towards the way of love. By his resurrection he broke the power of death, which the disciples believed to be the consequence of sin, and 'freed the multitude from the oppression of empire'.[326]

His life, death and resurrection from the dead, was for the early believers (and Christians now), a sure sign that this way of life-poured-out-love triumphs over death itself, making a spectacle of abusive power.[327]

The early Christians believed (and many still believe) that by accepting their own brokenness and need for salvation – trusting in Jesus and following in his way of love – they were set free from their own egocentricity, their helpless slavery to 'sin' and the fearful submission to empire, because Jesus had overcome them. Humanity was instead gifted with and invited into an altogether new life of freedom in a radically subversive community. A community reconciled with God and reorientated into a life of love-poured-out for the 'other'. A life which embodied substantial hope in the painful present and carried eternal potency.

But this did not fit with what Eusebius had come to believe. A suffering God? A weak and vulnerable God? A God against dominating imperial power? A God who undermined religious scholars? A God who valued friendship with ordinary people? A God who asked us to love our enemies and creatively resist violence? A God who actively sided with the poor and the marginalised? A God who demands social justice? No! How would the masses be controlled?

Eusebius instead depicted God as the *offended Sovereign*, unable to look on sinful humanity, who required the death of Jesus to satisfy his wrath and enable reconciliation between God and mankind.[328] The understanding of the death of Jesus became about appeasing an angry Imperial God. By submitting to 'the truth', the fallen sinner could now operate properly within a hierarchical order of the church and empire or society.[329]

This theology propped up hundreds of years of papal supremacy and the divine right of kings. If we follow this through history, we can see that it has led to the political structures of the West and the division of lands. This created and has perpetuated massive historical, social injustice, initially through the demarcation of the feudal system[330] and ongoingly through the power of the 'establishment'[331] and the development of the class system. The 'masses' had to submit to the 'individuals' or the 'powers', because this is apparently what God intended. As a result, some people think they are 'born to rule'.

• When the Age of Enlightenment broke out in the seventeenth century (following the utterly appalling and devastating Thirty Years' War in Europe, in which millions of men and women lost their lives over power struggles between various theological and imperial bases), the modern era emerged. Many people stopped believing in God. It was no longer considered rational and seemed to be the cause of war. However, with or without God, hierarchical dominance, centralised control, white supremacy and patriarchy remain pre-eminent in our collective psyche.

A MISPLACED FAITH?

We still believe, en masse, that peace is achieved through sovereignty and hierarchical power. That our problems are solved by electing the right government to protect our way of life and our borders. If only the right people are 'in charge', then everything will be OK.

This is made possible through the sacrifice of young men and women in war, and ensuring peace is maintained ultimately by the underlying threat of nuclear arms. Sadly, it is uncritiqued theology which lies behind this kind of thinking. This is why we witnessed the bizarre anointing of Putin by the Russian Orthodox Church. It is why so many evangelicals embrace Trump and Bolsonaro. It is what justified the appalling use of the atomic bombs in Hiroshima and Nagasaki, with the pilots who dropped them blessed by a priest beforehand.

The natural endpoint of Jesus' life and ministry amongst the poor and social outcasts was not the establishment of Christian nationalism. In fact, it is particularly strange as it is the antithesis of what Jesus was about. American actor, Rainn Wilson, of *The Office* fame ranted about this on X (previously known as Twitter). He lambasted 'Christian America' for the bizarre way in which Jesus

Christ has gone from being a 'humble servant of the abject poor' to someone who upholds the worst of our humanity. Instead, he says, Jesus has come to represent 'gun rights, prosperity theology', neglect of the destitute through uncaring government and 'fierce nationalism.'[332]

To be clear, the marriage of church and empire created a society built upon a theology and philosophy of sovereign power as *the* way of creating peace and order. However, what it has led to is staggering economic injustice, destruction of the environment, and increased global violence. All the while, the vast majority of political and economic decisions are made without any sense of relationship or participation.

Is the politics we have the best that we should hope for? Is this what we should expect or put up with? That people should assume positions of power, behave how they want to, call referendums and not worry about the consequences, drive through ideological agendas with devastating effects for the poorest in society, throw parties in a lockdown whilst banning others from seeing their dying relatives, try to change the rules when they don't suit them, prorogue parliament, lie to parliament, give peerages to party donors, award huge contracts to the tune of billions of pounds to people who don't deliver and are not held accountable, and hold the public in contempt? And we should shrug our shoulders and resign ourselves to it just being this way? OK, you might get barred from parliament for a while, but so what? You end up with a lucrative writing deal, a peerage or a directorship of some sort. Why do we put up with it? Are there no alternatives?

When we see our politicians 'toe the party line', it feels like they don't root for those of us they profess to represent. Maybe we are guilty of shrugging our shoulders and resigning ourselves to the status quo. Or maybe we'll accept things the way they are, as long as it doesn't interfere with our own sense of sovereignty.

Our politics is sick and broken. **We need something altogether different.** Are there any loving alternatives?

KENARCHY

If we go back and re-examine the actual politics of Jesus, we find a very different set of political priorities than those which currently shape the power-politics of the twenty-first century. We find a politics of non-violence as a counterpoint to military might. We find leadership that is compassionate and present, rather than uncaring and removed. We see stewardship among, rather than power over others. We find an economy which curtails our consumerist greed, freeing slaves rather than making them; sharing generously, so that no one is in need. We discover that people are cherished rather than used. We find a society in which those most marginalised, shamed and stigmatised are given the greatest honour.

'Kenarchy' is a word coined from two Greek words *kenosis* – to empty out, and *arche* denoting power – to describe an alternative politics of love. It is the idea of a self-giving, others empowering love. It is an antidote to hierarchical dominance. The politics of love are as radical today as they were in the face of the Roman Empire. They carry within them the potency to transform our current realities.

In his book, *The Faith of the Faithless*, Professor Simon Critchley, an atheist, describes this kind of love as 'the infinite demand to give what one does not have and receive that over which one has no power. The sort of demand that Christ made in the Sermon on the Mount when he said, "love your enemies, bless them that curse you, do good to them that hate you, and pray for them which despitefully use you, and persecute you."'[333]

Many of the anti-oppression movements over the last 150 years have been motivated by this kind of love. Perhaps, as we untangle the deeply intertwined root systems in the soil of our minds, revisiting the original politics of love is not a bad place to start our thinking about the kind of society we might cultivate together. If we consciously uncouple from our addiction to oppressive sovereign power, we make space for a fresh reimagining of political space.

Rooted in the principles of non-violence and economic justice, the priorities of kenarchy (the term I and others use as a shorthand for the politics of love) are found by simply following the journey of Jesus through first century Palestine and Israel. As outlined in the book *Discovering Kenarchy*, they fall into seven categories:[334]

- Advocating for the poor

- Instating women fully and equally

- Prioritising children

- Welcoming 'strangers'

- Reintegrating humanity with the environment

- Restorative justice for prisoners

- Healing the sick.

The politics of Christendom manifests as 'doing to' or 'doing for'. But the politics of love, is not even about 'doing with'. At its heart, the politics of love is about 'being with'.[335] **The politics of love is about a different kind of relationship,** where we cross the lines of discomfort to discover radical hospitality and friendship. It means deep listening. It takes humility. It requires compassion, or co-suffering.

Of course, the revolutionary power of a politics of love does not only belong to the Christian faith. Indeed, Christianity, as with any religion, wedded to a misaligned understanding of sovereign power is entirely unloving. It has led to huge abuses of power through the centuries and caused many to turn away from faith. There is much love to be found within other faiths and non-religious social movements. And some of what purports itself to be 'Christian' is sometimes horrifically unloving. That is not to say in a patronising way that 'all religions are the same'. They are not. But there is so much for us to learn from each other, across difference.

Valarie Kaur, who is a Sikh, a lawyer, filmmaker, educator, renowned speaker and civil rights activist, writes the most moving manual of how the politics of love works in practice, in her brilliant book, *See No Stranger: A Memoir and Manifesto of Revolutionary Love*. For her, revolutionary love calls us to refuse to 'other' our fellow human beings and learn to live from a place of deep compassion and kindness. Kaur invites us to reimagine the way we build society and practise our politics. 'This is our moment to declare what is obsolete, what can be reformed and what must be reimagined.'[336]

Likewise, Mohamed El Bachiri in his poetic reflections, *A Jihad for Love* asks this question: 'Would God really blame us for showing love towards people who think differently from us?'[337] **This call to love our neighbours and even our enemies as we love ourselves, is at the heart of a politics of love.** It has been taught and modelled through the ages, but our addiction to sovereignty pulls us back. Our misconstrued notion of sovereignty lies at the heart of all racism, nationalism and war. We cannot keep being pulled and shaped by the past. We must, rather, be transformed by the future ahead of us.

A LOVING CIVILISATION

In his essay 'A Loving Civilization: A Political Ecology that Promotes Overall Well-Being', theologian and philosopher, Thomas Jay Oord wrestles with the ideas of what a loving society needs at its foundations.[338] He defines love in this way: 'To love is to act intentionally, in relational (sympathetic/empathetic) response to others (including God), to promote overall well-being.'[339]

Our crisis is both environmental and social. Love motivates us to address both issues. We are no longer ignorant about them, but our individual and corporate greed has not yet been overcome. In fact, instead of electing leaders who might help us curb our excesses, we continue to vote for governments which allow us to behave in ways which are actively harmful to our fellow human beings, other species and indeed, the natural environment. Love assumes that all of life is intrinsically valuable. So, when we speak of 'overall wellbeing', it is not in the utilitarian sense of the greatest good for the greatest number. Rather, it is knowing that what we do for the least, for the weakest, for the smallest, for the seemingly insignificant, is the demonstration and substantial reality of love in action. Imagine if all our leaders were leaders of love.

What if God is not a sovereign ruler, who must be obeyed? But rather a leader of love, who holds space and time compassionately, looking to infuse all of life with love, to promote overall wellbeing, whilst bending the arc of history towards justice? What if having a God-complex (a description often given to megalomaniacal, narcissistic leaders) is not about wanting to rule over people but is instead about washing the feet of lepers and being the friend of the most ostracised in society? What does this mean for how we have historically understood and now understand leadership? What does it mean to build a loving society or civilisation? Let us be brave enough to break with our ideology of sovereign power as the means to peace and justice. Instead, as Cormac Russell invites us, let us rekindle democracy[340] through joined-up community participation. There are plenty of models available. It is time to embrace them and use the tools being developed to bring the priorities of the politics of love to the fore.

RECONSTITUTED POWER

If, like me, you work in public services, you may be used to the idea of engaging with communities. The idea is that before we make changes to a service provision or try and launch a new initiative, we consult with or engage with the community who will be affected by this. We are supposedly asking communities to participate in the decision-making and design process, so that what emerges is more able to meet their needs.

Jennie Popay, Distinguished Professor of Sociology and Public Health at Lancaster University, challenges the way this is done. For all the engagement taking place, little is changing when it comes to the inequalities and inequities experienced by the communities concerned. Popay and others argue that this is because of the difference between what she terms 'inward gaze' and 'outward gaze'. Inward gaze is when we go to a community with a problem and then supposedly empower them to change the internal circumstances within the community. These usually focus on psychosocial issues or the conditions within the neighbourhood. However, it does nothing to challenge or change the wider sociopolitical and economic structures which keep this community within the experience of inequity. In other words, nothing changes. It's a bit like telling the community what is wrong and then asking them to fix the issue, without them being able to influence what is actually causing their problems.

Outward gaze, on the other hand, is about listening to the intrinsic problems within a community, recognising their innate power, building community power to speak to and challenge the structural injustices they are experiencing, and working with them through community organising to bring about real action for change.[341]

The reality is, we need both – the ability to focus on both intrinsic and extrinsic issues. This is reconstituted power. This is flipping power on its head. Refusing to ride into a community to try and fix their issues, and rather, recognising how constituent power when joined together brings about meaningful change. So, rather than public sector organisations going to communities to engage with them about what needs to change and then fixing things for them, it is the public sector itself which must change.

THE POWER OF PARTICIPATION

If politics is fundamentally about the interconnectedness of human relationships and how we live well together, then it must be a participatory experience. The politics of love is, by definition, the invitation to participate in community. It is the antithesis of the hierarchical, dominating politics of Empire in its various guises through the centuries. In a first past the post system, the rights and opinions of so many people in our communities are ignored, overlooked, oppressed and forgotten. Increasingly, we see cronyism, chumocracy[342] and outright corruption at work. This further erodes trust in our 'politicians' and other public bodies.[343]

It's also true in our life together. Communities have become increasingly suspicious of each other. Indeed, one only needs to spend a short amount of time on X (previously known as Twitter), Facebook or any other social media platform to see just how our participatory experience can so easily become an almighty slanging match. Genuine conversation is largely replaced by loud shouting and increasingly entrenched points of view. It seems almost impossible to have kind discussions in which we explore the issues we face from a starting place of humility. Politics isn't binary. It is complex and therefore needs to be collaborative. We need collective sense-making. For example, we have created a damaging narrative around the 'sovereignty' of our own borders, with no acknowledgement of our complex and violent history of colonialism.

It's time for us to put love, inclusivity, forgiveness and kindness at the heart of our politics. It's time to recognise that it is the person we consider to be our 'other' who is utterly necessary to us if we are to become truly human. Learning to deeply and truly love the marginalised, the 'different' and those we currently consider our 'enemy' is the path to a new political future. There is an old Quaker saying: 'an enemy is one whose story we have not heard.' Learning to listen to the stories of our enemies will enable us to create a more integrated society. This is both an internal and an external journey – I myself must do this work, as must you. Together we must dismantle the oppressive systems of injustice and see new life and hope break through. We see glimpses of it all over the place. In fact, at the beginning of the first UK lockdown, due to Covid-19, we began to see what might be possible in a society where love and kindness are deeply at work. Just witness all the people who lovingly cut out material and sewed scrubs for those working in the NHS. Remember the extraordinary acts of neighbourliness and care shown to the lonely.

The ability to participate in our own reality, to feel like we're involved in something bigger than ourselves, and to have a sense of connection with those around us is at the heart of what it means to be human and to belong to a community. It is what lies at the heart of the 'politics of love'. This is beautifully framed by social thinker, Russell, when he talks about the connection between community and state.

The vast majority of decisions and initiatives should be by the people in their communities. Some things will be done by communities with help from other organisations including local and national institutions. A few things will be done for communities, but this will be decided by those communities. On occasion things will be done by institutions but only with the free, prior and informed consent of the community.[344] (emphasis added)

This is so beautifully radical. Empire looks at communities and decides what is wrong with them. It does things to them to make them better; or on the other hand, it withdraws its safety net of support and tells people that it's each for themselves. It believes the market will sort things out in the end.

Love, on the other hand, listens and recognises the innate capabilities within communities and cedes power and resources into them to enable them to thrive. **This calls for a radical reimagining and transformation of our political systems.**

It calls for a much greater focus on connectivity so that participation is possible. The reality is that poverty and inequality are terrible for health, both personally and corporately. Economist Amartya Sen argues it this way: 'It doesn't matter whether or not that poverty is absolute or relative, because relative inequality with respect to income translates into absolute inequality when it comes to capabilities: your freedom to be and to do.'[345] Professor Sir Michael Marmot shows that inequality strips people of opportunity, empowerment, security and dignity.[346] In other words, it is the ability to participate in society with dignity that begins to break the yoke of inequality and creates a society that is more whole.

Power does not necessarily corrupt, and absolute power need not corrupt absolutely. What power does is to expose what is in the hearts of those who hold the power.

We need leaders with the skills to hold power loosely and distribute it well.

We need those who can hold space for unlearning and the emergence of new and creative solutions for the problems we are facing.

We need people adept at holding tension and complexity, who can listen deeply and assimilate multiple perspectives.

We need leaders who are willing to stop trying to be the heroes or heroines of the hour and become hosts of political spaces in which all are welcome and able to participate.

We need leaders who enable us all to be part of the solution.

The opposite of sovereignty is not a world without leadership or full-on anarchy. Rather, it is the life-laid-down, loving, others-preferring politics of love.

LIFE-GIVING POWER

Mark, whom we met at the beginning of the chapter, was at the end of himself; the resources he was left to work with, based on political and societal ideologies, were insufficient to do what was asked of him. His team could not meet the needs of his community based on that model and he was burning out trying to do so. In fact, the model of care he had to provide was miles away from what those communities needed. Our top-down hierarchical, sovereignty-based models are broken. They are incapable of helping us discover a more caring future.

Do you remember the Parable of the Oak Tree in the Introduction? It seemed like that tree would stand for ever. But the wind began to blow in a different direction and its roots were found wanting. To put it another way: if we are wise and work together, each playing our part, we can say to this mountain of generational poverty and injustice, 'be uprooted and thrown into the sea.' Change can happen! Driven by compassion be outraged and intentional about the need for change, challenge the inevitability of systemic injustice and let's build some moral alternative economies, founded on love.

Self giving, others empowering love

- *What is your relationship with power?*

- *How often do you spend time with or relate to people who are different to you?*

- *What would it be like for you to participate more in the political issues affecting your local community?*

- *What might be possible if we embraced a more loving, collaborative and participative politics?*

- *How might we build this together?*

CHAPTER FIFTEEN
LOVE HOSPITALITY

EXCLUDED

It was a cold October day. The wind was blowing from the Irish Sea. The white horses were galloping on the waves and the mountains of south Cumbria formed our vista, as a bunch of unlikely companions gathered in The Alhambra Theatre, in Morecambe. This was our second 'Art of Hosting' (AoH) training in the area.

As I grabbed a cup of tea from the make-shift bar area, I scanned the room, amazed to see such a collection of people in one space together. Kerrie Higham walked in through the door with her big smile and always immaculate hair. With her husband Dave she runs 'The Well Communities', the Lived Experience Recovery Organisation (LERO) I have mentioned before. Behind her, walked a much shyer chap, in his early fifties, with a sun hat and dark glasses. His head was down, and he shuffled his feet awkwardly.

I bounded over, gave Kerrie a big hug and then introduced myself to the man with her. He took his glasses and hat off, tucked them into his bag and looked at me. He had a face that could tell a thousand stories. A few months sober, having been street homeless, he'd found himself at 'The Well Communities', and was beginning to get his life back together.

'Hello. I'm Alasdair,' he said in a broad Blackpool accent. 'I don't think I belong here. But I work with Kerrie, and she told me that I had to come along, cos this is what we're doing for the next two days.'

'OK!' I replied. 'Well, whether you think it or not, you're really welcome here, and it is so good that you're with us.'

'Well thanks. The only thing is, I've got to sign on at three, or else I'll be sanctioned. I'm feeling a bit nervous about that,' he admitted.

'No worries. I will make sure that you get there. Can I get you a cup of tea?' I asked.

In the room that day, we had 50 people from all across Morecambe and the surrounding district. People, like Alasdair, who had been street homeless and were recovering from addiction, a local GP, the local police sergeant and a couple of his constables (their chief inspector had done the previous training and decided his whole division needed to participate). Along with them, we had the chief nurse from the Clinical Commissioning Group, some teachers, some volunteers, artists, a playwright, a comedian, a cleaner, a foster mum, a local church pastor and an elected member of the city council, to name just a few examples. Such a beautifully diverse group of people, who under normal circumstances, would not usually be in a room together. They would almost certainly never otherwise be sitting down to a two-day conversation and immersive learning experience.

The fact that Alasdair did not feel like he 'belonged' shows that our society is love sick. **Everyone should feel included and able to participate.** That is the magic of the AoH, which I mentioned in Chapter 1. The AoH is not a thing that can be owned by anyone. In fact, rather annoyingly, it's very hard to pin down at all! It is a multitude of practices that belongs to everyone and enables people to work with and across a multiple of disciplines.[347] It has fundamentally shifted the way I think about my work. I believe it offers us some helpful ways of creating a more participatory and inclusive politics. **It invites us all to**

be part of the solutions we need to find together to the complex issues we are facing, like poverty, inequality, racism and climate change.

It took a while to start working in this way. It didn't just happen overnight. Slowly, through building relationships, having early morning coffee with colleagues before work, and demonstrating by example in public meetings, we began to build a coalition of practitioners. Together we began to spread the learning of the AoH with others in our own organisations and circles of relationships.

A FOUNDATIONAL PRACTICE

At the heart of the AoH, sit some key principles, which I learned from one of the UK stewards, Linda Mitchell.

- There is a basic human capacity to have meaningful dialogue/ conversation.

- Meaningful conversation (beyond the blah, blah, blah!) brings shared clarity and this leads to wiser action.

- To find wiser action, we need to build our capacity to unlearn and not know. In the space between the not knowing and solutions is innovation.

- New solutions are needed. We are in a time of fundamental change. For this we need co-creation.

- The paradox of polarity is always at play. We cannot afford to hide this. We must work with it.

One of the core tenets of the AoH is the Four-Fold Practice.[348] I find it a helpful way to think about our role in being part of community. It is about reconstituting the dynamics of power and creating spaces for altogether different kinds of conversation. The invitation is as follows:

1. Host yourself

2. Be hosted

3. Host others

4. Be part of a hosting community

I will now look at each of these practices in turn, as they form such a helpful framework.

HOST YOURSELF

Learning to host ourselves is key to becoming active participants in our community. It involves accepting and believing that who I am matters. It means learning that my contribution is important and that how I show up and interact with others makes a difference. To do this, I have to face up to my ego and the ego-projections I make to those around me.

It is impossible to build a healthy culture in which our egos constantly show up. I'm so grateful for the people in my life, not least my wife, but also mentors, elders and friends, who have consistently and lovingly called me out and highlighted to me where I have more work to do. Taking responsibility for this, being willing to face our past hurts, owning up to our behaviour patterns and getting help through therapy and coaching, is part of what it means to host ourselves.

As we explored in Chapter 3, it also includes self-care so that we don't burnout and collapse through exhaustion. We self-care for the sake of the wider whole. It means ensuring that we learn how to carry ourselves so that we learn to be present in the moment and available to that which is in front of us. My kids often tell me if I'm too distracted to listen to them, calling me to attention, presence and participation. Being present means that we are available to face the key issues of our day, rather than ignoring them or hoping they might just be dealt with by someone else. It nearly always means turning off our mobile phones!

BE HOSTED

When we hold AoH trainings in Morecambe Bay, we often talk about the Four-Fold Practice. This idea of being hosted, seems to be the concept that people struggle with the most. Perhaps it is because culturally we have it ingrained in us that it is better to give than to receive. Maybe there is an unconscious guilt attached to this. But to be hosted is to be humble. To be hosted is to accept the gift of another's hospitality. To be hosted is vital if we want to build community, because we cannot only do things on our own terms. We must be willing to be invited into unfamiliar, new territories and environments. When we do this, we allow ourselves to be the recipients of love unlooked for and enable others to practise the beauty of generosity. When Alasdair allowed himself to be hosted, he found that he did belong and that people from all walks of life cared about him.

One of the things I frequently challenge fellow leaders in the NHS over is how recently they allowed themselves to go and sit with people whom we make decisions for. How often do we allow ourselves to step out of the comfort of our board rooms and offices, with our posh suits and lanyards and accept the hospitality of others? Are we willing to share a park bench with someone who is street homeless? Will we let children in our local primary school take us by the hand and show us the way? Might we sit in the circle of a community of recovering addicts and learn what real vulnerability and humility is like?

Learning to host ourselves, whilst being hosted by others, creates an opportunity for us to let go of our power and cede it to our host. In turn, our host will give it back to us as we participate in the space created. I remember visiting Beeston, an inner-city estate in the City of Leeds, shortly after the 7/7 bombings took place. I was hosted by a devout Muslim man and visited the Mosque where the alleged bombers had attended worship. As I spent time with him, I realised that so much of the dominant press narrative was wildly inaccurate and only served to deepen the politics of exclusion. I was humbled by both the welcome and kindness of my host. **It allowed me to reorientate my heart and my head towards one of respect and love.** It gave me a new understanding of the Muslim faith and dispelled many of my misconstrued preconceptions. It was brave of Ali to welcome me and others into his community, especially at a time when they felt so vulnerable and misunderstood. His hospitality changed me. When we enter into conversation with our 'other', if we are willing to listen to each other, we are both changed in the process. We both become more fully human. We become more alive as a result.

HOST OTHERS

This is the space in which some people feel most comfortable. Whether it's the thought of having dinner parties, inviting people over to hang out or simply chairing a meeting, hosting others seems to be something that we can connect with quite easily as humans. Yet it is not always easy, at all. Remember Zoya, whom we met earlier in Chapter 5. She practised the gift of hospitality against all the odds. She made space for those who had wounded her own family in order to create the conditions for reconciliation and healing.

If we are to create new political spaces, we must learn to hold open spaces for others to come together. The 'Redeeming Our Communities' (ROC) charity, led by Debra Green OBE, is creating these kinds of places, across the UK.[349] We need to ensure that everyone knows they are welcome at the table, that every person has the right to be heard. This doesn't mean that everyone is right! And we must refute hate speech, whenever we hear it, and show solidarity. **We need to be good allies and advocates for each other.** However, if we are never interested in where the hate comes from, what the stories underneath might be and how they are being shaped by fear, then we will be unable to create a new story together.

We need to remain curious. Why do we hold certain fixed ideas about people? How do we make ourselves aware of unconscious bias? Why do we treat some people differently to others? What attitudes do we need to challenge in ourselves? We must find the deeper questions to the issues we are facing, grappling together to find a way through and enable truth to be spoken to power. These spaces must be ones of listening, at a deep level. We need to learn to hear each other. So many of our current societal conversations are fractious and divisive. This only leads to the politics of exclusion and hate.

One of the places I have seen hospitality done best is at The Rose Castle Foundation in Cumbria. Here, the 'hosts' bring together people from Orthodox Muslim, Jewish and Christian perspectives from regions around the globe where peace is not experienced between them. In the most beautiful way, each of the different religious texts are opened. A dialogic technique is then used to enable a space for deep listening, fresh perspectives and understanding, mutual respect and new friendships. The idea is not to say 'all are the same' – clearly, they are not. The hope is to create space for love in the midst of difference and so the potential for living well together in the fault lines of potential violence. In a society of increasing division, how might we be the kind of hosts who hold the space for truth and reconciliation?

This is the politics of love and the politics of peace in action.

It has been so moving to see the overwhelming response of the British public in wanting to host Ukrainian refugees. I wonder why our response has been less hospitable to the people of Afghanistan or the Yemen.

There are many challenges when it comes to hosting others.

- *What are our motives for showing hospitality? Do we do so primarily for our guests? Or is it more about what we are trying to get out of them? Is it about how it makes us look?*

- *When we think about the spaces we create, are they about connecting with people and building relationships or about focusing on 'getting the job done'?*

- *When we talk of hosting others, who is our other? Do we make space for them?*

- *So, who do we prioritise as our guests? Do we deliberately make space for those who might positively disrupt our safe worlds, call out our hypocrisy, challenge the status quo and rock the boat a little?*

- *Do we invite the marginalised, the rejected, the awkward guests, or is our hosting of others just the hosting of those who are in essence, just like us?*

- *How do we ensure we are not exclusionary and yet able to differentiate the right time and space and mix of people?*

When we think about our collective role to host refugees and asylum seekers in this country, are we as generous and welcoming as we might be? My wife and I have had the privilege of hosting destitute asylum seekers in our home. These are people who have not been given leave to remain, but cannot be sent home, due to the safety issues involved. Through the work of various charities, it is possible to host people in our homes, whilst they appeal their cases. One particular lady lived with us for a year. Honestly, it was like hosting an angel. The good she brought into our home was incredible at a time when we needed help.

Why would we tolerate shipping people off to Rwanda? Why do we let people drown in our seas? Why do we accept people being boarded up in our detention centres and having their human rights removed? Why do we deceive ourselves that we take 'more than our fair share' of refugees, when, in fact, our numbers are significantly less than Canada, USA, Germany and France?[350] We are not short of space. It doesn't mean no cap. It doesn't mean doing something we can't manage. And we don't have to be unwise about national security. We can welcome people into our country, with a sense of honour. We benefit so much in the process. Our country is so much richer for its diversity and inclusivity.

BE PART OF A HOSTING COMMUNITY

Hosting with others is both fun and complex! Settling into a team dynamic in which each one can play to their strengths becomes like a dance. One person doesn't have to do it all. Teams can hold space together. Different people can bring various gifts and create a sacred space between them. There are some complex situations that we are facing. Some really difficult and painful issues are at work in our communities that require time and attention. Away from the X (previously known as Twitter) spats or bun fights in the House of Commons, there are some solutions we need to find together.

Collaborative sense making, requires careful management of the space between us, to tend to what is important and ensure that all who are present are attended to. Wider than just community gatherings, we must also recognise our role as human beings in the wider ecology. What about our role in hosting and stewarding the environment? Are we good hosts of this for future generations? Do we care about the issues facing species at risk of extinction? What does it mean to take a collective sense of responsibility for these things?

SPACE TO PARTICIPATE

I try and use this in my work, wherever possible in working with communities around population health. I want to share with them the complex nature of the issues we might be facing. I want them to know that they are participants in the solutions, for example, around the loneliness of our elderly citizens, mental health problems in our young people, rising obesity rates and diabetes, or people walking around with uncontrolled blood pressures. Some of this, I can bring my expertise to, but some of it requires community sense making and a collaborative effort to bring about change. This is the politics of participation.

What if we had more political spaces like this? Well-hosted spaces which welcomed wide participation in an atmosphere of love, respect and kindness? There are so many tools and techniques available to enable large groups of people to actively participate in and contribute to important decision-making processes.

These include things like World Cafes, Design Cafes, Open Space, Triads, Samoan Circles, Fishbowls and a variety of others. Even more is possible now thanks to online solutions, like Miro boards, Jamboards etc. If we took more time, paid more attention and thought more creatively about how to curate new political spaces in our neighbourhoods, districts and cities, we could quite easily experiment with ways of building a politics of love.

HUMILITY IS OUR POLITICAL POSTURE

We often talk about having a sense of national pride. What if we flip that on its head and embrace humility as a core value; what might that mean? How would humility as a value influence relationships between individuals, communities, cities and across national boundaries?

Humility allows us to develop a posture of open heartedness and enables us to receive gifts and insights, which we would otherwise miss. Humility not only allows us to forgive but also enables us to receive forgiveness. Given some of the things we must tackle together around male privilege, white supremacy, inequality, inequity and clumsy policies – that may have been set up with good heart and intent but caused destruction and death – we need forgiveness. We need this maybe more than we allow ourselves to know or accept.

A politics of love requires humility.

Without humility, we never learn to listen. If we never listen, then we are never challenged. This leaves us unable to change. **Humility requires of us that we examine our relationship with power.**

What does humility call us to do in terms of emptying out our power for the sake of the other? Only true humility, that is genuinely willing to listen to the deeper pain undergirding the experience of so many in our communities, will allow ourselves to hear what fundamentally needs to change. As communities, cities and nations, it allows us to begin a process of healing. This is especially true when reconciliation and reparation are required. It also opens up the possibility of incredible grace. This is something that perpetrators of abuse and misusers of power almost certainly do not deserve. But then, that is the beauty of grace. No one deserves grace!

If in our local politics, we choose to listen to one another, rather than rely on our assumptions, what might that mean for our relationships? How might it affect those we love, those we work with or those who drive us crazy? When we cross the dividing lines of our life together and apply an ethic of care to those who experience social injustice, humility enables us to let go of ill-fitting ideologies, which no longer hold when we encounter our other.

Perhaps as a nation, we might want to ask ourselves whether we want to continue to be known as *Great Britain*. That's not to do us down. Rather it allows us to explore our identity at a deeper level, our insecurities and what kind of global reputation we want to have. Why in an age of such global complexity we think we are better to 'go it alone', breaking away from our Union with the rest of Europe, I struggle to understand. Brexit will sadly prove to be a terrible mistake.

The question of identity is profoundly going to shape the future of these British Isles in the years ahead. It is going to be vital that we hold onto humility and listen to each other as we find our way forward into a collective new future. This future may or may not allow us to think of ourselves as either a United Kingdom or Great Britain, as the Celtic nations explore independence. However, stronger borders are unlikely to be the answer. Rather, ceding power to the community levels and devolving as much power as possible to cities and regions is likely to be key in helping us find a new way. Therefore, as we enter these important community and national conversations our posture must be one of humility. As we try to build together a society that truly works for everyone, we need a politics and economics that are based on a foundation of love. So, let's have open ears and humble hearts as we seek that future together.

I BELONG HERE

If you met Alasdair today, you wouldn't recognise him as the man who walked into The Alhambra Theatre in Morecambe for the AoH training. He has become something of a community leader. He works in a hostel caring for people on their journey out of prison and addiction. He has been a key player in both rounds of our Poverty Truth Commission (PTC) – in fact he sits on the national board now, as an advisor. As part of the PTC locally, together with another amazing chap, he started an initiative called 'Let's BeFriends'.[351] It exists to build friendships with people who are street homeless, or isolated and lonely. It is helping to connect many people across our geography with a sense of mutual support and kindness. Alasdair is an active political participant in our area. He not only belongs here – he is integral to all our wellbeing.

Create space for

love

in the midst of difference

- *Can you imagine at a community level what it would be like if people were able to come together in creative spaces to work out how to find solutions to some of the complex issues they are facing? What if our district, regional and national political assemblies were not about a small cabinet trying to drive through a narrow ideological agenda?*

- *What if, instead of our traditional chambers, with people sat on opposing sides, we transformed these spaces into rooms full of round tables where the speaker, or host, could introduce the topics for discussion with powerful questions?*[352]

- *What if collaborative sense making through participation took place? I wonder how much more progress we'd be making on issues like climate change, poverty, social care and sustainable fishing.*

- *What if we were willing to unlearn what we think we know about how to do politics and entered into new collective conversations in which we were all changed in the process? What if we recognised strength in our diversity? What if coalition was the norm?*

A politics of love forms the foundation of how we begin to heal society. If we want to tackle the deep inequalities and inequities in society as a whole, then this is where we must begin. However, a reconstituted politics of love is not enough in and of itself. We also need a radical inclusivity.

CHAPTER SIXTEEN
LOVE UNITY

STIGMATISED

Judy, sixty-three-years old, walked uneasily into my room. I could see she was in pain. She was wincing and she held her abdomen gingerly. She looked gaunt and wasted, so much weaker than when I'd last seen her a few months ago. Judy was a nurse in our local care home. Originally from Zimbabwe, she had moved here years ago, with her husband, Cecil, who had since sadly died, following an unfortunate accident.

I'd first met Judy when doing the ward round at the nursing home, where she worked. I was blown away by her care and attention for every resident. She knew all of them so well and treated each one as if they were her own family. Her beautiful smile brought immediate comfort as we walked around the place – I was so impressed by her compassion.

Not only was she a brilliant nurse, but she was also a devoted mother. A few years ago, she had brought her youngest son to see me. She had two boys, Justice, now a nurse himself and Remi, who had been in the armed forces. I had seen Remi with the repercussions of war – PTSD and half a leg missing. He'd had good help from the military hospital in Birmingham, to sort out his prosthetic. But he continued with phantom pain (a condition in which the damaged nerves continue to make you feel pain in the part of the leg which is no longer there). However, he was even more troubled by his psychological trauma. War has so many costs attached to it and leaves deep scars imprinted in the memories of service men and women. We'd been able to get Remi help for this, and I watched Judy wrap love and support around him as she helped him find a way through and into a new career. He was himself now working with young people with mental health problems.

This time she was seeing me for herself. Scrolling through her notes before I called her in, there was very little of note – just some cervical smear and breast screening results, but not much else. She eased herself into the chair, looked me in the eyes and said, 'I am sick. Oh Andy, I am in pain.'

'Tell me more,' I replied, my face concerned and my eyes locked with hers.

She went on to detail about her lower abdominal pain, coupled with diarrhoea and some rectal bleeding. She'd been too busy to come and find time for an appointment, due to staff shortages in the care home. She simply didn't want to let her team or the residents down and there was huge pressure from the management team. Her symptoms had worsened over several months. I examined her. There was nothing that required an immediate admission to hospital. I took some blood tests and referred her on an urgent 'two-week wait' pathway to the General Surgeons. The news was not good. She had an aggressive bowel tumour, which had already spread to her liver and her lungs. The prognosis was very poor – months, at best. Justice's wife had a baby on the way, so she decided to give some chemotherapy a go. It would only be palliative, but it would buy her some time and help to reduce the pain, as the tumour decreased in size, a little.

Thankfully, Judy got her wish to see her first grandchild. Unfortunately, she did not have much time with him. Around three months after he was born, her health began to deteriorate. The chemotherapy was no longer effective, the cancer was stealing the resources her body needed and she was weakening by the day. I went to see her at home, on one of our local housing estates. We talked through what was important to her as her care became palliative, rather than curative. Within just a few weeks, she was bed bound, being cared for by her sons and our amazing Macmillan nurses, district nurses and Hospice at Home team. As I sat with her one lunchtime, during her final days, she took me by the hand.

She said, 'You know something, I waited a long time to come and see you in the first place, when I was ill. And it wasn't because I didn't know I was ill.' She paused, every sentence an effort for her, as her lungs were filling with fluid.

'When I first came to the UK, partly because it was so bad back home, and partly because there was an invitation to come and work in the NHS, my first job was in the hospital. I was looking after men on a urology ward one night. When I was handing out the medication, one of the men looked at me and he told me that I had only come to the UK because I wanted free healthcare, and I should go home. He didn't know anything about me. But his words stayed in my heart, and I was determined never to use the healthcare system unless I absolutely had to.'

'And now look,' she panted. 'Now I can't breathe. I should never have listened to him, but I didn't want people to think about me like that. I should never have listened. But those words stuck deep.'

Here was a woman, who had come to the UK on the invitation of the government, who had always paid her taxes. She had brought up two sons, pretty much on her own, one of whom was terribly injured serving his country and yet she felt like she had no real right to use the very health and care services that she worked within.

Although it was the cancer which killed Judy, she died so prematurely because of racism. A comment made to her by a patient, she was lovingly treating, so many years before, had somehow grown like a cancer inside her. She was made to feel like she was somehow less worthy of medical care than her fellow citizens. Words have power to bring life and to destroy. The ones spoken to her were poisonous. I wonder how many of the poor health outcomes for our minority ethnic communities in the UK are related to people feeling excluded from having a right to be full participants in society. Feeling that they shouldn't have access to the services which are available to all who live here. I wonder how the often derogatory, racist and appalling headlines in certain parts of the press, are contributing to the picture we see.

Judy died a few months before George Floyd was infamously killed by a white police officer in Minnesota, USA. As his neck was knelt on, Floyd cried out the same words that I'd heard Judy speak, 'I can't breathe.'

RACISM

The journal of the *BioMedical Centre for Public Health* discusses how racism in the UK affects both mental and physical health outcomes.[353] The Race Equality Foundation also demonstrates this troubling reality in their report on ethnic inequalities in health.[354] By being unfairly discriminated against, people of British minority ethnic groups end up in poorer housing, with fewer job opportunities, higher levels of poverty and poorer health outcomes. Covid-19 exposed for us the sad truth of this, as British citizens of Asian and African origin suffered poorer health outcomes and higher death rates. This was especially true in our economically more disadvantaged communities, particularly linked to overcrowded housing and low income.[355]

Prior to the Covid-19 pandemic, it should also be noted that the 'Hostile Environment' had a significantly negative effect on the health of migrants.[356] Compounding this issue further is the use of race as a form of stigmatisation for political gain. In her book *Stigma: The Machinery of Inequality*, Professor Imogen Tyler shows how the Leave campaign used deliberately racist language and tactics as part of their propaganda campaign to convince people that we must take back control of our borders.[357] Refugees and asylum seekers, people fleeing from war, were likened to cockroaches. This dehumanised them. Posters showing people of colour invading 'white Europe' were used. Whatever the government's recent independent report of the Commission on Race and Ethnic Disparities in the UK may claim,[358] the evidence demonstrates something altogether different. All the while, our human brothers and sisters drown in the seas surrounding these islands as they flee from wars that our failed foreign policies and cuts to aid budgets have contributed to.

According to Layla Saad, the system of white supremacy was not created by anyone who is alive today. But it is maintained and upheld by everyone who holds white privilege whether or not you want it or agree with it.[359] This is a hard-hitting perspective. But in the aftermath of the Black Lives Matter movement, it is one we cannot ignore. Nor can we rightly choose not to engage with it. Until recently, to my shame, I hadn't even realised that the concept of a 'white race' is something that was entirely made up. There is, of course, no such thing. But to justify the buying and selling of black African slaves to service the sugar plantations in Barbados, whiteness was invented as a concept. It has proven to be a very dangerous idea.[360] In the seventeenth century, whiteness became synonymous with being Christian and therefore superior to all those who were 'other'. Particularly strange, as Jesus was from the Middle East.

Facing the truth, not only about the horrors of the British Empire but ongoing institutional and systemic racism in the UK, is not easy. However, as was found through the Truth and Reconciliation Commission, in South Africa, post-apartheid, if you never face the truth, you can never be reconciled.[361] If we're serious about tackling inequality and creating equity in the UK, it is something we must collectively own and face together. We must stop whitewashing our history and see it for what it is. Only then can we move forward truly.

All political choices are moral choices.

If we're going to love people and create a loving society, then we must also **dare to imagine what it would be like if we put love at the heart of our political life together.**

In talking about politics in this chapter I mean it both in terms of politics with a small 'p' and politics with a big 'P'. Small 'p' politics refers to the relationships within a group or organisation that allow particular people to have power over others, or more simply, how we do life together. Big 'P' politics describes the activities of the government, members of law-making organisations or people who try to influence the way a country is governed.

THE POLITICS OF DIVISION

We are, as a society, perhaps more divided than we have ever been.[362] Our neighbourhoods,[363] workplaces[364] and schools[365] are divided along lines of income, equality and race. Very few of us have any meaningful relationships with people who are not 'just like me'. Some of this is our own fault. We have chosen it. We have also not adapted well to changing paradigms and work patterns.[366] But it has also been engineered to some extent as we shall see, through the politics of exclusion. The problem for us all is, that our increased division is having a profoundly negative effect on our wellbeing, and it is the driving force behind the widening gap in inequality in our society.

THE POLITICS OF EXCLUSION

We see the politics of exclusion around us in so many ways. **People excluded from the capability to participate in the**

decisions which affect them the most. People being done to, rather than *radically included.* Judy, whom we met at the beginning of the chapter, was the victim of a politics of exclusion.

Judy believed that the NHS was somehow not really for people like her. Racism in all its forms is a result of exclusionary politics. It can take several forms, from the barbaric and obvious, to the subtle and unnoticed. But it is wildly prevalent and devastatingly sinister. In his phenomenal book, *Exclusion and Embrace*, Professor Miroslav Volf demonstrates four ways in which the politics and practice of exclusion pervades our society. He sees exclusion as taking four particular forms: elimination, assimilation, domination and abandonment.[367] We will examine each of these in turn.

1. *Elimination* is the most brutal and barbaric form of exclusionary politics. It is something Volf experienced in the old Yugoslavia, during the genocide of the 1990s. It has been seen in recent times in Rwanda and Myanmar. So threatened by the 'other', the only way to protect freedom is to exterminate and annihilate those who threaten us. Beware the rhetoric that labels migrants as vermin or refugees as cockroaches. This is how the Third Reich began its propaganda. In a world in which fuel, water and food shortages become more apparent, too easily does this politics live in our psyches. We must refuse to see our fellow humans as anything which degrades their humanity. The beautiful adults and children who died in the English Channel[368] – trying to find their way to the UK, as the Home Office failed to fulfil its promises[369] – were none other than our human brothers and sisters. They were not dogs, nor rats nor any other kind of animal. The government policy to

send asylum seekers to Rwanda is a further form of elimination. It does violence to our sense of humanity. The UN questions its legality.[370] So too the Supreme Court.[371]

2. *Assimilation* is where we disregard and dishonour a people group's heritage and ensure that they become just like us. In this way they are no longer our 'other'. We see this with the Chinese Government in their treatment of the Uighur people.[372] Recent changes in British law may make it far more difficult for the Gypsy, Roma and Traveller communities to continue with their traditions, a more subtle form of assimilation.[373] It also occurs when we mock the cultural and religious practices we don't understand, like banning the burqa in several European countries.[374] When Boris Johnson referred to Muslim women as letterboxes,[375] some evidence suggests it led to a 375% increase in Islamophobic incidents across the UK.[376] By stripping people groups of their cultural norms and practices and assimilating them into our ways, rather than making room for them, we exclude them. We only allow them to participate if they participate on our terms. This is not hospitality. It is not the politics of love.

3. *Domination* describes how people groups are subjugated to extract value from them. They are allowed to live, but serve as an under-class to the rich, providing almost slave labour and with few legal rights. This is certainly the case with the caste system in India, was seen in Apartheid in South Africa, and describes the way in which the West uses cheap labour from overseas. This is also a type of abandonment, in which we turn our shoulder away so that we cannot see those who are enslaved by the corporate and individual life choices we make. Without knowing it, most of us have the equivalent of several

slaves. We just don't ever see them. But you can take a test to find out how many hidden slaves your lifestyle requires, if you can bear to face it, through the Slavery Footprint website.[377]

4. *Abandonment* can take several forms. A harrowing example of the politics of abandonment was seen in the Windrush scandal, through which hundreds of Commonwealth citizens were detained, deported and denied legal rights, some of whom died as a result.[378] More starkly we see exclusion through abandonment in the hundreds of refugees now lying at the bottom of the Mediterranean Sea.[379]

The politics of exclusion divides us and perpetuates cycles of violence and subjugation. It **gives us a false sense of security.** But it makes us more unwell because whether we like it or not, we are all connected. But it is also used cynically as a distraction technique. We blame the other that we're not getting the help we need. The Brexit campaign pulled on this kind of politics throughout its campaign, with its subtext of 'it's the migrants' fault that we are struggling'.[380] For sure, this is not the only reason people voted for Brexit. It was far more complicated than that, but the politics of division through exclusion, played a huge part.

STIGMATISATION

We stigmatise people when we brand them, mark them and 'other' them, making them less than human or less worthy of love. The politics of stigmatisation has produced a toxic climate of fear and hatred that is enveloping and dividing societies and communities. In 2016, Sail Shetty, then General Secretary of Amnesty International, warned that we are witnessing a far angrier and more divided politics globally. People groups being pitted against each other through fear, blame and stigmatisation. This causes us to see one another as less than human, taking our eyes off the real injustices being meted out by those who would cling to power; focusing instead on manufactured grievances.

Judy was branded and shamed by stigmatisation. It made her believe that she was somehow less worthy of the free health and care she herself provided to many other people. Every time we degrade or shame our fellow humans, we stigmatise them.

Our society is sick because our politics is sick. **It is love sick.** The politics of division is making it so.

The indigenous people of Australia reportedly have a saying: 'I cannot be well unless you are well. And we cannot be well unless the land is well.' Our true wellbeing depends on the wellbeing of those around us because we are interconnected with them to the ecology. However, like the travellers, in the Parable of the Good Samaritan, we walk on by the people who are beaten up or left for dead on the side of the road. We believe we must do this to maintain our own rights. Therefore, we allow the politics of exclusion through stigmatisation to remain. To maintain our freedom and sense of sovereignty, we turn away from uncomfortable truths.

The cost to us, of recognising the Syrian and Libyan refugees drowning in the seas of Europe as human beings, is too much. It threatens us. So, we are willing to allow our 'sovereign leaders' to make 'difficult decisions' on our behalf. All the while, we slightly uncomfortably carry on because we like our own sense of sovereignty. And we have just enough of it to make it feel worthwhile. Individualism and consumerism are alive and well. And so too, therefore is the politics and economics of exclusion.

THE POLITICS OF INCLUSION

Judy's story has exposed for us the deeper root issues of the politics of exclusion.

What are the options for our healing?

How can we find a way forward together?

Volf contends that we are all involved in upholding the status quo, either as oppressors or as victims. Those of us who benefit from the rules of the game are quite happy to keep on playing it. But those of us who are victims of our current politics often sit with the cards we are holding, wishing that the cards had been dealt differently. If they had been, we believe, then perhaps the game would be fairer.

The reality is this: **the game is unfair.** It will never be fair. It will never deliver equality or equity. It will only lead to cyclical violence, exploitation and retribution. So rather than keeping on playing it, **we need to put the cards away and choose an altogether different game.**[381]

If we are serious about getting to grips with the deeper issues of inequality in our communities, society and world, then we need to stop playing the game of exclusionary, neo-liberal, sovereignty politics. Instead, we need to discover an altogether kinder politics which upholds the wellbeing of all people and the planet. The alternative to a politics of exclusion is not undifferentiated inclusion. On the contrary, we need to recognise and celebrate difference.

We are first and foremost human beings, children of God – brothers and sisters. We each also carry other identities. Perhaps if we pay less allegiance to our flags, constitutions, borders, and political parties and hold them a little more lightly, we can embrace each other more completely – this is true inclusion.

Judy deserved to live in an inclusive, loving, kind and welcoming society. We must root out racism and all forms of exclusionary politics. It won't be easy, but we must be determined.

We are all connected and so when we are divided, we cannot be truly well. Where one suffers, all suffer. Without radical forgiveness, the cycle of exclusion will continue in other forms. We must cross the dividing lines and build a unified society.

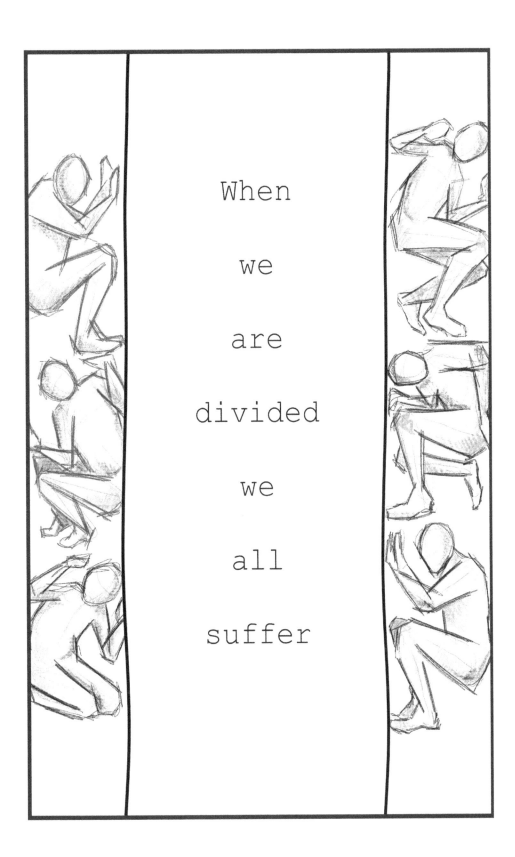

When

we

are

divided

we

all

suffer

- How does it make you feel when you reflect on Judy's story?

- Where do you experience exclusion in your own life?

- Where do you participate in the politics of exclusion?

- Are you able to challenge the inevitability of this thinking?

- What might an alternative, inclusive and embracing politics be like where you live?

CHAPTER SEVENTEEN
LOVE HOME

DAMP

I was just about to do a review with one of my medical students and fill in some forms with her before my lunchtime home visits, when Tracy barged in. Tracy is a member of the administrative team in my General Practice team. It was a cold winter's day, shortly after New Year. A time when we usually see many more people presenting with breathing problems.

'Andy, can you see this child please? Her mum's just brought her in and she looks really poorly,' Tracy asked anxiously.

Tilly was brought into my room by her mum. Stripped to the waist and wrapped in a blanket, I could see immediately that she was struggling to breathe. The muscles between her ribs were sucking in and out (what we call intercostal recession). She was using all her strength to help her little body get the air she needed. Her breathing rate was a breath a second. Her colour wasn't good.

I put my head round the door. 'Tracy, call an ambulance! I'll speak to them when you're through.'

This little two-year-old girl lived with her mum, dad and older brother. She had developed a condition called bronchiolitis. This is caused by a virus called respiratory syncytial virus (RSV). It causes the smaller airways of the lungs to become narrow, making it difficult for young children to breathe. It can affect any child but is more common in areas of poor-quality housing. Kids with bronchiolitis usually recover on their own, without needing any intervention. As long as the child remains well enough to keep eating and drinking, they can often be looked after at home.

This wasn't the case for Tilly. It was immediately clear to me that her breathing rate and heart rate were both too fast. She couldn't maintain her oxygen levels and was very unwell. She needed to be admitted to hospital for breathing support and close observation.

Tilly's parents wouldn't be considered 'poor'. But like many young families, they struggled to make ends meet. They lived in a top floor flat of a private-rented Georgian Townhouse, which was in need of some serious attention. The previous year, their roof had leaked quite badly, when we had particularly nasty storms across the UK. This had led to recurrent issues with damp in their home. There was mould on the walls. We know that this increases the risk of developing respiratory illnesses.[382] We also know that respiratory illnesses in children are much more common in areas of higher index of multiple disadvantage.[383] I use the term 'index of multiple disadvantage' here deliberately, instead of the more commonly used 'index of multiple deprivation'. That is because in the communities I am with, people don't like being called 'deprived'. They accept that they are disadvantaged and so I make no apology for making this change.

No matter how many times Tilly's parents had asked the landlord, help wasn't forthcoming. They tried to treat the walls themselves, but the damp kept recurring. They couldn't afford to move to somewhere else in the right location. Like so many young parents, they were unable to afford the deposit to get a mortgage to buy their own home. They were at the mercy of their landlord. It was affecting the health of their daughter.

But this is not an isolated case. More recently, the desperately tragic death of little Awaab Ishak, in Rochdale, has captured the national attention of the UK. He died as a direct result of recurrently inhaling mouldy spores in his family home.[384]

Taking a wider view, we can see the wider impact of housing on health outcomes. The quality of housing in which a child grows up can have profound consequences on their health. Poor housing can increase the chance of ill health in both childhood and adulthood by 25%.[385] In the UK, 20% of the population live with a long-term respiratory condition, based on data from 2012.[386] This is significantly worse in areas of economic poverty and leads to more ill health. These conditions are linked to air pollution, poor housing, and higher smoking rates.[387] Damp, mouldy housing leads to significantly higher rates of admission to hospital, for children with lung conditions.[388]

In coastal regions, like the towns of Morecambe and Blackpool, this is compounded by the reality of Houses in Multiple Occupation (HMOs). In his report into the health of our coastal communities, the Chief Medical Officer, Professor Chris Whitty, gives mention to the negative impact this is having on the wellbeing of people in places which should be our most healthy.[389] After the collapse of the seaside tourist trade in the UK, thanks to the expansion of cheap flights abroad, many old guest houses were turned into flats. These are often advertised as cheap and accessible places to live. Common also in the inner cities, they are often overcrowded and unsafe. They are filled with people who cannot afford to live anywhere else, but who find themselves at the mercy of sometimes uncaring landlords, who fail to upkeep the homes.

Indeed, Covid-19 exposed the problem of overcrowding. Easy spread of the virus in these environments led to significantly poorer health outcomes. There were higher death rates in communities where this kind of housing is commonplace. There are nearly a million people now living in this kind of situation in the UK. When you consider Ricky, whom we met in Chapter 2, and the plight of the homeless in the UK and the rise in housing rent prices,[390] our housing crisis is becoming even more concerning.[391]

Tilly's life-threatening lung condition was the result of a virus. It was severely worsened by the reality of both poor housing and the climate crisis. We know that flooding is becoming more common because of the impact of global climate change.[392] Yet globally, post-Covid, it is expected that there will be almost record increases in CO_2 emissions.[393] We continue to leave a legacy for Tilly's generation of likely irreversible climate damage.[394]

It's all too tempting to look at Tilly's tiny body, with her gasping for breath, and dive in to try and fix the problem there in front of us. We, in the NHS, fix the problems that walk in through the doors every hour of every day. However, more and more problems are coming through the doors with increasing complexity, and it's become harder and harder to fix the issues that we're seeing.

As a result of seeing Tilly that day, I offered to write to the family's landlord to explain the gravity of the situation. Thankfully he responded, the roof was fixed, and the damp proofing was sorted out. Tilly's life shouldn't have been put in danger. Much of the UK's housing stock is in a shocking state.[395] A large proportion of this is run by local councils, who are unable to afford to keep up with the number of repairs, following years of cuts to local government. The majority are in private owned, rented accommodation. Properties are crumbling. People are living in squalor. Nearly one third of the UK's population live in what is classed as 'bad housing'. This is 14.8 million people![396] It is estimated that the poor housing conditions people are living in is costing the NHS around £1.4 billion every year. **Good housing is a basic human right.** Yet, people suffer what they must.

If we think about Tilly's lungs for a moment, we see a body that was under trauma due to an assault from outside forces. In her case RSV, mouldy spores and damp air led to airways collapse. This left her struggling to get the oxygen that she needs.

When we walk out of Tilly's house, and we wander into the street we should also consider the flow of traffic through her neighbourhood. Poisonous gases are being pumped into the very atmosphere of the air that she breathes in daily. We can see that we're dealing with far more complexity than just one two-year-old girl fighting for her life. A study in New Zealand showed that if we were to get rid of damp from houses, we'd reduce the number of admissions to hospital caused by acute respiratory infections by 20%.[397] Let's pan out more widely still. Tilly, experiencing this trauma in her lungs speaks to us, of the trauma of our environment itself. We are cutting down the lungs of the earth in the shape of trees, and we are pumping the atmosphere full of pollutants. We have become wildly disconnected from the earth.

THE LUNGS OF THE EARTH

Deforestation is causing devastating consequences in health and wellbeing across the globe. In 2020 alone we lost 42,000 square kilometres of trees in our tropical regions, especially Brazil.[398] This is an area equivalent to the size of the Netherlands. It is having terrible consequences.[399] Our lungs connect directly with the outside world. The quality of the air we create is the quality of the air we breathe. The World Health Organization now calculates that 4.2 million people die every year as a result of air pollution.[400] Our lack of care for our environment is literally killing us, through lung cancer[401] and other respiratory diseases.[402]

Our society is sick because our home is sick. Planet earth is sick. **It is love sick.**

DISCONNECTED

Our disconnect from the land and our ecology has been long in the making. Most of the way our land is distributed was designed in the eleventh century and through the Middle Ages. The harrying of the land in the North of England[403] under William the Conqueror, through what some historians term a genocide, led to the instatement of Norman aristocratic families as the new landowners. Most of these families still own the vast majority of the land even today.[404] The land clearances in Scotland a few centuries later, had a similar effect.[405]

Our current housing crisis is really a consequence of our land system.[406] The historical feudal system means that most of the land is owned by a very few wealthy and influential families. Of course, many of the old aristocratic families are doing many good things to help care for and restore the environment. But many of them are not, and a sense of the commons is disappearing. Land is becoming hugely privatised, with no right to roam in

England, something the Scots are able to enjoy. To complicate matters further, increased foreign investment in new housing is also shaping the market adversely.[407] Of course, there are many vested interests; people in positions of significant power, who would resist us tackling this. But we must not let that stop us having some grown-up conversations about these complex issues of injustice and its effects. To be clear, I am not proposing some kind of communist redistribution of land. Rather, we must ask ourselves, 'to whom does the land belong?'

One way to frame the conversation is to change the emphasis from ownership to stewardship. In a world of abundance, perhaps we don't need to have a scarcity mindset, which is what drives consumerism.

The land and the wider ecology are not something for us to own or consume. It is a gift. It belongs to us all.

If we are to be good stewards of the environment, learning to own nothing but possess everything, what does this mean for how we care for our own back yard, local parks, city streets and waterways? If we happen to own some land, drawing on the ideas of a Doughnut Economy, as we explored in Chapter 13, how do we use this well for both social justice and environmental renewal? If we are 'landlords', how do we ensure we steward the resources we have for the wellbeing of the people who live under our roofs or on our land? Community land trusts, perhaps give us a more ethical way forward. These allow communities together to buy land and build affordable homes.[408]

RECONNECTING

Here in Morecambe Bay, we are eagerly exploring the potentials for a new curriculum in our schools, spearheaded by Professor Robert Barrett and the Eden Project Morecambe (formerly called Eden Project North). The Eden Project has worked here in the UK and now more globally, to try and reconnect us with the environment in which we live and embrace our role of stewardship with kindness.

As we have sat, listening to head teachers from around the Bay, I have been amazed by the number of stories about children who live less than two or three miles from the seaside, and have never visited it. Many of our young people have never climbed a mountain nor walked round a lake, even though we are a stone's throw from the Lake District National Park. This is especially true for children from our most disadvantaged communities. Yet in these places, obesity levels are highest, respiratory health is poorest, and mental health conditions are seen in far greater number. It is tragic that so many of us have become so disconnected from the beautiful surroundings in which we live. This is significantly worse for children who live in the cities.

One head teacher even told me a story about how they have a Cox apple tree in their school grounds. This year, they encouraged the children to pick the apples in the autumn and to eat them. But many children refused as they could not compute the idea that an apple came from a tree. When some of our local supermarkets run farm to fork afternoons with children, the children are absolutely baffled by where meat or crops come from. Our relationship with the land has become so broken and disconnected. Is it any wonder that we turned a blind eye to the reality of pesticides used on our crops?[409] Intensive farming practices of livestock[410] and arable crops[411] are causing the devastating pollution of our rivers. Not one of England's rivers are now deemed safe to swim in.[412] Water companies have also shamefully and deliberately dumped huge amounts of sewage into our waterways. This has been allowed due to government deregulation and cuts to the environment agency.[413] Our ecology is a mess.

Yet our bodies interact with the environment every single day. Our skin, the lining of our entire respiratory tract, from our nose to the tiny alveoli in our lungs and our digestive tract, are all membranes through which we relate to our environment. **Whether we are conscious of it or not, we are more intimately connected to our ecology than we dare to imagine.**

Tilly's lungs remind us of this. We will go on responding to the rising number of people presenting to the doors of our emergency departments with severe lung conditions. But we must also agree that it's time to make the world new, motivated by the love of each other and this precious planet we call home.

SOLUTIONS FOR OUR HOUSING CRISIS

Yes, we need to connect better to our wider ecology, as we shall explore more. But, taking us back to Tilly, whom we met at the start of this chapter, her little lungs tell us about the harsh reality of poor housing in the UK. It is something we must no longer tolerate in a loving society. But what can we do about it?

Firstly, we must remember the extraordinary power of people. The City of Bristol is one which knows the power of harnessing local passion for change, as they demonstrated when they toppled the statue of slave trader, Edward Colston.[414] When people begin to feel angry about something – challenging the inevitability of the situation and using their creative energy to try new ways of being – then exciting experiments can begin.

Bristol has also taught us an important lesson about how residents can group together to affect real change in the housing stock of a city.[415] People in rented accommodation are forming collaborative networks of support and taking on housing associations and landlords who are not treating them with kindness or justice. Communities do have more power than sometimes they allow themselves to believe. Community organising is such a vital skill in these situations.[416]

Secondly, through participatory politics, tenants can become part of the change that is needed. Mutual understanding between housing associations/landlords and tenants is vital if we are to find creative solutions. The National Housing Federation has developed a helpful charter which gives all housing associations a framework by which they can work in a more proactive and positive way with their residents.[417] The politics and economics of love is relational rather than combative.

Thirdly, those with 'big P' political power need to use it to form policies to bring more justice into the housing sector. Tim Farron, MP, in rural Cumbria, has been doing work in parliament to stand up for local communities who are being priced out of the Lake District National Park. Too many young families can no longer afford to buy their own homes because of rich second homeowners driving up the cost of housing. This has to change. There are also moves to change legislation around the role and responsibilities of landlords. For the sake of Tilly and millions like her, this agenda must not be lost.

Fourthly, we need new homes to be built. Our housing stock in the UK is old and in disrepair. Much of it isn't fit for human habitation. We need homes which help to create health and connect communities, enabling people to flourish.

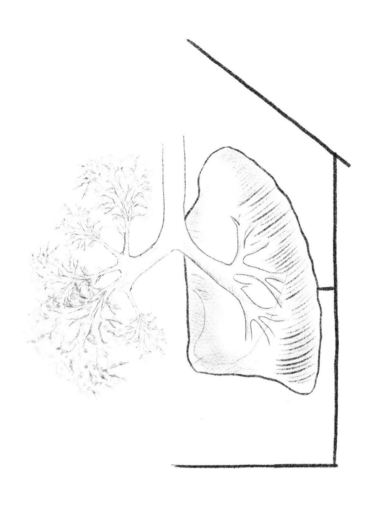

We are more intimately
connected to our
ecology then we dare to
imagine

REFLECTIONS

- How important is your home to you?

- If you own your own home, what do you need to change to help it become a place of wellbeing?

- Is your home a place of hospitality?

- If you are a landlord, are you behaving in a loving way towards your tenants?

- If you are a tenant, are you aware of your rights? How might you join with others to petition for better conditions? If you have a place to live, with a landlord who takes care of you, are you being loving towards your landlord in the way you live there?

- If you are a housing officer or work in the realm of housing policy, are you developing fair and just practices for children like Tilly and others who struggle with breathing problems?

- Why does it matter that we act on pollution in our ecology?

- What role might you play in helping our living environments become cleaner and greener?

CHAPTER EIGHTEEN
LOVE ECOLOGY

'I want you to act as if our house is on fire.
Because it is.' – Greta Thunberg[418] *(emphasis added)*

WORRIED

'I'm not sleeping.' The seventeen-year-old sat down in the chair next to my desk. He looked like he had the weight of the world on his shoulders.

'I'm sorry to hear that, Ben. How can I help?' I asked.

'I just want to be able to sleep,' he began. 'But I can't. I can't switch my thoughts off and I can't stop worrying.'

'Is there something in particular you are worrying about?' I questioned.

'Yeah, but I don't think there's anything you can do about that!' he replied.

'Try me!' I said. I see people with anxiety all the time I thought, and am highly experienced at helping them look at it and work out together what might help.

'You think you could fix climate change?' Ben asked, with a resignation and sadness in his voice.

It was the first time I'd seen a teenager with climate anxiety, but it wouldn't be the last. It felt like a punch in the stomach and like my heart suddenly expanded inside my chest. I felt this deep compassion for Ben and his generation, and a sudden new perspective of what they (and we) are facing. It was like when one of your children tells you something so big that they are facing and you know you can't fix it, though everything inside you wants to. I remember tears forming like big drops in my eyes and I swallowed hard. I had not expected this kind of reaction. The magnitude of what he was thinking about was staggering.

Yes, I could work with him to help with the anxiety and sleep. But the source of his worry – I felt like I understood climate anxiety in a new way that day.

I don't think it's possible for us to talk about being a sick society without exploring how disconnected we have become from our environment. We are sick because our ecology is sick. To be honest, I have less expertise in this area. However, I hope what I write in the pages ahead sparks conversations about what it means for us to engage with these issues soberly and urgently.

REPENT

When Greta Thunberg sat out in the cold and went on strike from school until her government decided to take climate change more seriously, I doubt that she could ever have imagined what would transpire. Never in her wildest dreams would she have thought that she would spearhead a global movement for climate justice. As she sat quietly, with her homemade placard outside her parliament, she could not have realised that one day she would be addressing the United Nations and global climate summits. She wouldn't have believed that she would be in X (previously known as Twitter) spats with a US president! Her ability to speak with such beautiful but intense prophetic clarity challenges us all to wake up, pay attention and repent. In its most basic form – this means change!

Her rallying call cut through the noise and clamour of our economic and political systems, resonated with the voices of many other activists and the groaning of the earth itself to provoke a worldwide awakening.

She cut through what the philosopher Giorgio Agamben would call *chronos* time. *Chronos* time is the timeframe of empire. The tick-tock clock to which we are all enslaved. It is like a railroad. The tracks of power, which have been laid down and ridden through the ages. These tracks ride roughshod over the earth, seeing it as a commodity to be extracted, rather than a life-source to be stewarded and cared for. Instead, Greta Thunberg, stepped into what Agamben calls *kairos* time.[419]

Kairos time cuts through and collides with *chronos* time and takes it off track. It pushes us into the zone of new possibility. Thunberg opened up a space for us to find another way together as humanity. The way of love, the way of justice, the way of gentleness, the way of peace. It's no wonder that she came up against such violent and vehement resistance from those who would maintain the status quo, putting money and profit above the wellbeing of all people and the planet.

As with so many prophetic voices through the years, her call for us to change comes with just enough time for us to make a difference. Many others have tried over the last several decades and yet it seems that it was an autistic, teenage girl who carried enough grace, fire and determination to cause us to finally pay attention. This is *kairos* time. The way of love has opened up a space for us to examine our ways and change before it is ultimately too late.

Our society is sick, and it is making our ecology sick. We have failed to steward and care for our environment. **It is love sick.**

STEWARDS

Ecology is the study of the relations of organisms to one another and their physical surroundings or environment. It is impossible to talk about creating a more loving society, without thinking about our planet and our relationship to it. We are just a small part of the expansive cosmos. You only need to look up at the sky on a starry night to realise how small and insignificant we are. This kind of experience helps us embrace more humility when we think about how we relate to the world around us.

Given the state of the climate crisis, humility allows us to view ourselves in our rightful place, not only as stewards of the environment but also as true participants in it. We are utterly dependent on the life-giving environment of the earth itself and the rich biodiversity within. Therefore, we need to act with more humility towards the environment which sustains us. If we allowed ourselves to listen to what the four elements – earth, wind, fire and water – are speaking to us right now, we would be taking more urgent action. What urgent action might this involve?

Global temperatures are on the rise, with terrible consequences. We are seeing massive changes in weather patterns. Wildfires have ravaged Australia and the Western United States. Hurricanes, storms, and cyclones are devastating communities across the globe. Our deserts are expanding, our rivers are polluted, our oceans are filled with plastic, and our ice caps are melting. Local ecologies are being destroyed and biodiversity is disappearing at alarming rates. Between 1970 and 2016, we have seen an average decrease of 68% of mammals, fish, amphibians, reptiles and birds globally.[420] These are creatures we exist together with – putting aside our call to steward the earth well, we actually need them to survive.

The World Health Organization now sees climate change as the biggest health threat facing humanity. It is affecting the safety of our drinking water and the quality of our air. It is making food and shelter less secure for billions of people. It puts us at far greater risk of global pandemics, and other preventable diseases, like diarrhoea and heat stress. It is estimated that between 2030 and 2050, climate change will cause an additional 250,000 deaths each year. The direct health cost is estimated to be $2–4 billion by 2030 and is already leaving health systems in many countries unable to cope or respond adequately.[421] Our society is sick because our ecology is sick. We have a symbiotic relationship.

IS THERE ANY HOPE?

In the face of such an enormous task ahead of us, it can feel like our little actions are pointless. I totally get that. It's true that we need governments to act urgently and collaboratively. I accept that unless Brazil, China, India, Russia, and especially the USA make huge changes to the way they use fossil fuels, along of course with the whole of Europe, we remain in deep trouble. This is one of the reasons we must reform our politics. It needs to be aligned with our planetary values at a global level. In the meantime, how we vote, does make some difference and we should radically critique all those who seek political office according to their climate credentials. In my opinion, we should only vote for those parties in our current political system who are taking this agenda seriously. It matters so much. Right now, we also urgently need governments to act together to keep fossil fuels in the ground and to clean the air of carbon dioxide and methane. This is going to take some brave policy decisions which on the surface may seem unpopular but would have the support of the vast majority of people, given the crisis that we face.[422]

I also recognise that changing our behaviour is tough, and we could just shrug our shoulders and leave it for the next generation. **But if the hearts of the fathers and mothers cannot turn to the children in this moment, then what kind of ancestors are we?**

I'm so grateful to Alastair McIntosh, Honorary Professor in the College of Social Sciences at the University of Glasgow, who has been hugely influential in helping me to connect with this issue rather than just think of it as some superfluous thing on the side. He offers three key ways – remembering, revisioning and reclaiming – in which we can learn to love our ecology, through what he calls the 'rubric of regeneration'.[423]

1. *Remembering* – we have forgotten our connection with all things. We have become separated, disconnected and

dismembered. If we are going to love our ecology, we must re-member it. We must include it in our lives and see ourselves as a living part of it. It is not there for us to extract from or consume, as the economics of capitalism would have it. It is something we are joined with synergistically and we need to remember this.

2. *Revisioning*, or what I might call reimagining – there is an ancient proverb which says that without vision, people perish.[424] This is certainly true when it comes to climate change. We need to create a fresh vision of what it means to live well in and with our ecology. We need to revision/reimagine what it would be like if we loved our ecology, tended it and took care of it.

3. *Reclaiming* – we need to reclaim it as ours. The ecology belongs to the people and the people belong to the ecology. We belong in, and with, a complex biodiverse sphere. Its wellbeing and ours are directly linked. It has become grossly privatised, but rightfully it belongs to the commons.

Decisions must always take into account the perspective of the ecology – the often unheard voice.

This would at least be a beginning to ensuring that we stop making rash and destructive political and economic decisions, which are detrimental to climate change. This voice must be a powerful counterbalance to the over-influential voice of the lobbyists.

US President Joe Biden made a wonderful and historic appointment in Deb Haaland as the US Secretary of the Interior, in the USA. He has ensured that for the first time indigenous people groups are included and represented at the highest level of government. There could be no one better to oversee the issues dealt with by her department, particularly when it comes to land rights and environmental sustainability.

RECONNECT

One of my favourite places to be is in my garden. I'm someone who has a busy mind. My mum would call it an 'overactive imagination'. My garden is one of the places where my mind does some ticking over and then learns to be still. I find it is a place of some of my greatest learning, insights, challenges and growth. I have found that by getting my hands into the soil, I am reconnecting to the earth. Sometimes I am arrested by a birdsong I do not recognise, or stilled by a robin, who comes to see what I am up to. I find that as I pull out the root systems of ground elder, that somehow, I'm able to process my own unhelpful thought patterns. When I wonder why unhelpful and damaging habits of behaviour in me die hard, the ground elder reminds me that it so easily regrows and needs constant attention and discipline.

I love noticing how the oak trees in our surrounding fields always awaken in the same order from west to east, each spring. I love the process of tending my vegetable beds and learning the consequences of not protecting my plants properly from a frost or a pest of some sort. We are using some of our land (we have a small field) to create a wildflower meadow. I had never understood the amazing job that cattle and sheep do in tending the land. And I can't tell you about the joy in seeing a multitude of butterflies and various other wildlife, like toads, stoats, slow worms, deer, hedgehogs, kestrels and buzzards on our land. Reconnecting with and tending our ecology is so good for the soul. It teaches us to love, and it brings us deep joy.

The living world around us, our ecology, offers us moments of deep joy every day. If we can learn to take notice and be present in the moment, we will experience it. The Quakers call this 'wonder'.

We find joy in the sound of a roaring waterfall, in the sight of penguins dancing on the ice, or dolphins jumping through the waves. We hear joy from goldfinches chirping in the early morning on our garden tables. Joy is found in the crackle of a bonfire, in kicking autumn leaves along whilst feeling the wind on our face, or sledging downhill in the freshly fallen snow. Joy is found after weeding our flowerbed or pulling up our first potatoes, or whilst catching our first fish. Joy is found in the scent of honeysuckle, on a summer's evening; or the sight of bluebells or daffodils in the spring. Joy is found in walking a springer spaniel down a country lane or listening to the hoot of an owl in the trees at dusk.

Every day is filled with countless moments of inexpressible joy. It is something to be deeply valued and treasured.

One of the things I have found interesting, as I have been part of hosting conversations around Morecambe Bay, is how regularly the desire to connect to our ecology is part of those discussions. People want green transport, for sure, but they also want spaces to be able to grow their own fruit and vegetables, keep bees, and connect with nature. So much of this comes back to how we design the spaces in which we live together and how we steward those spaces lovingly for each other and those who will follow us.

How much more exciting might our education be and how much more purposeful would it feel if we were building whole chunks of the curriculum around issues like climate change in really integrated ways? Why do we focus so much on our children needing to finish school having studied a Shakespearean play (I'm not against this at all by the way – I love Shakespeare) but without knowing how to build a shelter, purify rainwater and grow their own food? What if we took a problem-based learning approach to this? We could set our young people's minds alight with how different subjects could combine to enable them to get their heads around the issues.

They would learn to think collaboratively and creatively about solutions. They would learn to appreciate different skill sets; those with practical skills working together with those who are maybe more 'academic'. From an early age, our children and young people should be encouraged to get their hands into the soil, to plant seeds, to tenderly care for the seedlings. Watering them, seeing them grow, harvesting the fruit and vegetables and enjoying the produce should be essential learning practices. They could cook the food and practise hospitality with each other around the dinner tables in their school canteens.

Whilst doing this they would have the opportunity to understand the biology of plants, the ecology of soil, the history of farming practices, and the mathematics and economics of preparing meals. Our children and young people would understand the physical geography of weather patterns. They would learn about human geography of human slavery and how this supports and upholds our current global food markets. They would understand the reality that billions of people are on the brink of starvation, whilst the West maintains a greedy surplus. Building on this knowledge at each stage of their education, they will become more ambitious and purposeful in finding solutions. This is the stuff our education and learning should be filled with. An integrated and inclusive approach. It gives us all an opportunity to ask far better and deeper questions about the way that we build life together, the core values that we share, and the kind of future that we want to take hold of together.

RENEW

Our ecology is lovesick, and it is telling us so. But there are opportunities for each of us, every day to be part of the global movement for change.

Mike Berners-Lee, Professor and Fellow of the Institute for Social Futures at Lancaster University, has written several brilliant books on how we can make a difference. His latest one, *There Is No Planet B*, is excellent in helping us get to grips with the real and nitty gritty things we can do to be part of the seismic shift needed.[425]

Firstly, we need to try to 'drive and fly less'.[426] Covid-19 forced this upon us, for a while. It also led to record reductions in global fossil fuel emissions.[427] But keeping this up is easier said than done. We are a global community and many of us have family all over the world or simply love to travel. However, when we reflect that half of all emissions from air travel are caused by only 1% of the population, it makes you wonder how we can continue to justify this. The reality is it is primarily a certain section of the business community who are responsible for most of the pollution.

Driving less and moving more naturally is also good for our health. However, for those of us who live in places with terrible transport infrastructure, like many places in and across the North of England, driving less can be nigh on impossible. It's another reason why governments must take the building of good transport networks seriously, like in the Black Forest region of southwest Germany. This is good for the bits of economy which need to grow and good for the environment. We need road travel to become less necessary and this is going to take good and serious planning. We need to see global companies leading by example in the use of green technologies. We need governments to be more serious. They must stop funding fossil fuels and bowing low to the oil industry. New technologies are there to be invested in. This is where government can make the right kind of investment decisions.

Secondly, where we can, we need to try and reduce our home energy consumption. Although this is very important given the high costs and failed government schemes,[428] where possible, making green choices on how we heat our homes is a good thing to do. From better insulation to non-fossil fuel heating systems, those of us who can, need to get on with it. The invasion of Ukraine by President Putin has made this all the more urgent. As the technology catches up, and caring governments create better policies, more of us will increasingly play our part in this. However, it is incumbent on governments to make schemes work. Unfortunately, we've seen poorly thought through and half-hearted attempts in the UK fail.[429] This isn't good enough.

Thirdly, Berners-Lee suggests we should all try and eat less meat and dairy. We do need to be more mindful about what we're eating. Really? Is this just another thing to make us feel guilty? Won't we just feel like do-gooders but make little difference? I certainly thought so. But around 10% of all carbon emissions in the UK come from meat farming, primarily beef and lamb.[430]

I was struck recently by the brilliant TED Talk by journalist, Graham Hill.[431] He floated the idea of becoming a weekday vegetarian. This is something my family are now experimenting with. I have found that it is surprisingly highly doable. If we all did this, it would have a massive impact on our carbon footprint. Participative conversations on this are vital, though. There are important arguments for us to consider around the positive role grazing cattle can have when they are grass fed.[432] However, by significantly reducing my meat and fish intake, I can look forward to it more at the weekend. I can also afford to then buy higher welfare meat and fish, which means more sustainable farming practices. I can focus on knowing that my choices are both healthy and beneficial for the climate. Small steps, but not insignificant.

Alongside this, governments and the farming industry need to work together, nationally and globally. We have to radically change our intensive farming and fishing practices. We need to learn to let the land and seas rest and regenerate. We are destroying the quality of our soil, hugely damaging our waters, devastating our biodiversity, driving hundreds of species to extinction, and driving up global temperatures. If we eat less meat and fish, the practices will hopefully begin to change. That's part of how social movement works. It isn't just meat though, it is dairy farming too, plus the farming of certain grains, like rice, which contribute significantly when it comes to global warming.

What creative alternatives are there? The Borgen Project in places like Costa Rica and Zimbabwe, is one example providing some hopeful possibilities.[433] What if we learned to let the land and seas rest rather than ravishing them, and paid our farmers and fishers to rest too, using some of the time to work on repairs or other regenerative projects?

Fourthly, we need to make do and mend. In other words, we need to stop buying so much unnecessary stuff, especially when it comes to wasteful, fast fashion,[434] and be more satisfied with what we have. When you consider that it takes 10,000 litres of water to make one pair of denim jeans,[435] you can understand why. In fact, the fourth biggest lake in the world dried up, feeding this industry.[436] So, again, it might seem like a small act, but limiting our wardrobe size can be seriously worthwhile, if we all do it.

We could spend our money and resources on companies that fit with our values (like slave-free, living-wage chocolate) and have more to be generous with. What if we embraced the idea that there is an abundance available? There really is enough for everyone. Our fear of scarcity drives so much of our consumerist behaviour. If we relax into the idea that a well stewarded earth ensures that everyone is well fed and watered, perhaps we would embrace the notion of generosity more easily.

Fifthly, we need to make space for protest. This stuff matters! It matters for our children. It matters for their children. It also matters to our fellow inhabitants with whom we share this planet. So, where we see governments acting too slowly, or where we see companies acting in ways which are inherently unkind and selfish, then we need to act. We need to use our voice, our feet, our money, and our power to make it known that we will not stand by and let such staggering climate injustice continue. We also probably need to learn to do this in ways that don't upset the rest of the public and somewhat ruin the cause! Blocking motorways, although a powerful statement in some ways, isn't currently winning the argument.

Finally, we need to put our resources where our mouths are. If we care about our ecology, then there are plenty of initiatives we can get involved in. From charitable giving to fantastic organisations working on this agenda, to using our time to volunteer on various projects. We can help clean up beaches or plant trees in our national parks. We can create wildlife habitats in our gardens or start growing our own vegetables. Whatever we can do, we should do. **Billions of little actions together can make an enormous change.**

REVOLUTION

We see in the climate justice movement all the hallmarks of a social revolution. Remember the ingredients from Chapter 1: cultivate outrage, challenge inevitability and create moral alternative economies.

The anger and passion are certainly stirring. And so they should! When you consider that the oil, coal, auto, utilities, steel and rail industries together employed a PR guru to help them consistently brief against climate change, with great success,[437] we should be furious! The oil sector alone has been making profits of $3 billion every single day for the last 50 years.[438] This has given them huge power and influence in manipulating governments across the globe. It's utterly outrageous! Where was the regulation and the taxation? But now, the inevitability of our current situation is definitely being challenged, especially as we head towards unthinkably high household gas and electricity bills. Everywhere we see alternative ways of being beginning to emerge around us. Green technologies, sustainable food practices, the cleaning of our oceans and ethical fashion, to name but a few.

The more governments try to silence the voices of the revolution the more it will slip through their fingers, even when they fail to protect those killed for protesting.[439] It is ironic that those who protest for climate justice are called criminals[440] whilst those who actively destroy the world through uncaring businesses, are allowed to hide their wealth in tax havens.[441]

If we are going to have integrity on the issues of climate justice and restoration, then we need to radically align our behaviours with our beliefs. This means we need to become present to the realities we are now living with – no matter how difficult, inconvenient or painful they may be.

Love requires of us integrity and authenticity.

We find so much kindness at work in our relationship with the ecology. Countless organisations like the National Trust, The Wildlife Trust, Natural England, the World Wide Fund for Nature (WWF), and many others are trying to restore our biodiversity and treat the land with gentleness. They are helping us in restoring our relationship with it. Despite many intensive practices and the use of chemicals – which destroy the quality of the soil, the biodiversity of the species, pollute our rivers and destroy natural habitats – there are many who are experimenting with alternatives. They are trying to find a way through to more sustainable, and climate conscious practices. Where 10% of global emissions are currently caused by the fashion industry, companies like ASOS are genuinely trying to change their ways and treat the world with kindness. It is not too late for our ecology.

There is hope that if we act now across the globe through a multitude of loving initiatives, we can stem the tide of destruction and cede much restoration and regeneration.

We must seize the day!

We must show Ben and his generation that we care.

Act with humility towards
the environment which
sustains us

- *What will you do? What action can you feasibly take?*

- *What protests or campaigns might you join in with?*

- *How will you let the rising generation know that you stand with them?*

- *Or if you are already involved, whatever your age, how will you keep yourself resourced?*

- *How will you approach the sickness in our ecology with love?*

CHAPTER NINETEEN
LOVE HOPE

HEARD

When my daughter was three and a half years old, her schoolteacher, Mrs Sanderson, called my wife and me over for a chat in the playground one day, at pick-up time.

'Have you ever noticed anything about your daughter's hearing?' she asked.

We looked at each other a little puzzled. I was wondering if she was, perhaps, going to tell us that Amelia was a little easily distracted. This was often written in my school reports, and I assumed I had passed this unfortunate trait on to my offspring.

'Not really,' we replied, shaking our heads.

'OK, well I think it's possible that she might be struggling with her hearing a little. I've noticed a few things recently,' Mrs Sanderson began. 'She's very attentive when I talk to her and watches me intently. But if I call the children over and she's not facing me, she will continue playing. This is unlike her. So today, I did an experiment. I told the children that I was going to go outside and give them an instruction through the window. They all gathered round and stood on the carpet. I went out and mouthed an instruction to them. The whole class stood still, except for Amelia, who went and did exactly what I asked. I think she may be lip reading.'

We were stunned. We were simultaneously blown away by her teacher's brilliance and appalled at ourselves as parents. How had we not noticed this? Our daughter had had several ear infections since she was born, but I had never looked inside her ears afterwards myself, assuming that her eardrum was repairing itself each time. Yes, she was very affectionate and always got up close when we were talking to her and looked at our faces intently. But with a boisterous older brother and a newborn in our midst, we had simply missed this. We felt terrible.

We booked an appointment with our own GP. We were duly sent off to see the audiology team at the Royal Manchester Children's Hospital. The recurrent perforations of her eardrums had caused lasting damage and large holes. Her hearing on the left side was around 30% with 50% on the right. With lip reading, she could bolster this to around 85% accuracy. It was clear she needed hearing aids.

I will never forget the day we had them fitted. Children's hearing aids on the NHS in the UK are phenomenal. They are absolutely top of the range. The technology is so smart and adapts itself to the environment the child finds themselves in. When they were first turned on, her whole face lit up. I asked her how she felt.

'Daddy! You talk so loud!' Her face full of surprise and elation.

As we walked out of the department, she asked me to walk more quietly. As a musician and a doctor, I rely on my hearing so much. Never for one moment had I considered what it must be like to hear a car engine or a bird song for the first time, as my daughter did that day. Suddenly, her world was full of sounds she had never encountered. Everyday noise, which I had filtered out, became to her an experience of wonder.

LEARNING TO LISTEN

Deep listening, which we could also call transformative listening is vital if we're going to transform our community and political spaces. Listening is an art form and one that many of us never really learn, at least not to the deepest levels. According to Sue Mitchell, Art of Hosting (AoH) practitioner and life coach, listening is done at five levels.[442]

1. Level 1 is when we're thinking, 'Oh it's my turn in a minute.' It's when we're not listening at all and we're just waiting to jump in with whatever it is we want to say.

2. Level 2 is when something the speaker says sparks a memory in us and we start contributing about our own (perhaps) similar experience. We think about how it applies to our own lives. It's about us trying to make sense and find connection but can mean we miss what is actually being said.

3. Level 3 is about fixing. The listener steps in and tries to fix the problem, without listening or even acknowledging the other person's agency or own capabilities in sense making and solution finding. It's a level at which we don't want to connect too deeply, so we try and sort it and move on. Or perhaps we want to show off that we know what to do. We're the expert here thank you very much!

4. Level 4 is where it begins to be about real listening. It's where we allow ourselves to be truly with the person we are listening to. This is a sacred space. One where we allow ourselves to feel real empathy. To be with someone in their moment and experience, putting our own thoughts and experiences aside and creating a space for them.

5. Level 5 is where we begin not just to listen, but to hear the other person. It is the art of self-awareness. It is where we allow ourselves to be changed by the encounter and have our previously held perspectives and understandings changed. This is generative listening. It is the space in which we unlearn what we think we know and come into new understandings and therefore the realm of new possibilities.

If we are to connect within and across communities, we need to learn this art of listening. How might so-called 'public consultations' change if they did not have pre-determined outcomes, but were about real, deep generative listening?

We need to develop a way of doing politics and economics that tunes into what we are not currently hearing. We need to deliberately listen to the unheard voices, build relationships with those currently marginalised and include them in decision-making, so that we do not end up with a system which maintains the benefits for the few. In fact, we must listen even more deeply – not only to each other, but to the other species we share our ecology with and the land itself. What are they telling us?

A NEW PLUMB LINE

I grew up in the City of Coventry in the West Midlands. Much of the city centre was obliterated during the Blitz of World War II. This was due to the importance of Coventry as a place of manufacturing and industry. After the war, a new cathedral was built to replace the one that burnt down. It is a truly spectacular piece of architecture.

It is special because of its role in reconciliation, and was financed, in part, with money donated from both Germany and Japan. It happens to be probably my favourite building in the world, and it is where I asked my wife to marry me, one evening in 2001, when we had the place to ourselves.

To one side of the cathedral sits a remarkable sculpture by Clark Fitzgerald called 'The Plumb Line and the City'.[443] The sculpture asks a question of the city.

Is social justice found here?

It is based on a section of the book of Amos, in the Jewish and Christian Scriptures. Amos was a prophet of his day. He was deeply concerned with economic equity and social justice. He decried the religious people of his day – who were concerned only with appearing to be good, whilst allowing appalling economic inequity to continue. He was incensed by those who would gladly fatten themselves up whilst letting others starve. He was shocked at those who would follow the superficial rules, which made them look like good citizens, whilst perpetuating deep injustices. He challenged those who would deliberately silence the poor or keep them at such a distance that their cries for justice would be ignored. He had a vision of a plumb line being held over his nation and saw that it was crooked.[444]

Like Amos, it's time for us to apply a new yard stick, a new plumb line, a new set of measurements to our own situation. If we keep on with the same economic values and continue to measure things in the same way, we will continue to get the same inequities, injustices and destructive behaviours. To put it another way, our current models have been weighed in the scales and found wanting.

Our towns, cities and the surrounding regions are sick because our society is sick. **They are love sick.**

It's time to be brave enough to realign our vision with our values. It means we can't only point the finger at others – these values have to align within us. It requires honesty and relational participation. Together we must experiment with new ways of thinking and acting with the resources we have available. We must be willing to forgive previous wrongs, let go of old mindsets, broken systems and dysfunctional addictions, and dare ourselves to reimagine a future of interconnected economic wellbeing and climate justice. So, like Amos, we speak to our economic system, and we say it is time for justice and goodness to be built on the foundations of love and kindness.

After all, the economy is our servant, not our master! It's time to let love rule.

THE POWER OF LOVE

To create **a politics of love** we must stop talking of ceding power into local communities and instead recognise the power and innate capabilities **already at work within them.**

It must be true for everyone in a town, city and the surrounding region that 'Nothing about us, without us, is for us'[445] becomes the guiding principle. In their superb book, *New Power*, Henry Timms and Jeremy Heimans explore the huge shift in power which is occurring globally and why we need to pay attention to this and learn to work differently.

They demonstrate the difference between what they term 'old power' and 'new power'.

> *Old power works like a currency. It is held by few.*
> *Once gained, it is jealously guarded, and the powerful*
> *have a substantial store to spend. It is closed, inaccessible*
> *and leader-driven. It downloads and it captures. New power*
> *operates differently, like a current. It is made by many.*
> *It is open, participatory and peer-driven. It uploads and*
> *it distributes. Like water or electricity, it's most forceful*
> *when it surges. The goal with new power is not to*
> *hoard it, but to channel it.*[446]   (emphasis added)

The journey they take us on ends with them asking us to consider the future and how we might create a 'full-stack society'. This is a coding term which speaks of how multiple layers within a software product come together to form a coherent whole – both those we see and those we don't. **In other words, we need to create together the kind of world in which people can more meaningfully participate in and feel true ownership for every aspect of their lives,** rather than feeling like the pawns of the elite, unable to affect any change, except through the occasional election or referendum. The truth is that issues like poverty are complex, ingrained and pervasive. We all need to play our part if we are to see the kind of change we need. This will be a people movement; perhaps like we have never experienced before.

People need to be able to engage with technology platforms, their work, their health, education, political and economic decisions, and the workings of government itself. To create a full-stack society, Timms and Heimans argue that we need to dream up entirely new models that make us feel powerful and more connected to one another in all our guises: as patients, taxpayers, consumers, neighbours, voters, students and parents.[447]

What would we prioritise if we were to take a 'full-stack' approach to renewing and restoring our towns and city regions motivated by a politics of love? **The politics of love is outworked, in the action of compassionate care.** In order to create compassionate cultures, we need people who are committed to help embed this kind of change.

KEY PLAYERS IN SOCIAL CHANGE

John Paul Lederach, one of the world's leading peace builders, writes in his book, *The Moral Imagination*, that there are four types of people who become key to enabling social change to occur. He terms them critical yeast, anchors, networkers and web watchers.[448]

Firstly, we need *critical yeast*. Lederach uses the word 'yeast' rather than 'catalyst' because a catalyst is not necessarily itself changed when it sparks a reaction. He says that we need 'yeasty' people in our communities; we need people who have experienced hardship, been changed by love, done their work, let go of their ego, and become agents of gift to those around them. Critical yeast people are not usually leaders or people with titles or a sense of self-importance. Critical yeast people are marked by humility. They have an edginess that comes through the life experience of some kind of suffering – be that poverty, trauma or marginalisation. Critical yeast people aren't afraid to challenge the inevitability of the status quo.

Secondly, we need critical yeast people to connect with *anchors*. Anchors are people who are rooted in a place, committed to it for the long term. They are steadfast in their love of the area and the people who live there. They might be community leaders in a traditional sense or perhaps recognised as elders, who hold the wider community in their hearts.

Thirdly, anchors are often connected together through *networkers*. These are people who love building relationships and connecting people together. The space between the anchors becomes like a web.

Fourthly, *web watchers* then guard that space, ensuring those relationships function and flow well together. They sooth over any disgruntlements or hurts that might develop. They help create a web of relationships which becomes a flexible structure. This then enables and gives permission for the moral alternative economies and experiments to develop. This might be through innovative funding mechanisms, commissioning new services or new ways of thinking about governance, for example. These people all co-exist within neighbourhoods and wider political spaces.

We need to think more about space.

THE NEW POLITICAL SPACE

In a statement after the EU referendum, Sadiq Khan, Mayor of London and Anne Hidalgo, Mayor of Paris said this: 'If the nineteenth century was defined by Empires and the twentieth century by nation-states, the twenty-first century belongs to cities.'[449]

In the UK, 82.9% of us are now 'urban dwellers',[450] whilst globally 56.2% of us live in cities.[451] Cities and their surrounding regions (city regions) have become the most common ecology for human beings and carry enormous political and economic importance. They are heterogeneous and complex. This is where so much of our life happens. We need to live life well. Like we really exist. Like our lives count for something. So, our city regions need to be places in which we can flourish. Where we can know that we are loved, we are seen, we belong and we are welcome.

City regions are multidimensional and have the potential to be places of participation, integration, inclusivity and collaboration in a way that nation states cannot. They are an environment in which the politics and economics of love can be outworked, and society can be healed and rebuilt. How do we release this potential? If we are going to create participative cities and city regions, then we are going to have to learn to listen to each other across our current divides in a way that we certainly do not at present. When we talk about city regions, we also need to ensure that we do not forget or neglect smaller towns and rural areas.

THE POLITICS OF HOPE

Now, perhaps more than ever, we need fresh hope. When we look at all of the global issues we are facing, it can feel hard to find any sense of hope. Hope might even be considered futile or false. Rebecca Solnit is so helpful here. She says, 'Hope is not a lottery ticket you can sit on the sofa and clutch, feeling lucky. It is an axe you break down doors with in an emergency.'[452]

One of my favourite parts of my job is to host conversations alongside others in various places. A few years ago, we were running an AoH training in the town of Barrow-in-Furness. Some people rudely call it the longest cul-de-sac in England, but it is a truly wonderful place with some significant inequalities.

We co-hosted a conversation about the dreams people held in their hearts for their town. The truth is, no matter how hard life is, no matter how tough the current reality may be, people still have the capacity to dream. Imagination is what sets us apart as a species. Therefore, we simply created some space and allowed people the opportunity to get creative. We asked them to dream individually and collectively about what they would love their town to be like. We wanted to know how they would like it to develop over the following decades. Unsurprisingly, people were not short of ideas and had great imaginings of what that could be like.

Following on from this event and some further conversations, Sam Plum – then Chief Executive at Barrow Borough Council, now Chief Executive of the newly formed Westmorland and Furness Council, and a truly excellent leader – invited Professor Hilary Cottam, author, innovator and social entrepreneur, to come and help. She hosted a series of workshops with her academic partners called 'constellations'. The idea is for people to lie down, look at the stars and begin to think about how their dreams can become a reality. The stars inspire them to plot their course to the future. That process in Barrow-in-Furness has been beautiful to behold.[453]

People from all walks of life, from all kinds of backgrounds and communities, have come together and created a future vision for their town, which is quite honestly extraordinary. It has not remained something held only within peoples' hearts. The people who came together have been able to share that dream and vision with their local council, with public sector leaders, business leaders, and politicians. Their manifesto is becoming the working plan for all of those groups and organisations, to practically shape the future together.

A recent survey of young people across the UK showed significant levels of hopelessness and fear about the future.[454] Yet when I listen to my children's generation, I find them to be a group of people that fill me with hope. My daughter has taught me so much about listening with attention, so that I really hear. Due to her need to lip read, when she is listening to me, she is fully engaged and fully focused, so that she ensures she is hearing me. I wonder if we are listening to our young people. Are we hearing the questions they are asking us? Are we willing to respond?

Collectively they are causing us to wake up to face the realities of climate change and mental health issues. They are causing us to have braver conversations about how we might face these issues together. I am so grateful for their tenacity and strength in calling us into something far better. They must be included as active participants in shaping the future with love. It is why we must, in my opinion, lower the voting age to sixteen and make voting compulsory within a system of proportional representation. Some politicians, like the Mayor of Manchester, Andy Burnham, are calling for this.[455]

We find hope, when we choose to listen deeply to each other and awaken new possibilities together.

Now is not a good time to let go of hope. When we begin working across boundaries, there is hope. Hope that we can experience community like never before.

When we start collaborating with each other and become gifts to one another, there is hope. Hope that we can learn from each other and find love in the interstitial spaces between us.

When we bring our hopes together, we begin to create a sense of collective vision. So many of our cities, towns, villages and regions are floundering because they lack vision. When the people of Barrow-in-Furness brought their hopes together, they began to find fresh vision for their town.

From this hopeful vision, town, city and national leaders are presented with the exciting challenge of cultivating this new and affirming landscape. This wonderful dance of creativity reframes the blueprint of what our politics might look like. From this eye-opening vista, leaders can respond by using their gifts, resources and power to make these hopes and dreams into living realities.

THE RIVER AND THE CITY

In the Preface of this book, I quoted Archbishop Desmond Tutu: 'There comes a point where we need to stop just pulling people out of the river. We need to go upstream and find out why they are falling in.'[456]

We do not need to spend our lives pulling people out of polluted rivers. The river need not be something that people fall into and are left to drown. Rather, the river should be something which brings life to all in the city. The trees on its banks bring shade and shelter for the people, and the leaves contribute to their healing.

Let the river of hope flow through our cities!

Listening is
an art form

- *How might you wield the axe of hope?*

- *What are you hopeful for?*

- *What might the politics of hope be like where you live?*

- *What is the vision for the place you live that people are rallying around?*

- *How will you contribute in a meaningful way to the social change we need to see?*

- *What action might you take?*

CHAPTER TWENTY
LOVE SOCIETY

Throughout this book, we have engaged with the stories of people for whom society is not working. Our society is sick, but it doesn't have to be. It is within our power to reimagine a society, built on love, which truly works for everyone and regenerates our ecology.

In this penultimate chapter, I want to give some space to that imagining.

LOVING SOCIETIES CREATE HEALTH, WELLBEING AND CARE

Healthy societies are those which create the conditions in which people experience health and wellbeing as much of the time as possible. For a society to be healthy, it must build healthy communities. Healthy communities are those which are able to focus on their assets and build from what is strong, not what is wrong. They are participatory and able to co-create services they need with local institutions.

Healthy societies create the circumstances in which people can live healthy lives. Policies therefore need developing to make this possible for everyone. True population health takes a life-course approach from conception to grave. There should be no apology for deliberately focusing on health inequalities and ensuring those with the worst health outcomes have increased support and investment. Creating healthy societies requires shared vision and collaboration across all parts of the public sector. There is, as we have previously discussed, no point telling people to eat healthily and then surrounding them with advertising for unhealthy foods, taking sport out of school curriculums, putting takeaways in local neighbourhoods, and making sugary food cheap and easily available.

Loving societies care about the environment people are living in.

They create a sense of safety and security, including good housing for all. Healthy societies are regenerative for the ecology. The physical spaces inspire and encourage health in all its forms, rather than separating and dividing communities. Careful design can curate the experience of belonging within a loving community and enable healing even across old lines of separation and stigmatisation.

Of course, loving societies need health and care systems in place which prevent ill health, detect when people are becoming unwell early, protect them from becoming more unwell, manage their conditions in a person-centred way in line with best practice, are as close to home as possible, and help them recover well into community when they suffer a setback. Healthy societies are places where people can start well, live well, work well, age well and die well – no matter who they are or where they live, and ensure there is a safety net for those who fall on hard times.

Love makes this possible.

LOVING SOCIETIES CARE FOR THE POOR

If a society is loving, then it must prioritise the needs of those who are struggling with poverty.

In our society, the level of inequality is growing.[457] What would an economic policy be like if it was truly focused on ending poverty, by tackling inequality and inequity? The issue of land and the lack of affordable housing has a huge effect on people being locked in cycles of poverty. It creates massive health inequalities. In the worst-case scenarios, there is gentrification.[458] Rising house prices and the cost of living is pushing people out of areas in which they have lived as a family for many years, often out of their community or region altogether.[459]

In Chapter 1, we explored the terrible effect of abuse on human development. When we expand our view from the individual to society as a whole, we can see that whole communities in the UK are being serially neglected: emotionally, psychologically and physically.

Loving societies create an ethic of care.[460]

This means that everyone in the society has a voice, has the chance to be listened to, heard and respected. Love means that every person has a warm home. Love ensures people are paid enough to live well. This includes the kind of good work being available which makes a positive contribution to society and the ecology. Love ensures a good safety net of welfare that helps pick people up when they have fallen. Love provides long-term support to those who need it, without stigmatisation and shame through societal fair taxation schemes. We see this at work in some cities. Manchester has something to teach us about homelessness through the Manchester Homelessness Charter.[461] The example of Leeds can help us adopt Poverty Truth Commissions.[462] London has made public transport so much more affordable in a way which connects people together. If we are to create a loving society, it must begin with those who are currently the most neglected.

LOVING SOCIETIES CREATE EQUITY FOR WOMEN

A loving society must instate women at the heart of its economic policies and practices. Women continue to carry the main strain of child rearing, and yet suffer economically for it. They are paid less, valued less, and experience more exploitation.[463] Loving societies will not only end basic inequalities like period poverty but must examine patriarchy in all its forms and how it leaves women picking up the vast majority of care, often to their own detriment.[464] They must also focus on ending violence against women and all forms of sexual harassment. A society that cares about women must therefore be one in which women enjoy true equality and equity with men.

There are currently very few global cities where this is even beginning to happen. Vienna is considered to be the most gender equal city.[465] Toronto currently fares well among leading business cities,[466] but still leaves much to be desired. Ensuring equality of opportunity and access to leadership spaces is going to be vital in making this happen.

LOVING SOCIETIES PRIORITISE CHILDREN

A society which truly prioritises children ensures children get the best start in life,[467] and can live in safety, knowing they are unconditionally loved, seen and belong within a community. This especially applies to those who are 'looked after' by the state.

Loving societies teach children the way of love.

UNICEF[468] and World Vision[469] have both set helpful visions and criteria to help societies focus on how they can become places where children thrive.

If a society is going to care for all its children and young people, we need to start during pregnancy with learning circles of women and their partners. These are deliberately created spaces with time for them to build relationships, and wherever possible, across difference. To learn to be mutually supportive of one another. To be given space to process their own experience of childhood trauma and together enable healing. This would allow them to develop a clear sense of how they themselves would like to nurture their own children. After birth we could see these learning circles – or hopefully now friendship circles – develop and continue to support one another. Creating a sense of togetherness in the process of child rearing, while celebrating the differences of cultural backgrounds and life experiences, immediately begins to create a sense of cohesiveness, mutual love and respect. Those who are struggling with postnatal depression can more easily get help from both community and professionals – such as their community midwife, GP and mental health teams – because stigma is broken down.

Where it is noticed that a child is having some developmental delays, appropriately funded health visitors, speech and language therapists (SALT), school nurses and other allied professionals can reach into their communities and can ensure that early help is given in a way that is helpful. This allows preventative measures to be brought in. Cuts in health visiting services,[470] SALT and long waits for diagnostic and supportive help from autism services, for example, have been detrimental, especially for families who are struggling. More involved and holistic support can be given, based on what children and their families feel they need.

Early diagnosis and intervention are proven to be more cost effective in the long run. I believe that such an approach would be far better at reducing the number of children who are currently taken into care. We have seen a 28% rise in the number of looked after children in the UK, over the last decade.[471] Recent reports show many are experiencing terrible abuse in this so-called 'care system'.[472] Wouldn't it also be better if we could foster whole families, rather than children alone?[473]

We need to listen to families who are struggling and find out what it is that they need, building our social care around them. Taking children into care is always traumatic, and ideally should be rare in a loving society. However, when a child is removed from an abusive and dangerous situation because it is the most loving thing to do, they should be treated with the utmost care. Adoption of a child is one of the most beautiful acts of love.[474]

And a loving society ensures long lasting support to all involved.

Let's face it. Parenting is the hardest job in the world. No one can press our buttons like our own children. They have this ability to hold a mirror up to all our own personal failings like no one else on earth! I agree with Jon Yates, who suggests in his book *Fractured*, some form of parenting class for the parents of pre-school children.[475] His view is that this should be mandated by local and national government and supported through workplaces and/ or welfare state. Again, this would help to solidify relationships, whilst also ensuring parents have the tools and skills necessary for the task of raising their children.

I would add in help from our Violence Reduction Units (VRUs) with a focus on relationships, and stress and anger management. VRUs are collaborative partnerships between the police, local councils (including social care and education), and the NHS.[476] This is vital in both preventing non-accidental injury in children and in decreasing domestic violence against women. Creating places for people where they can talk about difficult experiences and enable teams to intervene early – for example, allowing couples to work through significant difficulties and finding a way through to a more wholesome relationship – creates a framework for more restorative justice. Maintaining relationships and raising children is hard!

We need to create a society of mutuality and support.

Likewise, when behavioural issues arise with children at any point through their development process, a loving approach would be to work with the whole household. This would be better than simply delivering the child over to some kind of mental health team or support services in the school environment. Whenever a child is experiencing distress, it can be hard for their parents or carers to know what to do to help them. This is true in the child's own family context or when a child has been removed from a home situation into foster care. Actively providing help for all concerned is a kinder and more holistic approach.

Dr Cathy Betoin, a clinical psychologist in Morecambe Bay, has developed the I Matter Framework.[477] It recognises that there is little point in working with a distressed child in isolation and then sending them back into a stressful environment, whether it is, for example, home or school. That is not to say that children don't benefit hugely from therapeutic interventions, like play therapy; they do. But most behavioural issues in children come from what they are experiencing within a home, school or other environment. So, working with the child alone usually does very little to change the behaviour in the short or long term. Involving the parents or carers and school staff in the process is vital. It helps the adults learn to manage their own reactions and stress in the situation. This enables them to create loving and safe frameworks for their children. This leads to significantly improved outcomes in the child's own processing and wellbeing and an overall happier home.

Alongside all of this, we must work with our children from a young age – investing in the personal development of their character – so they grow in kindness, gentleness, forgiveness and love. We need to nip bullying in the bud at a very early stage, creating safe environments for children to talk about their experiences and emotions, normalising this for boys especially and developing good practices for their own psychological and spiritual wellbeing. We need to create a healthy focus on children learning to live well within their own bodies. This means compassionate and specially tailored help for those who do not feel at home in their body, due to issues such as gender dysphoria, body dysmorphia and neurodiverse conditions. All of this begins to build some positive foundations for the future. This must include good learning opportunities through later teen years and into the world of work. They must grow in the ability to participate in the issues affecting their future.

Societies which love young people need to think about youth provision. Clubs and voluntary organisations are on the wane. Teenagers are becoming increasingly screen bound. We are seeing an increase in all kinds of issues, including mental health problems, gang violence and sexual exploitation. We need stronger legislation to protect our children and young people from the vaping industry. We need braver conversations, creative alternatives and communities which invest in our young people so that they feel loved, seen, welcome and secure.

There are many incredible things happening already, like 'Escape 2 Make' in Lancaster.[478] But we need so much more. Our young people are too precious to be left as fodder for those who prey on their vulnerability and elastic minds.

LOVING SOCIETIES WELCOME 'STRANGERS'

Our society has become increasingly segregated, separated and divided. Recent race riots from Oldham[479] to Portland (Oregon),[480] display just how fractured our communities are. We must think about how to bring people together. The use of space to create environments for peace, rather than hate, requires serious attention. Architects, like Aisling Rusk, are working to see how the liminal spaces of our cities can become places of healing and connection.[481] If it can be reimagined in Belfast, then there is hope it can happen anywhere.

Loving societies are inclusive and integrate migrants.

They celebrate and care about diversity, rather than trying to assimilate people. Loving societies are anti-racist. They welcome refugees and asylum seekers with generous hospitality. They contribute to ending the inhumane, degrading treatment of these precious human beings in our outsourced detention centres.

According to the UN Refugee Agency, there are four cities which are doing this really well. They are Milan in Italy, São Paulo in Brazil, Victoria, BC in Canada, and Vienna in Austria.[482] The City of Sanctuary UK movement is also trying to do similar work.[483] The 'East meets West' initiative I explored in Chapter 5, provides us with ways of bridging the divide and stewarding the spaces needed to create friendships that unify.

LOVING SOCIETIES REGENERATE THE ECOLOGY

Loving societies have an integral relationship to the wider ecology. They must therefore invest in regenerative farming and fishing practices, reforestation, recycling and green technologies. They need to experiment increasingly with new ways of doing things, like vertical farming, where crops are grown in multistorey buildings akin to car parks. They must do all they can to keep carbon in the ground and clean it from the air. Healthy societies cannot exist if the environment is unhealthy. So, if we want to become healthy, we must care about this deeply. There are many cities leading the way in becoming truly eco-friendly, with the top ten currently considered to be: Copenhagen, Amsterdam, Stockholm, Berlin, Portland (Oregon), San Francisco, Cape Town, Helsinki, Vancouver and Reykjavik.[484]

LOVING SOCIETIES PRACTISE RESTORATIVE JUSTICE

Dr Cornel West tells us that justice is what love looks like in public.[485] In a loving society, this means that we must choose to use a trauma-informed lens for those who perpetrate crimes, to enable their restoration.

We must also recognise that in a loving society, justice must mean something for those who are on the receiving end of injustice. It isn't loving to let people get away with crime. It isn't loving to let gangs drive fear through our streets. It isn't loving for people not to face the consequences of their actions. However, programmes led by the Violence Reduction Networks (VRNs), like ours in Lancashire,[486] make an ethic of care possible, even in the face of significant wrongdoing. Rather than being on the back-foot with violent crime, restorative justice is a proactive approach seen in loving communities, as we learned from Zoya in Chapter 5. Working with young people and gangs to break the destructive cycles involved, enables the possibility of building positive peace. Glasgow and London also have VRUs and are looking to learn from one another how to do this well.[487]

CONNECTED COMMUNITIES

Local neighbourhoods are becoming our prime place for a connected, participatory politics and economics. In order for citizens to be able to participate fully, technology, which can be divisive or even dangerous, will need to be harnessed for good. However, communities in neighbourhoods do not and cannot exist in isolation. They connect to form our society. Whether locally, regionally, nationally or globally, it is vital for communities to connect.

At a global level, this is happening in an increasing variety of ways. Mayors of world-leading cities connect through the C40[488] and offer reciprocal learning about how they can take their role in climate change seriously. The Resilient Cities Network is trying to connect cities across the globe, collaborating for a 'safer, more equitable, and sustainable future for all'.[489] Doughnut cities are actively exploring how to apply Professor Kate Raworth's thinking on Doughnut Economics and create cities which take the dual task of social justice and climate sustainability seriously, outside the dominant narrative of free market capitalism.[490]

Creating relational networks of friendship, accountability, learning, and enterprise creates real hope for the future in how we help each other face into the complexities and enormity of the task ahead of us. It also recognises that some networked cities can provide services and help to each other, based on need and particular kinds of expertise.

Locally and nationally, cities and their regions need connection through far better and affordable green transport infrastructure. The Freiburg city region in southern Germany is one of the best examples I have ever seen. The North of England, by contrast is a disgrace. The current train franchise model is ludicrously expensive, unreliable and leaves vast part of the North entirely disconnected. Any government serious about 'levelling up' must correct this farcical reality. How otherwise will people be able to participate in the new 'green economy' we are promised?

CONTRIBUTING COMMUNITIES

Communities which are loving and are connected to one another become filled with a collective purpose to contribute meaningfully to the global issues of our day. The citizens and communities have a responsibility to call their town/city/region to align with the values of love.

There is much we need towns, cities and regions to pioneer in the days ahead. This must include dynamic political and economic models, which are participatory and regenerative. We need to see how coalitions and collaborations across lines of difference create spaces for new imaginings of how we live well together. We need to ensure the flow of resources through our towns, cities and regions matches the needs of the communities with them. If we are going to help build places which are healthy in nature, this isn't going to happen by accident. We need to use design very deliberately to help us. Perhaps the most important contribution towns, cities and regions need to make into the world at large currently, is around the climate crisis. At a time of such a global emergency, we must act together and act now. We must resolutely change our ways. Our political and economic policies and strategies must become actions because love is a verb. Love requires of us that we do not stay the same.

Look at the stars and
wonder how dreams can
become reality

- *What might it be like if our society became truly compassionate and caring?*

- *How might the very fabric of your village, town or city be used to create better health?*

- *How loving is our society when it comes to prioritising the poorest in society? Are there any groups of people who need particular attention?*

- *How well does your community welcome those who are 'other', and how cohesive is your community across lines of difference?*

- *How are you going to ensure that your community is one in which women enjoy true equality and equity with men?*

- *How child friendly is your region? Do all children manage to thrive where you live? If not, why not? What needs to change?*

- *What is youth provision like? How might it be improved? Why is this important?*

- *What could be done to support parents and carers more?*

- *How is your community, town or city contributing to turning the tide on climate change? What needs to happen to make climate change more of an urgent priority?*

- *How will you call local and national government to account on climate change?*

CHAPTER TWENTY-ONE
LOVE ACTION

My hope in writing this book has been three-fold.

Firstly, I wanted to ask why our health and care services are so overwhelmed. As I followed my patients out of my clinic and into society, I discovered so much inequality, inequity, and social injustice. I began to uncover why we tolerate this, by digging down beneath the signs and symptoms to expose the values which underpin our society, politics, and economics.

Secondly, I appealed to the ancient and foundational idea that all of life is held together by transcendent love. I wanted to make the case that love – and the core values which flow from it – gives us a substantial alternative on which to build a society that works for everyone.

Thirdly, I therefore wanted to stoke the fire of the conversation about how we make the world new. The story we are living in is one which is no longer working for the vast majority of humanity and the planet we live on.

We need to write a new story together, which takes stock of our past and weaves a new future built on the foundation of love.

I know that our current reality is a long way from where we want to be. But I hope I have asked some provocative questions and offered some practical thoughts about what might help us get ourselves unstuck and move us to action. We ourselves must change and we must change our systems by infusing them with values based on love.

A BRIEF RECAP

Everything that exists is because of love, and love holds it all together.

Love is the foundation and without it, there can be no wellbeing. We are never well outside of love, or without love. If we do not love, we are not well. If we are not loved, we are not well. It is, however, possible to be loved and unwell and to be unwell and loving. Fundamentally, we all need to know that we are unconditionally loved, that we are seen and that we belong.

Peeling back the layers underneath our current status quo, we discover values and ideologies, which perpetuate our societal injustices, through our political and economic systems. We have uncovered the problems of the politics of division and sovereignty and exposed the oppressive realities of our 'freedom'. We have revealed the broken economics of capitalism, fuelled by consumerism. We have weighed all these things in the scales of love and found them wanting. The writing is on the wall; whatever does not flow from and into the way of love cannot last.

We have also begun to reimagine what life might be like if love was at the fore.

When we learn to love ourselves and receive the love of others; we learn to love those who are different to us and dare to dream of a more loving world.

We need to be part of building community power and take part in the social movement for change. We need to listen deeply to one another and create new frameworks of justice, built on love. If we allow our outrage towards injustice and passion for change to stir, to challenge the inevitability of the way things are – and together, build alternative moral economies – then we begin to find a way forward.

As we create space for critical yeast to challenge our thinking and practices (Chapter 19), we connect our anchors and weave a new web on which to build a loving society.

By politically prioritising the poor, women, children, 'foreigners' (migrants, refugees and asylum seekers), those in the criminal justice system (or at risk of entering it), the sick and our environment, we find a way of deliberately working to tackle the social injustices they experience.

In resetting the measures and reframing the boundaries of our economy, we stop being obsessed with greed-driven growth and focus instead on human flourishing and wellbeing, and environmental sustainability.

We develop this kind of economy with a new set of values.

Reconnecting with our ecology allows us to repent of harmful attitudes and behaviours, and join the revolution needed to renew it through real care.

WHAT DOES THIS MEAN FOR US?

Whilst we are all in this together, we have different roles to play in creating a more loving world. How will we respond to the challenges ahead? We will do so through 'love action'! Below I address and challenge different groups separately. It's not an exhaustive list, but I hope you will resonate with what is written.

If you are a *grandparent*, *parent* or *carer* of any kind, what legacy will you leave for those who follow in your path? Your love is a potent force on this planet. It is your responsibility to ensure that those you care about know that they are loved; that they are seen and that they belong. How can you make your love even bigger? What will you do to share it even more widely? How will you use it to embrace even more people? What will you do to instill your core values into the rising generation? How will you care for the environment you will leave behind?

If you are a *young person*, or even *young at heart*, then I hope you have seen that things do not have to remain as they are. There are other ways that we can remake the world together. We are recovering from the shock of a global pandemic. It has been disruptive, distressing and traumatic. Now, as we face into the grim realities of climate change and social injustice, we need to find a new way together. There are ways that we can go about building the future our hearts long for that are not dependent on the old ways of empires past.

So, how do you want us to shape the future, built on love? What will your role be in your own neighbourhood and community?

How will you make sure that you do your own work, so that you become a person of love and a life gift to those around you? What positive practices will you develop to help you do this? How will you ensure that you do not burnout? What will you do to build relationships, very deliberately, with those who are different to you? How will you honour those who are your elders? How will you participate in the politics of your city or region? What will you contribute to the economy? Will you live generously and wholeheartedly? How will you help to renew the ecology where you live? What will be your resource of love to replenish your tank?

If you are *someone who feels like you are on the margins* and there doesn't seem to be much of a place for you, then I hope you can see now how much you belong. Your participation in society is vital. You are the critical yeast we need to bring a transformative reaction. You are more valued and valuable than you have been allowed to know or dared to dream. What will you do with your power? It is potent. No decision about you, without you, is for you. What will you do with your voice? It is OK to speak truth to power. When your voice shakes, it brings a resonance to the airwaves and has the potential to change the atmosphere. You belong to both the family of humanity, and the world in which we live together.

If you are a *teacher*, or work in *education*, you have one of the most important jobs on earth. I hope you know how honoured you are. I hope you have discovered even more passion for the kind of education you want to deliver. I hope you are reconceptualising the learning environments you want to create. You have the tools and skills needed to spark the imagination of future generations. You can equip them with what they need for the task ahead. I hope you find new grace and patience to practise your craft in a way that brings you deep joy.

How will you respond with love to those who are in your classrooms? What is the culture you will embed in your team to enable this? How will you co-create the supportive dynamic you need so that you don't burnout? What action will you take to ensure the wider community participates with you in building a more inclusive society? What will you do with them to bridge our current divides? How will you bring peace within your workplace? How will you create a truly trauma-informed approach in how you work?

If you work in the sphere of *health* and *social care*, how will you make space to do your own work? Will you practise self-compassion so that the love and care you give flows from a full tank? What will you do to work more proactively with the community you serve? How will you listen to the uncomfortable truth of health inequality and inequity and act to do something about it? How will you use your power to collaborate with other organisations to tackle the core determinants of health? How will you ensure that the most powerless get the very best care, provided with excellence, kindness and joy? What will you do differently to ensure an inclusive and socially just work environment?

If you are a *student* or participate in *academic research*, how will you make the world a better place, especially for those on the margins? What will your contribution be to climate justice and making the world more sustainable for future generations? How will you make your wisdom available in a way that helps us all create a society that tackles social injustice and creates the good life for all?

If you are a *politician* or *civil servant*, how are you going to build a political system, which is truly collaborative, inclusive and kind? How will you transition from an abusive 'sovereign' power to one aligned with a politics of love? What will you do to devolve power from the dominant centre, cede it into local communities and recognise their innate capabilities? How will you enable people to use their freedom for good? How will you ensure that our corporate life is a participatory experience, which prioritises those who currently suffer the greatest injustices? What decisions will you take to safeguard and renew the environment? What policies will you make to reimagine radically how the economy serves the values of a loving society? How are you going to foster and cultivate the new political spaces we need?

If you work in the realm of *law and order*, how will you change the way you see people to view them through trauma-informed lenses? How will you help us build restorative justice in society? What will you do to work more proactively with communities who are currently on 'the wrong side of the law' through stigmatisation and systemic racism? How will you ensure that your team functions with the utmost honesty, integrity and truth? What will your contribution be to bringing positive peace across society? How will you cross the lines of division and build unity? What will you do about ingrained violence against women? What will you do to end child sex trafficking? How will you break open county lines? How will you ensure our streets feel safe?

If you are a *journalist* or a *communicator*, I hope you feel encouraged and provoked to continue to uncover the stories that matter. Will you shine a light on that which seeks to hide in dark places to retain its power? What will you do to change the culture, which consumes people's lives as though they were prey for the masses? How will you ensure that the invisible is made visible? What will you do to magnify the untold stories that could change society, for the better?

If you work in the *food and drink industry* or *service industry*, be that in farming, fishing, manufacturing, sales or advertising, how are you going to ensure you bring life to our environment? How will you play your part in regenerating our ecology? What will you do differently to ensure your practices are sustainable for future generations? How will you promote the wellbeing of all people over profit? How will you care deeply about the way you go about your work?

If you run a *business*, how can you create a real anchor in your local community? What will your contribution be to the generative economy we need to build together? How will you ensure your practices are ethical, sustainable, environmentally gentle and good for society? What kind of culture will you create amongst your team to bring joy to all your work? How will you invest in and develop the people in your teams? What salary scales will you set that mean no one has to use a food bank or choose between eating and heating? What differences could you make through apprenticeship schemes? How will you ensure that you positively employ people from areas of greater disadvantage? How might a more deliberately diverse team be good for your business and your community?

If you are a *community leader of any sort*, how will you create the kind of culture that creates a flow of life and enables your community to be full of love? What acts of service are needed to ensure that the needs of the community are met? Who is on the margins or forgotten about that needs to be radically included?

What are the strengths and assets in your community which can be built on? Where can you foster joy and kindness?

If you work with your hands, in any kind of manual work, how does love inspire excellence in you? How will you use your skills and abilities to foster joy in the people you work with or for? How will you use your conversations to bring hope and encouragement to people? How will you participate fully in the life of your community and city or region? What would you love to see change? How can you be a part of shaping that?

If you work in the *transport industry*, the way you connect people really matters! How can you ensure that the way you go about your work encourages deeper, richer and more cohesive community? What will your part be in helping transport to become greener and more sustainable for the future?

If you work in the world of *digital technology* or *artificial intelligence*, I hope you see the impact you can have for good. How will you develop algorithms and platforms that lead to a creative and participative society? How will you use your skills to help us build collective sense-making of and collaborative solution-making to the issues we face? What does it mean for you to take responsibility and play a part in the end of exploitative practices of oppression through this liberating technology? How will you steward your power well for those at risk of abuse, manipulation and addiction? What does an ethic of love and care call you to in this virtual shared space?

If you are an *architect, designer, city planner, builder* or *engineer of any kind*, how will you help to conceptualise, design, create, and build the kind of spaces we need to live well together in and across our communities? How will you do this in a regenerative way? What materials will you use? How will you infuse our neighbourhoods with beauty? What will you do to use your gift to help us find each other and come together?

If you are a *musician,* an *artist,* a *poet,* a *maker,* a *creator,* a *writer* or *social media influencer,* how will you use your gift to inspire us? How will you use your influence for good? Remember, it is you who help us dream. You help us to see that which is not yet. You make it possible for us to imagine new ways. You have the ability to unlock us from our current prison and discover how to use our freedom in line with the way of love. What will you do to show us the way? How will you help us participate in a new dance? What are the songs we need to be singing together? What stories do you need to tell to set us on the path of regeneration?

ABOVE ALL LOVE

Love is a verb. Love demands something of us; it requires action. Love alone is not enough. To make the world new, we need accountability, authenticity and bucket loads of courage. We need compassion, determination, empathy, faith, forgiveness, gentleness, goodness, grace, hope, humility, inclusivity, integrity, joy, justice, kindness, mercy, nurture, patience, peace, resilience, self-control, tenacity, vulnerability and wisdom.

Above all else, we need to love like never before.

Loving people is not always easy. In fact, loving people genuinely costs us, whatever type of love it may be.

The truth is that to love people we must learn to deal with our own ego. There are no two ways about this. Life would be so much easier if we didn't have to do our own work! We can't keep excusing bad behaviours. We can't hide behind excuses. We have to let go of the pretence and the projections that we make to those around us, so that we are somehow more acceptable. We need to become our authentic selves. This helps us become integrated human beings – body, soul and spirit. We only become well in the context of relationship. This is how we learn to become people of transcendent love.

When we decentre our ego, then what do we put there instead? I believe the answer is love.

We become love-centric, instead of egocentric. Love at the centre of who we are.

This enables us to deeply value every other person as uniquely important and utterly sacred. Love awakens us to live intentionally for the good and wellbeing of everybody and the world we co-habit.

TIME FOR A REVOLUTION

In this apocalyptic moment in which the facades are peeled back, we see the stark reality of how (love) sick our world is. So many of us are experiencing overwhelm from trying to stem the tide that flows from the inequality, inequity and injustice in our society.

Our task is not to escape our current reality into the world of dreams. On the contrary, if our vision for a more socially just and environmentally sustainable future is ever to become a substantial reality, we must do something! We must act with love in the painful present and **bring the transformation we long for** into the here and now.

This happens through simple acts of revolutionary love.

It happens when we do our own, difficult, internal work and become agents of love.

It happens when we refuse to 'other' our fellow human beings, and cross over the lines of division to build relationships, creating a society in which everyone can participate, contribute and know they are innately valued.

It happens when we reframe our politics to prioritise those who are currently recipients of oppression.

It happens when we re-evaluate how and why we allocate our resources as we do in our economy, and realign them with our core values.

It happens when we reconnect with and renew our ecology through simple, everyday choices and major policy shifts.

Let us refuse anything less than this because after everything else, one thing will surely remain and that is love. So let us begin to act like it.

**Let us
love action.**

Start well, live well, work well, age well, die well

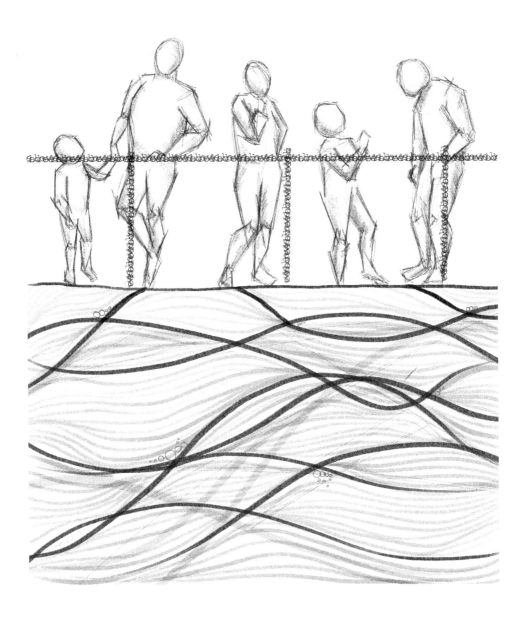

EPILOGUE

LOVE IN ACTION

A few years ago, I met a head teacher called Gill Wood from Little London, in Leeds. One year, she decided that the SATs tests done by all eleven-year-olds would be detrimental for the children and provided no real benefit. She had some good reasons for this. Many of the children in her school did not speak very much English, were experiencing high levels of adverse childhood experiences (ACEs), and were living with the reality of hunger every day. They were experiencing significant stress in preparing for these exams. Teachers have a far better knowledge of a child's skills and abilities than any arbitrary test can show on one day. With all this in mind, she woke one morning with the word 'enough' in her head. With the backing of her governors, she decided a more loving world would mean to stop treating the children in her school as statistics and fodder for the economic machine.

So, rather than do their SATs, she took them all from inner city Leeds to the beach at Whitby, North Yorkshire. Most of the children had never been. They had never felt the sand between their toes before. She ended up hounded by the press and threatened with all kinds of things, but she stood her ground and did what she believed to be more loving. As I reflected on her story, it inspired me to write this poem, which I hope helps us to entertain the possibility of a more loving world.

ENOUGH NOW!

Enough now, I heard it in sweet Yorkshire tones
From the mouth of Gill Wood, a head teacher, who roams
Through the corridors of old Little London, in Leeds,
A place which she loves with her heart 'til it bleeds.
For the children, their futures, their hopes and their dreams,
Their wellbeing, their nurture, their low self-esteem.
The traumas through which many live every day,
And the stress of the SATs is the price they must pay
To populate league tables marking their score,
The competitive culture demanding ever more.
And who needs to know a subordinate clause?
Could we just stop a moment, reflect with a pause?
What are we doing? What is achieved?
What kind of dragon does this biopower feed?
SATs scores improve, well hip hip hooray
But our mental health crisis is growing by the day!

Enough now! Enough now! Enough of it all
The ideology's broken – this beast must now fall.
Its vile underbelly exposed in plain sight
And we must resist it with all of our might.

Enough now of economy driven by greed
Where profit beats people with mouths we can't feed.
Enough now of the backhanded contract awards
To companies promising such great rewards
To our public services whose assets they strip
And then hand back the contract and its 'toodle-pip!'
And who pays the price of these outrageous bailouts?
Oh, that would be us – there are no doubts!

This unbridled, deregulated monster
Spits out its venom and billions suffer.
They literally live on the crumbs and the scraps
That fall from the table of the elite, and the cats
Who have all the cream, lick from the laps
Of their luxury living whilst, the trickle-down taps
Leak just enough out to convince us to go
And uphold, yes maintain this sick status quo.

Enough now of the hoarding of trillions offshore
Miserly hiding resource from the poor.
Enough now of destruction of beautiful earth
Selfish pollution releasing its curse,
Whilst plastic smothers and suffocates seas;
Deforestation and genocide of bees.

Enough of our weapons! Enough of our wars!
Enough of our arms deals and conflicts they cause.
Enough of the cover-ups and dodgy trade deals,
The threats and the violence of power that wields.
Its sword of destruction on innocent lives
And twists the true story with dangerous lies.
Enough now of division and building of walls,
The pointing of fingers and the hating of all
Who aren't just like us, who don't dress our way
Who we blame for our problems and don't want them to stay.

Enough now of the gangs and the drugs and the fear.
Enough for the mothers weeping their tears
For the ones they have lost so young in their life
To the gun or the needle, or the sharp stabbing knife.
Enough now of trafficking people as slaves
Or the drowning of refugees deep in the waves,
As we protect our own borders and turn a deaf ear
To the cries of the children whose hope disappears.

Enough now of reviling the poorest of poor
Whose help we are cutting and trapping them more.
Enough now of our judgements before we have heard
The truth of the stories that truly undergird
The pain and complexity, weighing heavy like lead
Holding them stuck in a tangling web;
Whilst the welfare they need is broken and lacks
The relationship required to truly tack
This wild, unkind and tumultuous sea
Of joblessness, addiction or disability.

Enough now of the media, throwing its weight
Around all our psyches and stirring up hate.
Enough now of the lie of supposed democracy.
No, what we have is multiplied sovereignty!
And that does not represent the rich tapestry
Of the views and opinions and perspectives we see.

Where's your enough now? What makes you care?
Don't now be silenced, speak up, don't be scared!
The empire is over, colonialism's dead!
It's time that we find a better future instead.

There's a time to pluck up, to tear down and overthrow
There's a time to build up, to plant and to sow.
So, let's dream of a future that's built on the power
Of love and of kindness and of peace in this hour.

An economy distributive and regenerative by design
A politics that cuts through the old party lines.
The bravery to tackle environmental need.
A gentler way of living to ensure that we feed
Every hungry belly and every mouth that knows thirst
Might have clean water, yes, let's get the basics right first.
Education that releases potential and life

To a world that needs healing and an ending of strife.
Healthcare regardless of ability to pay;
Parks in which all kids find safety to play.
Welfare that is well fair and breathes wholeness to all.
A justice system that restores those who fall.
Homes for the homeless, freedom for slaves.
Welcome for refugees, a livable wage.
Wrongs to put right, but together we can,
If we choose now to draw a line in the sand.

We'll need conversations involving all ears and voices
To collate the wisdom, we need to make difficult choices.
Life-giving green energy that keeps us all warm.
Reconciling peacemakers helping us form
Connected communities where all can stand tall,
In their place of equality and their unique call
To shine like a star in the darkness and leave
A legacy for the future that continues to weave
Love upon hope upon life upon peace.
This is the future that we must now release!

Before all and above all, my friends: love! (emphasis added)

THE END

ABOUT THE AUTHOR

Andy Knox is a husband, a dad, a son, a brother and a friend. He is also a GP Partner at Ash Trees Surgery in Carnforth, Associate Medical Director of the Lancashire and South Cumbria ICB – focused on Population Health and Health Inequity; Population Health Associate at The King's Fund; Associate at the Centre for Population Health; Honorary Senior Lecturer at Lancaster University in Sociology and Health. He's an author, a blogger, a member of the NHS Assembly, part of the Poverty Truth Commission, executive coach, a facilitator, Art of Hosting practitioner, and general enthusiast. Andy is a member of the Royal College of General Practitioners and the Faculty of Public Health.

He is usually heard before he is seen due to his ridiculously loud laugh and can often be found singing, whilst walking with his springer spaniel Lola, around the glory that is Morecambe Bay. He relaxes by playing the piano, reading books, cooking good food and being in and around water. He was recently awarded an MBE in the King's first Birthday Honours List for services to Primary Care and tackling Health Inequalities. His claim to fame is that his Grandpa invented Fairy Liquid and his cousin won *The Great British Bake Off!*

ENDNOTES

1   https://www.janehanson.com/blog/2020/desmondtutujanehanson

2   https://www.quantamagazine.org/einsteins-parable-of-quantum-insanity-20150910

3   https://www.greatbritishlife.co.uk/homes-and-gardens/places-to-live/22609337.meet-michael-wilson---queens-guide-sands-morecambe-bay/

4   https://www.etymonline.com/word/apocalypse

5   https://www.kingsfund.org.uk/publications/what-are-health-inequalities

6   https://www.local.gov.uk/marmot-review-report-fair-society-healthy-lives

7   Marmot, M., *The Health Gap: The Challenge of an Unequal World* (London: Bloomsbury Publishing, 2015), p.7

8   https://www.nuffieldtrust.org.uk/news-item/is-the-nhs-at-breaking-point

9   https://www.nursingtimes.net/news/workforce/level-of-staff-burnout-real-concern-for-nhs-trust-leaders-06-10-2020/

10   https://www.bbc.co.uk/news/health-61598158

11   https://www.bma.org.uk/advice-and-support/nhs-delivery-and-workforce/pressures/pressures-in-general-practice-data-analysis

12   https://www.health.org.uk/publications/reports/level-or-not

13   https://www.england.nhs.uk/publication/nhs-long-term-workforce-plan/

14   https://www.thelancet.com/journals/lancet/article/PIIS0140-6736(15)60921-7/fulltext

15   https://bjgp.org/content/68/669/168

16   https://post.parliament.uk/mental-health-impacts-of-covid-19-on-nhs-healthcare-staff/

17   https://www.personneltoday.com/hr/third-of-nurses-plan-to-quit-nhs-in-emerging-crisis/

18   https://www.nuffieldtrust.org.uk/resource/the-nhs-workforce-in-numbers

19   https://www.nursingtimes.net/news/workforce/rcn-survey-suggests-half-of-nursing-staff-thinking-about-quitting-04-01-2022/

20   https://time.com/6233694/nurses-strike-nhs-rcn-hospitals/

21   https://www.gponline.com/sharp-rise-gps-reporting-worsening-mental-health-covid-19-pandemic/article/1692460

22   https://www.kingsfund.org.uk/publications/caring-change

23   https://nhsfunding.info/nhs-crisis-making/

24   https://www.health.org.uk/news-and-comment/charts-and-infographics/taxes-and-health-care-funding-how-does-the-uk-compare

25   https://www.gov.uk/government/speeches/the-future-of-health-and-care

26   https://www.gov.uk/government/publications/build-back-better-our-plan-for-health-and-social-care

27   Hooks, b., *All About Love: New Visions* (USA: William Marrow and Company Inc, 2000), p.4

28   Kaur, V., See *No Stranger: A Memoir and Manifesto of Revolutionary Love* (London: Octopus Publishing Group Ltd, 2020)

29   Crisp, N., *Health is Made at Home, Hospitals are for Repairs: Building a Healthy and Health-Creating Society* (UK: Salus Global, 2020), p.21

30   Royal College of General Practitioners

31   https://theworldcafe.com/key-concepts-resources/world-cafe-method/

32   Fournier, V., 'Utopianism and the Cultivation of Possibilities: Grassroots Movements of Hope', *The Sociological Review* 50 (2002), 1_suppl, 189–216; https://doi.org/10.1111/j.1467-954X.2002.tb03585.x

33   https://medialectic.wordpress.com/2016/12/15/processing-anger-a-conversation-with-dr-maya-angelou-dave-chappelle/

34   https://www.birthrights.org.uk/2021/11/11/new-mbrrace-report-shows-black-women-still-four-times-more-likely-to-die-in-pregnancy-and-childbirth/

35   https://www.ons.gov.uk/peoplepopulationandcommunity/healthandsocialcare/childhealth/articles/birthsandinfantmortalitybyethnicityinenglandandwales/2007to2019

36   https://www.runnymedetrust.org/blog/the-weaponisation-of-the-left-behind-white-working-class-harms-us-all

37   https://england.shelter.org.uk/professional_resources/legal/homelessness_applications/homelessness_and_threatened_homelessness/legal_definition_of_homelessness_and_threatened_homelessness

38   https://www.legislation.gov.uk/ukpga/1996/52/contents ss.175–177HousingAct1996

39   https://worldpopulationreview.com/countries/cities/united-kingdom

40   https://england.shelter.org.uk/media/press_release/274000_people_in_england_are_homeless_with_thousands_more_likely_to_lose_their_homes

41   https://www.crisis.org.uk/ending-homelessness/about-homelessness/

42   https://www.theguardian.com/society/2021/feb/22/uk-homeless-deaths-rise-by-more-than-a-third-in-a-year-study-finds

43   https://acestoohigh.com/2012/10/03/the-adverse-childhood-experiences-study-the-largest-most-important-public-health-study-you-never-heard-of-began-in-an-obesity-clinic/

44   https://warrenlarkinassociates.co.uk/wp-content/uploads/2021/03/03-Feb-2021-ACEs-trauma-and-system-change-slide-pack.pdf (p.4)

45   https://warrenlarkinassociates.co.uk/wp-content/uploads/2021/03/03-Feb-2021-ACEs-trauma-and-system-change-slide-pack.pdf (p.7)

46   van der Kolk, B., *The Body Keeps the Score: Brain, Mind and Body in the Healing of Trauma* (UK: Penguin Random House, 2015), pp.74–86

47   https://www.bbc.co.uk/news/uk-politics-59365725

48   https://www.cycj.org.uk/news/aces-distance-resilience/

49   https://bmjopen.bmj.com/content/10/6/e036374

50   West, M.A., *Compassionate Leadership: Sustaining Wisdom, Humanity and Presence in Health and Social Care* (Swirling Leaf Press, 2021)

51   Date: 27 October 2006, Source: created this work using Inkscape. Author J. Finkelstein; https://www.physio-pedia.com/index.php?title=File%3AMaslow%27s_hierarchy_of_needs.svg.png&veaction=edit&section=2
The diagram is redrawn to fit in with the style of the book.

52   Maslow, A.H., 'A Theory of Human Motivation', *Psychological Review* 50 (1943), 4.430–437

53   Author's own diagram.

54   1 John 4:7–12, *The Bible*

55   https://www.bbc.co.uk/news/uk-england-leeds-59599884

56   https://www.bbc.co.uk/news/uk-england-birmingham-59494448

57   https://www.childrenscommissioner.gov.uk/2020/11/11/thousands-of-children-in-care-being-failed-by-the-state-because-of-a-broken-residential-care-home-market/

58   https://blackpoolbetterstart.org.uk/

59   Baginsky, M., 'Evaluation: New Beginnings Greater Manchester – Peer Mentoring Project', (London: NIHR Policy Research Unit in Health and Social Care Workforce, The Policy Institute, King's College London, 2020); https://kris.kcl.ac.uk/portal/en/publications/evaluation-new-beginnings-greater-manchester--peer-mentoring-project(36790932-11de-4a89-b31d-36a9f731eea2).html

60   Bethell, C., J. Jones, N. Gombojav, J. Linkenbach and R. Sege, 'Positive Childhood Experiences and Adult Mental and Relational Health in a Statewide Sample: Associations Across Adverse Childhood Experiences Levels', *JAMA Pediatrics*, 173 (2019), 11; https://jamanetwork.com/journals/jamapediatrics/fullarticle/2749336

61   https://www.ons.gov.uk/peoplepopulationandcommunity/birthsdeathsandmarriages/deaths/bulletins/suicidesintheunitedkingdom/2020registrations

62   https://www.samaritans.org/how-we-can-help/if-youre-worried-about-someone-else/supporting-someone-suicidal-thoughts/

63   Riso, D.R. and R. Hudson, *The Wisdom of the Enneagram: The Complete Guide to Psychological and Spiritual Growth for the Nine Personality Types* (New York: Bantam Books, 1999)

64   https://www.mind.org.uk/workplace/mental-health-at-work/taking-care-of-yourself/five-ways-to-wellbeing/

65   Chatterjee, R., *The 4 Pillar Plan: How to Relax, Eat, Move and Sleep Your Way to a Longer, Healthier Life* (UK: Penguin Random House, 2018), pp.72–141

66   https://www.psychologytoday.com/gb/blog/comfort-gratitude/202007/gratitude-helps-curb-anxiety

67   Comer, J.M., *The Ruthless Elimination of Hurry: How to Stay Emotionally Healthy and Spiritually Alive in the Chaos of the Modern World* (UK: Hodder & Stoughton, 2019)

68   Yates, J., *Fractured: Why Our Societies are Coming Apart and How We Put Them Back Together Again* (Manchester: HarperNorth, 2021), pp.153–169

69   https://www.nia.nih.gov/news/social-isolation-loneliness-older-people-pose-health-risks

70   https://www.churchill.com/press-office/releases/2013/do-you-know-your-neighbours-name

71   https://www.edenprojectcommunities.com/we%E2%80%99re-no-longer-a-nation-of-nattering-neighbours

72   Yates, J., *Fractured: Why Our Societies are Coming Apart and How We Put Them Back Together Again*, p.131

73   https://www.brookings.edu/blog/techtank/2021/09/27/how-tech-platforms-fuel-us-political-polarization-and-what-government-can-do-about-it/

74   https://health.clevelandclinic.org/why-giving-is-good-for-your-health/

75   https://www.civilsociety.co.uk/news/volunteering-levels-fall-by-15-per-cent-in-a-decade-finds-office-for-national-statistics.html

76   https://www.thirdsector.co.uk/volunteering-levels-reach-new-high-proportion-givers-down-major-government-survey-shows/volunteering/article/1723682

77   https://livingwell.org.au/well-being/five-ways-to-mental-wellbeing/keep-on-learning/

78   https://www.healthline.com/health/fitness-exercise/benefits-of-dance#benefits

79   https://www.ncbi.nlm.nih.gov/pmc/articles/PMC6368928/

80   https://iwillteachyoualanguage.com/blog/9-health-benefits-of-learning-a-foreign-language

81   https://www.bmj.com/company/newsroom/insomnia-disrupted-sleep-and-burnout-linked-to-higher-odds-of-severe-covid-19/

82   Walker, M., *Why We Sleep: The New Science of Sleep and Dreams* (UK: Penguin Books, 2018)

83   The 12-step programme is used by 'The Well Communities' to help people recovering from all kinds of addiction; https://www.alcoholics-anonymous.org.uk/about-aa/the-12-steps-of-aa

84   https://warrenlarkinassociates.co.uk/portfolio-items/routine-enquiry-about-adversity-in-childhood-reach-programme/

85   Pearce, J., C. Murray and W. Larkin, 'Childhood Adversity and Trauma: Experiences of Professionals Trained to Routinely Enquire about Childhood Adversity', *Heliyon* 5 (2019), 7; https://www.cell.com/heliyon/fulltext/S2405-8440(18)34785-6

86 Felitti, V.J., 'Health Appraisal and the Adverse Childhood Experiences Study: National Implications for Health Care, Cost, and Utilization', *The Permanente Journal* 23 (2019); https://www.ncbi.nlm.nih.gov/pmc/articles/PMC6326558/pdf/18-026.pdf

87 Wells, S., *A Nazareth Manifesto: Being with God* (UK: John Wiley & Sons, Inc, 2015), p.89

88 Wells, S., *A Nazareth Manifesto: Being with God*, pp.93–97

89 https://researchbriefings.files.parliament.uk/documents/CBP-8537/CBP-8537.pdf

90 https://www.mayoclinic.org/healthy-lifestyle/adult-health/in-depth/forgiveness/art-20047692

91 https://moretolife.org/

92 Hopwood, H., 'Welcoming Strangers: East Meets West', *The Kenarchy Journal* 2 (2021); https://kenarchy.org/wp-content/uploads/2021/03/Kenarchy_Volume2.3.pdf

93 https://www.carehome.co.uk/advice/care-home-stats-number-of-settings-population-workforce

94 Gawande, A., *Being Mortal: Illness, Medicine, and What Matters in the End* (London: Profile Books Ltd, 2014)

95 https://www.sueryder.org/news/hospice-funding-crisis

96 https://deathcafe.com/

97 https://www.health.org.uk/sites/default/files/NHS-70-What-Can-We-Do-About-Social-Care.pdf

98 https://www.nuffieldtrust.org.uk/resource/care-home-bed-availability

99 https://ageing-better.org.uk/summary-state-ageing-2022#

100 https://www.goodlifedeathgrief.org.uk/content/compassionate_communities_networ/

101 https://www.learningwithexperts.com/wellbeing/blog/live-longer-better-with-the-optimal-ageing-programme

102 https://www.manchester.gov.uk/info/200091/life_over_50/8388/find_out_about_age_friendly_manchester#

103 https://www.agedcareinsite.com.au/2021/05/culture-shock-challenges-for-migrants-in-their-end-of-life/

104 https://evidence.nihr.ac.uk/themedreview/help-at-home-use-of-assistive-technology-for-older-people/

105   https://theconversation.com/heres-why-some-dutch-university-students-are-living-in-nursing-homes-68253

106   https://www.theguardian.com/society/2018/nov/12/children-care-homes-residents-feel-more-human

107   https://faithbeliefforum.org/wp-content/uploads/2020/08/Cohesive-Societies-Faith-Belief.pdf

108   'Care and Support Reimagined: A National Care Covenant for England', Commissioned by and with a Foreword by the Archbishops of Canterbury and York; https://www.churchofengland.org/about/archbishops-commissions/reimagining-care-commission

109   https://ageing-better.org.uk/blogs/how-do-we-bridge-uks-age-divide

110   Condon, L., J. Curejova, D.L. Morgan, G. Miles and D. Fenlon, 'Knowledge and Experience of Cancer Prevention and Screening Among Gypsies, Roma and Travellers: A Participatory Qualitative Study', *BMC Public Health* 21 (2021); https://bmcpublichealth.biomedcentral.com/articles/10.1186/s12889-021-10390-y

111   https://www.ons.gov.uk/peoplepopulationandcommunity/healthandsocialcare/healthinequalities/bulletins/healthstatelifeexpectanciesbyindexofmultipledeprivationimd/2017to2019

112   https://publications.parliament.uk/pa/cm201719/cmselect/cmwomeq/360/full-report.html#heading-10

113   https://www.gypsy-traveller.org/wp-content/uploads/2019/07/discrimination-facing-gypsies-roma-and-travellers-in-the-uk-today-2.pdf

114   https://www.theguardian.com/culture/2022/feb/04/jimmy-carr-condemned-for-joke-about-gypsies-in-netflix-special

115   https://www.wearecocreate.com/

116   https://www.kingsfund.org.uk/publications/wigan-deal

117   Cottam, H., *Radical Help: How We Can Remake the Relationships Between Us and Revolutionise the Welfare State* (Great Britain: Virago Press, 2018), pp.49–80

118   Cottam, H., *Radical Help: How We Can Remake the Relationships Between Us and Revolutionise the Welfare State*, pp.196–240

119   New Local, X (previously known as Twitter), 29 January 2022; https://twitter.com/wearenewlocal/status/1487376222430580739

120   Hewitt, N.A., *Radical Friend: Amy Kirby Post and Her Activist Worlds* (USA: The North Caroline University Press, 2018)

121   https://www.edenprojectcommunities.com/the-big-lunch

122   https://www.theguardian.com/society/2021/feb/21/uk-17-year-olds-mental-health-crisis

123   Gruber, E. and J.W. Grube, 'Adolescent Sexuality and the Media: A Review of Current Knowledge and Implications', *West J Med.* 172 (2000), 3; https://ncbi.nlm.nih.gov/pmc/articles/PMC1070813/

124   Hornor, G., 'Child and Adolescent Pornography Exposure', *Journal of Pediatric Health Care* 34 (2020), 2.191–199; https://www.jpedhc.org/article/S0891-5245(19)30384-0/fulltext

125   https://www.bbc.co.uk/news/uk-wales-54194093

126   https://www.bbfc.co.uk/about-us/news/children-see-pornography-as-young-as-seven-new-report-finds

127   https://www.endviolenceagainstwomen.org.uk

128   https://www.theguardian.com/uk-news/2022/apr/23/three-cabinet-ministers-reportedly-facing-allegations-of-sexual-misconduct

129   https://www.independent.co.uk/life-style/women/office-national-statistics-women-safety-b1907807.html

130   https://www.openaccessgovernment.org/social-media-is-harming-young-peoples-wellbeing/95646/

131   https://www.thesocialdilemma.com/the-dilemma/

132   https://www.girlguiding.org.uk/what-we-do/our-stories-and-news/news/exam-stress-is-part-of-a-perfect-storm-of-pressures-on-girls-finds-new-girlguiding-research/

133   Foucault, M., *The History of Sexuality, Volume 1: An Introduction* (Australia: Penguin Group, 2008), pp.140–141

134   https://www.theguardian.com/commentisfree/2021/apr/08/gavin-williamson-education-secretary-behaviour-hubs-children-schools

135   https://www.theguardian.com/world/2022/jan/02/more-than-half-of-uks-black-children-live-in-poverty-analysis-shows

136   https://publications.parliament.uk/pa/cm5802/cmselect/cmeduc/85/8502.htm

137   https://www.the-educator.org/poor-white-boys-worse-schools-black-asian-muslim-youngsters-girls-especially-worse-jobs/

138   Weedon, B.D., F. Liu, W. Mahmoud, et al., 'Declining Fitness and Physical Education Lessons in UK Adolescents', *BMJ Open Sport & Exercise Medicine* 8 (2022), 1; https://bmjopensem.bmj.com/content/8/1/e001165.info

139   https://www.forbes.com/sites/nickmorrison/2019/04/09/how-the-arts-are-being-squeezed-out-of-schools/?sh=56a50327aaf4

140   Wang, S., H.W. Mak and D. Fancourt, 'Arts, Mental Distress, Mental Health Functioning & Life Satisfaction: Fixed-Effects Analyses of a Nationally-Representative Panel Study', *BMC Public Health* 20 (2020) 208; https://doi.org/10.1186/s12889-019-8109-y

141   Yates, J., Fractured: *Why Our Societies are Coming Apart and How We Put Them Back Together Again* (Manchester: HarperNorth, 2021), pp.95–100

142   https://www.independent.co.uk/news/education/education-news/school-funding-gap-ifs-report-b1934075.html

143   https://www.philanthropydaily.com/tax-breaks-for-private-schools-are-a-bad-use-of-the-u-k-s-public-money/

144   https://ifs.org.uk/articles/long-long-squeeze-teacher-pay

145   https://www.tes.com/magazine/archive/third-teachers-leaving-profession-within-5-years

146   https://www.theguardian.com/education/2022/apr/11/teachers-england-plan-to-quit-workloads-stress-trust

147   https://witton.atctrust.org.uk/

148   https://clf.uk/

149   https://www.oasiscommunitylearning.org/

150   https://www.theguardian.com/commentisfree/2022/mar/03/fathers-children-poverty-child-maintenance-biased-against-women

151   https://medium.com/iipp-blog/introducing-the-work-project-reimagining-work-and-life-989beefa9a2d

152   https://www.bbc.co.uk/news/business-57139434

153   https://medium.com/iipp-blog/the-work-project-reimagining-work-and-time-5dedf27c4508

154   https://medium.com/iipp-blog/the-work-project-reimagining-work-and-care-b324056f4be7

155   https://carersuk.org/policy-and-research/key-facts-and-figures/

156   https://medium.com/iipp-blog/the-work-project-imagining-transition-d3d56c4e7b4e

157   https://www.unilever.com/planet-and-society/responsible-business/employee-wellbeing/

158   https://www.buurtzorg.com/about-us/

159   https://www.businessinsider.com/benefits-of-four-day-work-week-global-study-2022-12?r=US&IR=T

160   Perlo, J., B. Balik, S. Swensen, et al., *IHI Framework for Improving Joy in Work*. IHI White Paper (Cambridge, Massachusetts: Institute for Healthcare Improvement, 2017)

161   https://fabnhsstuff.net/

162   https://www.youtube.com/watch?v=J16Zyknu9Mw

163   https://hbr.org/2016/11/why-diverse-teams-are-smarter

164   https://fabnhsstuff.net/fab-stuff/15-seconds-30-minutes

165   https://inews.co.uk/news/most-deprived-areas-uk-list-ranking-blackpool-north-jaywick-343952

166   https://www.blackpooljsna.org.uk/Home.aspx

167   https://www.health.org.uk/news-and-comment/blogs/a-worrying-cycle-of-pressure-for-gps-in-deprived-areas

168   https://www.independent.co.uk/news/health/gps-nhs-england-health-foundation-patients-b598324.html

169   https://www.kingsfund.org.uk/publications/health-people-ethnic-minority-groups-england

170   Takeshita, J., S. Wang, A.W. Loren, et al., 'Association of Racial/Ethnic and Gender Concordance Between Patients and Physicians With Patient Experience Ratings', *JAMA Netw Open.* 2020;3(11):e2024583; https://jamanetwork.com/journals/jamanetworkopen/fullarticle/2772682

171   https://www.gpsmycity.com/attractions/chinese-arch-42777.html

172   I recognise that all ways of talking about race are clumsy. By landing with the term 'minority ethnic' I am reflecting that this is generally preferred to Black, Asian and Minority Ethnic (BAME), by the majority of minority ethnic communities. I could have used the term 'global majority' instead, though at the time of writing this is not yet in wider use.

173   Otu, A., B.O. Ahinkorah, E.K. Ameyaw, A.A Seidu and S. Yaya, 'One Country, Two Crises: What Covid-19 Reveals About Health Inequalities Among BAME Communities in the United Kingdom and the Sustainability of its Health System?', *International Journal for Equity in Health* 19 (2020); https://equityhealthj.biomedcentral.com/articles/10.1186/s12939-020-01307-z

174   https://digital.nhs.uk/news/2019/ae-attendances-twice-as-high-for-people-in-the-most-deprived-areas-as-in-the-least-deprived

175   https://www.newstatesman.com/spotlight/healthcare/2023/02/how-save-nhs-health-funding?

176   https://www.ippr.org/news-and-media/press-releases/revealed-midlands-and-the-north-endure-biggest-public-health-cuts-in-england

177   https://www.kingsfund.org.uk/publications/what-are-health-inequalities

178   https://www.n8research.org.uk/media/Child-of-the-North-Report-2021.pdf

179   https://coronavirus.data.gov.uk/details/deaths

180   Marmot, M., J. Allen, P. Goldblatt, E. Herd and J. Morrison, 'Build Back Fairer: The COVID-19 Marmot Review. The Pandemic, Socioeconomic and Health Inequalities in England' (London: Institute of Health Equity, 2020). The Health Foundation was also involved in the work of the Review; http://www.instituteofhealthequity.org/resources-reports/build-back-fairer-the-covid-19-marmot-review/build-back-fairer-the-covid-19-marmot-review-executive-summary.pdf

181   Marmot, M., J. Allen, P. Goldblatt, E. Herd and J. Morrison, 'Build Back Fairer: The COVID-19 Marmot Review. The Pandemic, Socioeconomic and Health Inequalities in England'

182   https://www.ons.gov.uk/employmentandlabourmarket/peopleinwork/labourproductivity/articles/sicknessabsenceinthelabourmarket/2021

183   https://assets.publishing.service.gov.uk/government/uploads/system/uploads/attachment_data/file/644090/work-health-and-disability-green-paper-data-pack.pdf

184   https://www.kingsfund.org.uk/publications/anchor-institutions-and-peoples-health

185   Brown, M. and R.E. Jones, *Paint Your Town Red: How Preston Took Back Control and Your Town Can Too* (London: Repeater, 2021)

186   https://www.health.org.uk/news-and-comment/charts-and-infographics/the-nhs-as-an-anchor-institution

187   https://www.uhmb.nhs.uk/news-and-events/our-campaigns/flourish

188   https://echalliance.com/hospitals-produce-tonnes-of-plastic-waste-annually-how-can-they-reduce-this/

189   Yasny, J.S. and J. White, 'Environmental Implications of Anesthetic Gases', *Anesth Prog.* 59 (2012), 4.154–158; https://www.ncbi.nlm.nih.gov/pmc/articles/PMC3522493/

190   https://www.newcastle-hospitals.nhs.uk/content/uploads/2021/02/Climate-Emergency-Strategy-2020-2025.pdf

191   de Mooij, L.D., M. Kikkert, J. Theunissen, et al., 'Dying Too Soon: Excess Mortality in Severe Mental Illness', *Front Psychiatry* 10 (2019); https://www.ncbi.nlm.nih.gov/pmc/articles/PMC6918821/

192   https://www.mencap.org.uk/learning-disability-explained/research-and-statistics/health/health-inequalities

193   https://www.england.nhs.uk/author/dr-bola-owolabi/

194   https://www.england.nhs.uk/about/equality/equality-hub/national-healthcare-inequalities-improvement-programme/core20plus5/

195   This abridged version of David's speech was used with permission from David and Imogen. The speech was first published in Imogen Tyler's book. Tyler, I., *Stigma: The Machinery of Inequality* (London: Zed Books, 2020), pp.160–162. Imogen uses David's words to demonstrate how the stigmatisation of people in poverty is an integral part of austerity cuts to welfare.

196   David is not his real name but has been changed.

197   'Love Society' - Session 1 - Prof Bev Skeggs - Morecambe Bay; https://www.youtube.com/watch?v=kzAwv07QKuQ

198   'Love Society' - Session 1 - Prof Bev Skeggs - Morecambe Bay; https://www.youtube.com/watch?v=kzAwv07QKuQ

199   Thatcher, M., 'Interview for *Woman's Own* ("No Such Thing as Society")', 1987, in *Margaret Thatcher Foundation: Speeches, Interviews and Other Statements* (London); https://newlearningonline.com/new-learning/chapter-4/neoliberalism-more-recent-times/margaret-thatcher-theres-no-such-thing-as-society

200   Taylor-Goody, P., *The Double Crisis of the Welfare State and What We Can Do About It* (Basingstoke: Palgrave Macmillan, 2013), p.viii

201   https://www.newstatesman.com/business/economics/2012/10/george-osbornes-speech-conservative-conference-full-text

202   https://www.gov.uk/government/speeches/chancellor-george-osbornes-budget-2015-speech

203   Tyler, I., Stigma: *The Machinery of Inequality* (London: Zed Books, 2020), pp.159–210

204   https://www.ohchr.org/en/documents/country-reports/ahrc4139add1-visit-united-kingdom-great-britain-and-northern-ireland

205   https://www.jrf.org.uk/sites/default/files/jrf/migrated/files/Summary-Final.pdf

206   https://www.kingsfund.org.uk/blog/2015/10/nhs-spending-squeezed-never

207   https://www.kingsfund.org.uk/publications/whats-happening-life-expectancy-england

208   https://www.bbc.co.uk/news/uk-politics-48503170

209   https://www.dw.com/en/uk-food-banks-outnumber-mcdonalds-restaurants/a-56952232

210   Tyler, I., Stigma: *The Machinery of Inequality*, pp.159–210

211   https://www.icij.org/investigations/pandora-papers/global-investigation-tax-havens-offshore/

212   https://www.theguardian.com/business/2021/may/21/number-of-billionaires-in-uk-reached-new-record-during-covid-pandemic

213   https://www.bigissue.com/news/social-justice/uk-poverty-the-facts-figures-and-effects/

214   https://www.economist.com/britain/2020/07/30/why-britain-is-more-geographically-unequal-than-any-other-rich-country

215   https://povertytruthnetwork.org/commissions/what-is-a-poverty-truth-commission/

216   http://www.morecambebaypovertytruthcommission.org.uk

217   http://lovemorecambebay.co.uk/?CONVERSATIONS:Love_Economics

218   The speech was first published in Imogen Tyler's book. Tyler, I., *Stigma: The Machinery of Inequality* (London: Zed Books, 2020), pp.160–162

219   Marmot, M., *The Health Gap: The Challenge of an Unequal World* (UK: Bloomsbury, 2015), p.46

220   Mazzucato, M., *Mission Economy, A Moonshot Guide to Changing Capitalism* (UK: Penguin Random House, 2021), p.22

221   Mazzucato, M., *Mission Economy, A Moonshot Guide to Changing Capitalism*, p.23

222   https://www.bbc.co.uk/news/health-44642027

223   https://eco18.com/how-food-has-changed-in-the-past-50-years/

224   https://www.hsph.harvard.edu/obesity-prevention-source/obesity-causes/diet-and-weight/

225   http://obesityhealthalliance.org.uk/2019/02/28/protect-children-junk-food-advertising-say-health-experts-parents-agree/

226   https://www.milbank.org/quarterly/articles/guns-obesity-and-opioids-a-population-health-science-perspective-on-3-contemporary-epidemics/

227   https://www.gov.uk/government/publications/the-eatwell-guide

228   https://foodfoundation.org.uk/sites/default/files/2021-10/Affordability-of-the-Eatwell-Guide_Final_Web-Version.pdf

229   Godfrey, K.M., R.M. Reynolds, S.L. Prescott, et al., 'Influence of Maternal Obesity on the Long-term Health of Offspring', *Lancet Diabetes Endocrinol* 5 (2017), 1.53–64; https://www.ncbi.nlm.nih.gov/pmc/articles/PMC5245733/

230   https://thedailymile.co.uk

231   Thread from T. Lawrie on X (previously known as Twitter), 25 October 2020 (used with permission); https://twitter.com/trina1982t/status/1320493301842280448

232   https://www.trusselltrust.org/wp-content/uploads/sites/2/2021/04/Trusell-Trust-End-of-Year-stats-data-briefing_2020_21.pdf

233   https://www.bigissue.com/news/social-justice/universal-credit-what-is-it-and-why-does-the-20-increase-matter/

234   https://www.theguardian.com/society/2019/sep/23/people-england-living-unsuitable-housing

235   https://www.bbc.co.uk/news/disability-58550010

236   https://www.theguardian.com/society/2022/jan/16/englands-north-south-divide-is-deepening-says-new-report

237   https://www.amnesty.org.uk/press-releases/uk-home-office-forcing-people-live-squalor-repeated-scandal

238   https://www.trusselltrust.org/news-and-blog/latest-stats/end-year-stats/

239   https://www.bbc.co.uk/news/science-environment-44634122

240   https://www.jrf.org.uk/work/uk-poverty-2019-20-work

241   https://www.ageuk.org.uk/latest-press/archive/over-3-million-older-people-are-concerned-about-staying-warm-in-their-own-home-this-winter/

242   https://www.ft.com/content/747a76dd-f018-4d0d-a9f3-4069bf2f5a93

243   https://www.unhcr.org/uk/figures-at-a-glance.html

244   https://www.youtube.com/watch?v=T19YqLQ5aLg

245   https://journals.kent.ac.uk/index.php/feministsatlaw/article/view/65/187

246   https://www.jrf.org.uk/report/end-benefit-freeze-stop-people-being-swept-poverty

247   https://www.trusselltrust.org/news-and-blog/latest-stats/

248   Fitzpatrick, S., G. Bramley, J. Blenkinsopp, et al., 'Destitution in the UK 2020', Joseph Rowntree Foundation (2020); https://www.jrf.org.uk/report/destitution-uk-2020

249   https://www.theguardian.com/education/2020/oct/28/marcus-rashford-petition-to-end-child-food-poverty-signed-by-over-1m-people

250   https://www.trusselltrust.org/news-and-blog/latest-stats/end-year-stats/

251   https://www.jrf.org.uk/report/destitution-uk-2020

252   Thomas, C., A. Round and S. Longlands, 'Levelling Up Health for Prosperity', Institute for Public Policy Research (2020); https://www.ippr.org/files/2020-12/levelling-up-health-for-prosperity-dec-20.pdf

253   https://www.rcplondon.ac.uk/projects/inequalities-health-alliance

254   https://www.instituteofhealthequity.org/in-the-news/news-coverage/jaw-dropping-fall-in-life-expectancy-in-poor-areas-of-england-report-finds

255   Skeggs, B., 'Exchange, Value and Affect: Bourdieu and the "Self"', *Sociological Review* 52 (2005), 2; https://journals.sagepub.com/doi/abs/10.1111/j.1467-954X.2005.00525.x

256   Mazzucato, M., *The Value of Everything: Making and Taking in the Global Economy* (UK: Penguin Random House, 2019), pp.279–280

257   Mazzucato, M., *The Value of Everything: Making and Taking in the Global Economy*, pp.233–234

258   Love Economics - Part 4 - Prof Katherine Trebeck; https://www.youtube.com/watch?time_continue=1&v=7OuL8BERmd8&feature=emb_title

259   https://wellbeingeconomy.org

260   https://apps.who.int/iris/bitstream/handle/10665/338915/Eurohealth-26-3-6-9-eng.pdf

261   https://www.ted.com/talks/nicola_sturgeon_why_governments_should_prioritize_well_being?language=en

262   https://www.disabilityrightsuk.org/news/2018/september/disability-benefit-spending-reduced-£5-billion-over-last-decade

263   https://www.trusselltrust.org/news-and-blog/latest-stats/end-year-stats/

264   https://www.gov.uk/government/statistics/abortion-statistics-for-england-and-wales-2020/abortion-statistics-england-and-wales-2020

265   https://www.politico.com/news/2022/05/02/supreme-court-abortion-draft-opinion-00029473

266   https://commonslibrary.parliament.uk/research-briefings/cbp-8909/

267   https://www.abortionrightscampaign.ie/abortion-law-in-ireland/

268   Thread from R. Cunliffe on X (previously known as Twitter), 4 May 2022; https://twitter.com/RMCunliffe/status/1521802347319541762

269   https://www.theguardian.com/us-news/2022/may/07/enforced-childbirth-is-slavery-margaret-atwood-on-the-right-to-abortion

270   https://www.guttmacher.org/fact-sheet/induced-abortion-worldwide

271   https://www.kingsfund.org.uk/publications/whats-happening-life-expectancy-england

272   https://www.theguardian.com/society/2019/mar/27/womens-life-expectancy-in-poor-areas-falls-by-almost-100-days

273   Criado Perez, C., *Invisible Women: Exposing Data Bias in a World Designed for Men* (UK: Chatto & Windus, Penguin Random House, 2019), pp.244–245

274   https://www.bbc.co.uk/news/uk-scotland-scotland-politics-51629880

275   https://www.ohchr.org/sites/default/files/Documents/Issues/Poverty/EOM_GB_16Nov2018.pdf

276   https://www.bbc.co.uk/news/uk-48354692

277   https://publications.parliament.uk/pa/cm201919/cmselect/cmworpen/51/51.pdf

278   https://www.bigissue.com/latest/philip-hammond-cant-see-the-uk-poverty-brought-up-in-un-report/

279   https://www.theguardian.com/society/2019/jun/03/philip-hammond-accused-of-being-blind-to-scale-of-uk-poverty

280   https://www.ageuk.org.uk/latest-press/articles/2021/number-of-pensioners-living-in-poverty-tops-two-million/

281   https://www.theguardian.com/society/2019/aug/18/elderly-poverty-risen-fivefold-since-80s-pensions

282   Volf, M., *Exclusion and Embrace: A Theological Exploration of Identity, Otherness, and Reconciliation,* revised and updated (Abingdon Press, 2019), pp.99–104

283   Brueggemann, W., *Gift and Task, A Year of Daily Readings and Reflections* (USA: Westminster John Knox Press, 2017), p.92

284   Brueggemann, W., *Gift and Task, A Year of Daily Readings and Reflections*, p.92

285   https://assets.grenfelltowerinquiry.org.uk/GTI%20-%20Phase%201%20report%20Executive%20Summary.pdf

286   Trebeck, K. and J. Williams, *The Economics of Arrival: Ideas for a Grown Up Economy* (Bristol: Policy Press, 2019), pp.11–64

287   https://www.chemistanddruggist.co.uk/news/antidepressants-dispensed-almost-quarter-last-five-years

288   Mazzucato, M., *Mission Economy: A Moonshot Guide to Changing Capitalism* (UK: Penguin Random House, 2021), pp.11–25

289   https://www.ippr.org/files/2019-06/public-health-and-prevention-june19.pdf#page=8

290   Mazzucato, M., *Mission Economy, A Moonshot Guide to Changing Capitalism*, p.19

291   Mazzucato, M., *Mission Economy, A Moonshot Guide to Changing Capitalism*, pp.26–59

292   https://inequality.org/facts/inequality-and-health/

293   Mazzucato, M., *The Value of Everything: Making and Taking in the Global Economy* (UK: Penguin Random House, 2019), pp.189–228

294   https://www.theguardian.com/commentisfree/2020/may/07/outsourcing-coronavirus-crisis-business-failed-nhs-staff

295   Mazzucato, M., *Mission Economy, A Moonshot Guide to Changing Capitalism*, pp.39–40

296   https://www.nao.org.uk/report/pfi-and-pf2/

297   https://www.nhsforsale.info/sector/public-health-new-copy/

298   https://www.theguardian.com/society/2020/may/05/private-covid-19-tracing-disaster-councils

299   https://www.disabilityrightsuk.org/news/2022/may/care-home-discharges-during-covid-ruled-%E2%80%98unlawful%E2%80%99

300   https://www.independent.co.uk/news/uk/politics/covid-unusable-ppe-burnt-fast-track-b2030820.html

301   https://www.theguardian.com/politics/2019/nov/21/priti-patel-says-tory-government-not-to-blame-for-poverty-in-uk

302   Mazzucato, M., *Mission Economy, A Moonshot Guide to Changing Capitalism*, p.112

303   Raworth, K., *Doughnut Economics: seven ways to think like a 21st century economist* (London: Penguin Random House, 2017)

304   Raworth, K. (2017), *Doughnut Economics: seven ways to think like a 21st century economist*. London: Penguin Random House.

305   The Doughnut of social and planetary boundaries. Kate Raworth and Christian Guthier. CC-BY-SA 4.0   Raworth, K. (2017), *Doughnut Economics: seven ways to think like a 21st century economist*. London: Penguin Random House. The diagram is taken from p.51 of Doughnut Economics and redrawn to fit in with the style of the book. Used with permission by the author.

306   https://www.kateraworth.com/2020/04/08/amsterdam-city-doughnut/

307   https://doughnuteconomics.org/stories/4

308   https://www.yesmagazine.org/issue/ecological-civilization/2021/02/16/cities-life-affirming-economies

309   https://www.climateactionleeds.org.uk/leedsdoughnut

310   https://doughnuteconomics.org/members/12613

311   https://doughnuteconomics.org/stories/71

312   https://www.communitycare.co.uk/2020/12/11/coronavirus-75-social-workers-feeling-negative-work-life-last-year-survey-finds/

313   Department for Education, 'Children Looked After in England (Including Adoption), Year Ending 31 March 2019', 2019; https://assets.publishing.service.gov.uk/government/uploads/system/uploads/attachment_data/file/850306/Children_looked_after_in_England_2019_Text.pdf

314   https://www.theguardian.com/society/2019/dec/25/revealed-thousands-children-care-unregulated-homes

315   https://www.nationalcrimeagency.gov.uk/what-we-do/crime-threats/drug-trafficking/county-lines

316   https://www.bbc.co.uk/news/uk-england-leeds-59637683

317   https://www.probonoeconomics.com/a-decade-of-change-for-childrens-services-funding

318   https://www.ncb.org.uk/about-us/media-centre/news-opinion/more-children-risk-councils-forced-halve-spending-early-support

319   https://www.theguardian.com/uk-news/2021/dec/17/scariest-place-ive-worked-social-worker-recalls-stint-in-bradford

320   https://www.lgcplus.com/idea-exchange/how-we-went-from-inadequate-to-outstanding-in-three-years-29-09-2021/

321   https://www.independent.co.uk/news/uk/politics/david-cameron-accused-hypocrisy-after-complaining-about-counter-productive-tory-cuts-a6730986.html

322   https://www.ted.com/talks/simon_sinek_how_great_leaders_inspire_action?language=en

323   Mitchell, R.H., *The Fall of The Church* (Eugene, Oregon: Wipf & Stock, 2013), pp.10–11

324   Brueggemann, W., *Gift and Task, A Year of Daily Readings and Reflections* (USA: Westminster John Knox Press, 2017), p.84

325   Mitchell, R.H., *The Fall of The Church*, p.12

326   Mitchell, R.H., *The Fall of The Church*, p.12

327   Colossians 2:15, *The Bible*

328   Mitchell, R.H., *The Fall of The Church*, p.13

329   Mitchell, R.H., *The Fall of The Church*, p.13

330   https://alastairparvin.medium.com/a-new-land-contract-684c3ba1f1b3

331   Jones, O., *The Establishment: And How They Get Away with It* (UK: Penguin, 2015)

332   R. Wilson on X (previously known as Twitter), 3 August 2019; https://twitter.com/rainnwilson/status/1157736650274828288?lang=en

333   Critchley, S., *The Faith of The Faithless: Experiments in Political Theology* (London; New York: Verso, 2012), pp.6–7

334   Mitchell, R.H. and J. Tomlin Arram (eds), *Discovering Kenarchy* (USA: Wipf & Stock, 2014)

335   Wells, S., *A Nazareth Manifesto: Being with God* (UK: John Wiley & Sons, 2015), pp.11–20

336   Kaur, V., *See No Stranger: A Memoir and Manifesto of Revolutionary Love* (London: Octopus Publishing Group Ltd, 2020), pp.202–203

337   El Bachiri, M., *A Jihad for Love* (Head of Zeus, Ltd, 2017), pp.23–24

338   Oord, T.J., 'A Loving Civilization: A Political Ecology that Promotes Overall Well-Being', *The Kenarchy Journal* 2 (2021), 1–18; https://kenarchy.org/wp-content/uploads/2021/03/Kenarchy_Volume2.1.pdf

339   Oord, T.J., *Defining Love: A Philosophical, Scientific, and Theological Engagement* (Grand Rapids, Michigan: Brazos, 2010)

340   Russell, C., *Rekindling Democracy: A Professional's Guide to Working in Citizen Space* (Oregon: Wipf & Stock, 2020)

341   Popay, J., M. Whitehead, R. Ponsford, M. Egan and R. Mead, 'Power, Control, Communities and Health Inequalities I: Theories, Concepts and Analytical Frameworks', *Health Promot Int.* 36 (2021), 5.1253 –1263; https://pubmed.ncbi.nlm.nih.gov/33382890/

342   https://www.theguardian.com/world/2020/nov/15/chumocracy-covid-revealed-shape-tory-establishment

343   https://reutersinstitute.politics.ox.ac.uk/trust-uk-government-and-news-media-covid-19-information-down-concerns-over-misinformation

344   Russell, C., *Rekindling Democracy: A Professional's Guide to Working in Citizen Space*, p.214

345   Sen, A., 'Poor, Relatively Speaking', *Oxford Economic Papers* 35 (1983) 2.153–169

346   Marmot, M., *The Health Gap: The Challenge of an Unequal World* (London: Bloomsbury Publishing, 2016), p.44

347   http://artofhosting.ning.com/video/art-of-hosting-story-and-lineage

348   https://www.wedialogue.com/gifts-from-the-art-of-hosting/

349   https://roc.uk.com/

350   https://fullfact.org/immigration/asylum-seeker-november-2021/

351   http://www.thecornerstonelancaster.org.uk/Lets%20BeFriends%20Handbook.pdf

352   http://artofhosting.ning.com/profiles/blogs/shaping-powerful-questions

353   Hackett, R.A., A. Ronaldson, K. Bhui, A. Steptoe and S.E. Jackson, 'Racial Discrimination and Health: A Prospective Study of Ethnic Minorities in the United Kingdom', *BMC Public Health* 20 (2020) 1;

https://bmcpublichealth.biomedcentral.com/articles/10.1186/s12889-020-09792-1

354   https://www.nhsrho.org/research/ethnic-inequalities-in-healthcare-a-rapid-evidence-review-3/

355   Iacobucci, G., 'Covid-19: Increased Risk Among Ethnic Minorities is Largely Due to Poverty and Social Disparities, Review Finds', *BMJ* 2020;371:m4099

356   https://www.jcwi.org.uk

357   Tyler, I., *Stigma: The Machinery of Inequality* (London: Zed Books Ltd, 2020), p.134

358   https://www.gov.uk/government/publications/the-report-of-the-commission-on-race-and-ethnic-disparities

359   Saad, L.F., *Me and White Supremacy: How to Recognise Your Privilege, Combat Racism and Change the World* (UK: Quercus Editions Ltd, 2020), pp.12–14

360   https://www.theguardian.com/news/2021/apr/20/the-invention-of-whiteness-long-history-dangerous-idea

361   https://www.justice.gov.za/trc/

362   Yates, J., *Fractured: How we Learn to Live Together* (Manchester: HarperNorth, 2021), pp.18–27

363   https://www.oecd.org/cfe/divided-cities.pdf

364   https://www.tuc.org.uk/research-analysis/reports/still-rigged-racism-uk-labour-market

365   Moody, J., 'Race, School Integration, and Friendship Segregation in America' *American Journal of Sociology* 107 (2001), 3.679–716

366   Yates, J., *Fractured: How we Learn to Live Together*, pp.18–27

367   Volf, M., *Exclusion and Embrace: A Theological Exploration of Identity, Otherness, and Reconciliation,* revised and updated (Abingdon Press, 2019), pp.69–71

368   https://www.nytimes.com/live/2021/11/25/world/migrants-drown-france-uk

369   https://www.independent.co.uk/news/uk/home-news/refugee-resettlement-home-office-coronavirus-b1799714.html

370   https://www.independent.co.uk/news/uk/politics/rwanda-asylum-seekers-uk-priti-patel-b2059064.html

371   https://www.lawsociety.org.uk/contact-or-visit-us/press-office/press-releases/supreme-court-ruling-end-of-the-line-for-rwanda-policy#:~:text=The%20Supreme%20Court%2C%20the%20highest,the%20Court%20of%20Appeal%27s%20judgment.

372   https://www.amnesty.org/en/latest/research/2021/03/the-nightmare-of-uyghur-families-separated-by-repression/

373   https://www.politicshome.com/thehouse/article/gypsy-roma-and-traveller-groups-fear-new-government-measures-could-harm-their-nomadic-way-of-life

374   https://www.dw.com/en/where-are-burqa-bans-in-europe/a-49843292

375   https://www.bbc.co.uk/news/uk-politics-45083275

376   https://www.independent.co.uk/news/uk/home-news/boris-johnson-muslim-women-letterboxes-burqa-islamphobia-rise-a9088476.html

377   https://slaveryfootprint.org/

378   https://www.jcwi.org.uk

379   https://www.bbc.co.uk/news/world-europe-53764449

380   https://www.aljazeera.com/features/2016/6/28/brexit-ukips-unethical-anti-immigration-poster

381   Volf, M., *Exclusion and Embrace: A Theological Exploration of Identity, Otherness, and Reconciliation*, pp.110–119

382   Fisk, W.J., E.A. Eliseeva and M.J. Mendell, 'Association of Residential Dampness and Mold with Respiratory Tract Infections and Bronchitis: A Meta-Analysis', *Environmental Health* 9 (2010), 72; https://ehjournal.biomedcentral.com/articles/10.1186/1476-069X-9-72

383   Foley, D., E. Best, N. Reid and M.M.J. Berry, 'Respiratory Health Inequality Starts Early: The Impact of Social Determinants on the Aetiology and Severity of Bronchiolitis in Infancy', *Journal of Paediatrics and Child Health* 55 (2019), 5.528–532; https://pubmed.ncbi.nlm.nih.gov/30264506/

384   https://www.theguardian.com/uk-news/2022/nov/15/death-of-two-year-old-awaab-ishak-chronic-mould-in-flat-a-defining-moment-says-coroner#:~:

385   Cohen, S., D. Janicki-Deverts, E. Chen and K.A. Matthews, 'Childhood Socioeconomic Status and Adult Health', *Ann N Y Acad Sci.* (2010), 37–55

386   https://statistics.blf.org.uk/lung-disease-uk-big-picture

387   https://indepth.nice.org.uk/respiratory-reducing-emergency-pressure/index.html

388   Ingham, T., M. Keall, B. Jones, et al., 'Damp Mouldy Housing and Early Childhood Hospital Admissions for Acute Respiratory Infection: A Case Control Study', *Thorax* 74 (2019), 9.849–857

389   https://www.gov.uk/government/publications/chief-medical-officers-annual-report-2021-health-in-coastal-communities

390   https://www.bigissue.com/news/housing/rents-in-the-uk-are-rising-at-the-highest-rate-for-14-years-will-they-keep-going-up/

391   https://www.kingsfund.org.uk/blog/2020/09/poor-housing-covid-19

392   https://www.unep.org/news-and-stories/story/how-climate-change-making-record-breaking-floods-new-normal

393   https://www.bbc.co.uk/news/science-environment-56805255

394   https://www.un.org/press/en/2019/ga12131.doc.htm

395   https://www.itv.com/news/2021-09-12/britains-housing-shame-shocking-conditions-and-despair-at-a-lack-of-action

396   https://england.shelter.org.uk/professional_resources/policy_and_research/policy_library/people_living_in_bad_housing_-_numbers_and_health_impacts

397   Ingham, T., M. Keall, B. Jones, et al., 'Damp Mouldy Housing and Early Childhood Hospital Admissions for Acute Respiratory Infection: A Case Control Study', *Thorax* 74 (2019), 9.849–857

398   FAO and UNEP, *The State of the World's Forests 2020. Forests, Biodiversity and People* (Rome, 2020); https://www.fao.org/documents/card/en/c/ca8642en

399   FAO and UNEP, *The State of the World's Forests 2020. Forests, Biodiversity and People*; https://www.fao.org/documents/card/en/c/ca8642en

400   https://www.who.int/health-topics/air-pollution#tab=tab_1

401   https://www.cancerresearchuk.org/about-cancer/causes-of-cancer/air-pollution-radon-gas-and-cancer/how-can-air-pollution-cause-cancer

402   Jiang, XQ., XD. Mei and D. Feng, 'Air Pollution and Chronic Airway Diseases: What Should People Know and Do?' *J Thorac Dis.* 8 (2016), 1; https://pubmed.ncbi.nlm.nih.gov/26904251/

403   https://www.historyextra.com/period/anglo-saxon/william-conqueror-war-criminal-story-harrying-north/

404   https://www.dailymail.co.uk/news/article-6935577/HALF-Britain-owned-ONE-population.html

405   https://scottishhistorysociety.com/the-highland-clearances/

406   https://alastairparvin.medium.com/a-new-land-contract-684c3ba1f1b3

407   https://www.thetimes.co.uk/article/revealed-how-china-is-buying-up-britain-t7njdhhc5

408   https://www.communitylandtrusts.org.uk/

409   https://www.pan-europe.info/issues/pesticides-and-loss-biodiversity

410   https://www.theguardian.com/commentisfree/2021/jul/21/britains-rivers-suffocating-industrial-farm-waste

411   https://www.theguardian.com/environment/2021/dec/06/how-arable-farming-sows-the-seeds-of-river-pollution

412   https://www.thetimes.co.uk/article/pollution-no-river-in-england-is-safe-for-swimming-q8thdx678

413   https://www.greenpeace.org.uk/news/raw-sewage-discharge-water-pollution/

414   https://www.theguardian.com/uk-news/2022/jan/05/four-cleared-of-toppling-edward-colston-statute

415   http://s3-eu-west-1.amazonaws.com/doc.housing.org.uk/Editorial/Bristol_Votes_Housing.pdf

416   https://www.corganisers.org.uk/

417   https://www.housing.org.uk/our-work/together-with-tenants/

418   Thunberg, G., 'Our house is on fire': Greta Thunberg, 16, urges leaders to act on climate, *Guardian*, 25 January 2019

419   Delahaye, E., 'About Chronos and Kairos. On Agamben's Interpretation of Pauline Temporality through Heidegger', *International Journal of Philosophy and Theology* 77 (2016) 3.85–101;
https://www.tandfonline.com/doi/full/10.1080/21692327.2016.1244016

420   https://cms.zsl.org/sites/default/files/2022-10/ZSL%20Annual%20Report%202021-22.pdf

421   https://www.who.int/news-room/fact-sheets/detail/climate-change-and-health

422   https://www.theguardian.com/environment/2021/jan/27/un-global-climate-poll-peoples-voice-is-clear-they-want-action

423   Love Ecology - Part 1 - Alastair McIntosh;
https://www.youtube.com/watch?v=eOLuXKu-2FE

424   Proverbs 29:18, *The Bible*

425   Berners-Lee, M., *There Is No Planet B*, revised and updated (Cambridge: Cambridge University Press, 2021), pp.226–227

426   Berners-Lee, M., *There Is No Planet B*, p.226

427   https://www.carbonbrief.org/global-carbon-project-coronavirus-causes-record-fall-in-fossil-fuel-emissions-in-2020

428   https://www.theguardian.com/environment/2021/sep/08/audit-office-blames-uk-government-for-botched-15bn-green-homes-scheme

429   https://www.bigissue.com/news/environment/home-insulation-stalled-last-year-during-slam-dunk-fail-green-homes-grant/

430   https://ahdb.org.uk/knowledge-library/carbon-footprints-food-and-farming

431   https://www.ted.com/talks/graham_hill_why_i_m_a_weekday_vegetarian?language=en

432   https://climatenexus.org/climate-issues/food/grazing-cattle-climate-change/

433   https://borgenproject.org/sustainable-agriculture-in-zimbabwe/

434   https://www.climatecouncil.org.au/resources/fast-fashion-climate-change/

435   https://www.thefashionlaw.com/how-many-gallons-of-water-does-it-take-to-make-a-single-pair-of-jeans/

436   https://ethicalmadeeasy.com/the-fourth-largest-freshwater-lake-the-aral-sea-dried-up-but-what-does-this-have-to-do-with-clothing/

437   https://www.bbc.co.uk/news/science-environment-62225696

438   https://www.theguardian.com/environment/2022/jul/21/revealed-oil-sectors-staggering-profits-last-50-years

439   https://www.humanrightspulse.com/mastercontentblog/killing-of-climate-activists-on-the-rise

440   https://www.theguardian.com/environment/2021/aug/21/wrong-to-label-extinction-rebellion-as-extremists-says-home-office-adviser

441   https://www.imf.org/external/pubs/ft/fandd/2019/09/tackling-global-tax-havens-shaxon.htm

442   http://lovemorecambebay.co.uk/?TRAININGS:Lancaster_2019 ; Sue Mitchell draws her material here from Otto Scharmer's work in *Theory U*. Scharmer, C.O., *Theory U: Leading from the Future as It Emerges*, 1st edn (San Francisco: Berrett-Koehler Publishers, 2009)

443   https://commons.wikimedia.org/wiki/File:The_Plumb_Line_and_the_City_-_Coventry_Cathedral.jpg

444   Amos 7:7, *The Bible*

445   https://poverty-truth.org.uk/

446   Timms, H. and J. Heimans, *New Power: How it's Changing the 21st Century – and Why You Need to Know* (London: Macmillan, 2018), p.2

447   Timms, H. and J. Heimans, *New Power: How it's Changing the 21st Century – and Why You Need to Know*, pp.253–254

448   Lederach, J.P., *The Moral Imagination: The Art and Soul of Building Peace* (Oxford, MA: Oxford University Press, 2005)

449   https://www.icorn.org/article/together-cities-can-and-will-shape-century-ahead

450   https://www.gov.uk/government/publications/trend-deck-2021-urbanisation/trend-deck-2021-urbanisation

451   https://www.weforum.org/agenda/2020/11/global-continent-urban-population-urbanisation-percent/

452   Solnit, R., *Hope in the Dark: Untold Histories, Wild Possibilities* (Edinburgh: Canongate Books, 2010), p.29

453   https://newconstellations.co/listen/barrows-journey-the-light-is-in-everyone-in-this-town/

454   https://www.independent.co.uk/life-style/young-adults-anxiety-stress-future-uk-b2191457.html

455   https://www.theguardian.com/politics/2022/jun/25/why-its-time-for-labour-to-back-proportional-representation

456   https://www.janehanson.com/blog/2020/desmondtutujanehanson

457   https://www.sciencedaily.com/releases/2021/08/210817193019.htm

458   https://www.nationalgeographic.org/encyclopedia/gentrification/

459   https://www.ft.com/content/98f5e207-98b0-4221-b7b3-c5cd12d048f1

460   https://ethicsofcare.org/carol-gilligan/

461   https://charter.streetsupport.net/

462   https://www.leedspovertytruth.org.uk/

463   https://wbg.org.uk/wp-content/uploads/2015/02/Gender-and-Poverty-Briefing-June-2015.pdf

464   https://www.ons.gov.uk/employmentandlabourmarket/peopleinwork/earningsandworkinghours/articles/womenshouldertheresponsibilityofunpaidwork/2016-11-10

465   https://www.bbc.com/travel/article/20210524-how-vienna-built-a-gender-equal-city

466   https://www.bloomberg.com/features/best-business-cities-women-ranking-2021/

467   Marmot, M., J. Allen, P. Goldblatt, E. Herd and J. Morrison, 'Build Back Fairer: The COVID-19 Marmot Review. The Pandemic, Socioeconomic and Health Inequalities in England' (London: Institute of Health Equity, 2020), pp.50–77; https://www.instituteofhealthequity.org/resources-reports/build-back-fairer-the-covid-19-marmot-review/build-back-fairer-the-covid-19-marmot-review-full-report.pdf

468   https://childfriendlycities.org/initiatives/

469   https://www.childinthecity.org/2021/01/15/cities-for-children-framework-promoting-just-and-inclusive-cities-where-children-thrive/

470   https://nursingnotes.co.uk/news/clinical/government-fails-to-take-concerns-seriously-as-health-visitors-raise-concerns-about-funding/

471   https://www.local.gov.uk/about/news/number-children-care-reaches-10-year-high

472   https://www.bbc.co.uk/news/uk-61709572

473   Rapsey, C.M. and C.J. Rolston, 'Fostering the Family, Not Just the Child: Exploring the Value of a Residential Family Preservation Programme from the Perspectives of Service Users and Staff, *Children and Youth Services Review*, 108 (2020), 104505; https://doi.org/10.1016/j.childyouth.2019.104505

474   https://homeforgood.org.uk

475   Yates, J., Fractured: *Why Our Societies are Coming Apart and How We Put Them Together Again* (Manchester: HarperNorth, 2021), pp.277–292

476   Violence Reduction Units (VRU) form part of the Home Office's targeted approach to serious violence. They are the multi-agency delivery body for areas across England and Wales most affected by serious violence. Each VRU brings together essential partners to reduce local violent crime and address the underlying causes. Some VRUs have chosen to call themselves a Violence Reduction Network (VRN), like the one in Lancashire, to emphasise the multi-agency and partnership approach needed.

477   https://www.imattertraining.com/

478   https://escape2make.org/

479   https://www.bbc.co.uk/news/uk-england-manchester-57249659

480   https://www.bbc.co.uk/news/world-us-canada-57532258

481   Shannon, A., 'Mouth-Pieces of the Limit: Liminal Spatial Praxis in Israel / Palestine and Northern Ireland', July 2020; https://pure.qub.ac.uk/en/studentTheses/mouth-pieces-of-the-limit

482   https://medium.com/@UNHCR/4-cities-that-embrace-refugees-yours-should-too-10b43903d2be

483   https://cityofsanctuary.org/

484   https://www.openaccessgovernment.org/top-10-eco-friendly-cities-around-the-world/53998/

485   Cornel West: Justice is What Love Looks Like in Public; https://www.youtube.com/watch?v=nGqP7S_WO6o

486   https://www.lancsvrn.co.uk/

487   https://blogs.lse.ac.uk/politicsandpolicy/patterns-of-violence-glasgow-london/

488   https://www.c40.org/

489   https://resilientcitiesnetwork.org/our-story/

490   https://smartcityhub.com/governance-economy/doughnut-cities/

TRADE MARK ACKNOWLEDGEMENTS

Sick Society refers to many companies' products throughout. All trade marks, service marks and company names are the property of their respective owners.

While the author has made every effort to provide accurate internet addresses at the time of publication, the author and publisher do not assume any responsibility for errors or changes that occur after publication.

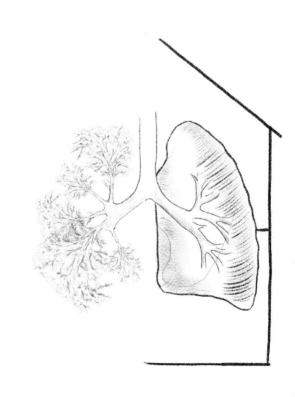